Life at the Texas State Lunatic Asylum,

1857–1997

∞

NUMBER EIGHTY-TWO:
*The Centennial Series*
*of the Association of Former Students,*
*Texas A&M University*

# Life at the
# Texas State Lunatic Asylum,
# 1857–1997

SARAH C. SITTON

*Texas A&M University Press*

COLLEGE STATION

The paper used in this book meets the minimum requirements
of the American National Standard for Permanence
of Paper for Printed Library Materials, z39.48-1984.
Binding materials have been chosen for durability.

∞

Library of Congress Cataloging-in-Publication Data

Sitton, Sarah C., 1943–
    Life at the Texas State Lunatic Asylum, 1857–1997 /
Sarah C. Sitton. — 1st ed.
        p.   cm. — (Centennial series of the Association of
Former Students, Texas A&M University ; no. 82)
    Includes bibliographical references and index.

    1. Texas State Lunatic Asylum (Austin, Tex.)—History.
2. Austin State Hospital (Austin, Tex.)—History.   3. Psychiatric hospital care—Texas—History.   I. Title.   II. Series.
RC445.T4A817   1999
362.2'1'0976431—dc21                                    98-45348
                                                                       CIP

ISBN 978-1-60344-739-3 (paper)

# ᴠ᷄ CONTENTS ᴥ

# ❧ ILLUSTRATIONS ~

# ✥ PREFACE ✥

I first became interested in the history of Austin State Hospital in 1990 while researching my neighborhood, Hyde Park, which is adjacent to the hospital. Several people who had grown up in the neighborhood described playing on the grounds of the hospital during the early years of this century. They had fished, ridden bicycles, played baseball and "rag-knot" football, watched outdoor movies, and talked with the patients. Courting couples had visited the beautifully landscaped grounds of the asylum for Sunday outings. Many of these stories appear in *Austin's Hyde Park: The First Fifty Years, 1891–1941.* The early permeability of the boundaries between hospital and neighborhood, which had disappeared by the time I moved to Austin in the 1960s, intrigued me.

As a psychologist, the scant training I received in the history of mental health care had not indicated that such casual interaction between patients and the community could occur. Others were equally surprised. Carol Gibbs, assistant director of Community Relations for the hospital, read those early accounts and asked if I would be interested in preparing a history of the hospital. She offered to facilitate my access to all of the hospital's archival materials and to provide a list of potential interviewees from long-term and retired employees.

I accepted her offer and was able to reach more than fifty individuals from her list. They, in turn, provided additional names. Approximately 30 percent of those I contacted from this source declined to be interviewed.

In addition, I placed a notice in Jane Greig's popular column in the *Austin American-Statesman* requesting that anyone with knowledge of the hospital as either an employee, patient, or visitor contact me. This notice netted more than forty responses. Unlike the first group, those who responded to this request tended to be short-term employees, including students who had worked there while attending the University of Texas; people with childhood memories of the hospital, often those whose parents had worked there; and a few former patients.

To create as full a history as possible of daily life at Texas' first mental institution, I examined it from as many different angles as possible. Such an approach proved necessary, since former inhabitants' accounts of the asylum differed greatly in perspective and content depending upon these persons' status in "our little town," as some spoke of it. The Texas State Lunatic Asylum (later Austin State Hospital) was a complicated place, and patients, attendants, medical staff, superintendents, and neighborhood children playing on the grounds all offered important information to help explain the complex reality.

Consequently, in my attempt to recreate the daily life of the hospital, I studied patient records from the nineteenth century, minutes from staff meetings, the correspondence of various superintendents, staff memos, training manuals and films, superintendents' annual reports to the governors, reports of legislative investigations, newspaper accounts, transcripts of interviews with former employees, biographical sketches of superintendents, personal memoirs, and other histories of the institution. Oral history interviews, superintendents' reports, and a penetrating 1950s study by sociologist Ivan Belknap perhaps provided the most telling information, but no relevant sources were neglected.

In the account that follows, I try to present the viewpoints of the various groups associated with the hospital and at the same time to weave them into a portrait of the whole. Naturally, each of these groups had a somewhat different view of hospital life, but their combined perspectives allowed me to reconstruct a complex social history of the place.

In this study of the Texas asylum, I attempt to tell what life was like for the many thousands of people who lived and died there. A social history is always a mix of chronological and synchronic elements, and in this case two chronologically organized sections bracket an essentially synchronic core. My first and second chapters set the stage and follow the first twenty years of the asylum from 1861 to 1880, when it became overloaded with patients and heavily custodial. Likewise, the last chapter chronicles the period of rapid change that began during the 1960s and led to deinstitutionalization by the 1980s—the end of asylum.

However, the core chapters dealing with superintendents, medical staff, ward attendants, and patients are basically topical, and with good reason. For the better part of a century, superintendents, medical staff, modes of treatment, and patients came and went, but life in the wards and on the grounds went on much the same. Secure behind its fences, the self-contained world of the asylum cycled through its daily and yearly rounds and passed on its way largely unchanged. The experience of living and working in the asylum altered little until deinstitutionalization emptied its halls. Presently, the hospital houses fewer than three hundred inpatients. Most of its spacious grounds have been leased for commercial and residential development, and its historic administrative building is in dire need of restoration. By the time of my study, many of the hospital's records had been lost or destroyed, and much evidence resided only in living memory. Between 1994 and 1996, I conducted more than sixty oral history interviews with individuals who had been connected with the hospital in various capacities. Many of these people also shared with me their personal archives of information about the hospital, and their comments appear intact except for stylistic editing. Tapes of these interviews and other donated material now reside in the Austin–Travis County Collection of the Austin Public Library.

I would like to thank all of those who gave so generously of their time and materials. Especially, I want to thank Carol Gibbs for first suggesting the idea of a history of the hospital and for providing access to the hospital's files, films, and other archival records. She and Susan Adair, director of Community Relations, introduced me to other employees interested in the institution's history, such as Linda Campbell, director of Clinical Services, who provided me with much useful information; Marvin Chamberlain, the head of Maintenance, who arranged a meeting with several long-term employees; and Adolph Supak, assistant superintendent, who helped locate photographs. Virginia Meehan, director of Human Resources, and Woody Woodruff, a trainer in Human Resources, also shared old records from their department and directed me to many helpful sources. Pat Gooding, director of Personal Care, generously provided both childhood recollections and rare photographs. Austin State Hospital's superintendents Kenny Dudley and Diane Faucher facilitated my access to many of the institution's old records and were helpful in other ways as well.

Reference librarians at St. Edward's University, the Texas Research League, and Barker Texas History Center at the University of Texas were unfailingly helpful and patient. I particularly want to express my appreciation to the Austin History Center's director Biruta Kearl, who always graciously facilitates historical investigations, and to Clare Maxwell and Grace McEvoy of the Austin–Travis County Collection for their help in reproducing the photographs. Portions of this research were supported by a grant from the New College Faculty Development Fund of St. Edward's University.

I also wish to thank Joe Pearce for his insightful analysis of conditions at Austin State Hospital, for sharing his collection of materials concerning the hospital, and for a painstaking reading of the manuscript. Thad Sitton also read the manuscript, offered many good suggestions, and provided much-needed editorial assistance and encouragement. Any errors of fact or of interpretation are my own.

# Life at the Texas State Lunatic Asylum, 1857–1997

∞

# ⌁ CHAPTER I ⌁

# Introduction

*"The Cult of Curability"*

The asylum movement, which dominated mental health care in the United States for nearly a century, grew out of a belief that certain forms of mental illness could be cured if treated within an institution especially designed to provide a respite from the stresses of life. Proponents of this "cult of curability" maintained that a daily routine of exercise, social contact, and other structured activities in conjunction with a well-balanced diet, adequate rest, and attention to physical health could restore sanity.

Reformers such as Phillipe Pinel in France, William Tuke in England, and Benjamin Rush in America all encouraged humanitarian treatment of the mentally ill and reported remarkable effectiveness using this approach. Certainly, many reformers of the time came to believe in the possibility of controlling and even curing insanity. In his history *The Discovery of the Asylum,* David Rothman noted, "They would try to create—in a way reminiscent of the founders of utopian communities—a model society of their own, not to test a novel method for organizing production or making political decisions, but to exemplify the advantages of an orderly, regular, and disciplined routine."[1] While some modern social control theorists like Foucault and Scull argued that the controlling class created asylums to keep disruptive elements of society in line, others saw the asylum movement as growing out of nineteenth-century social utopianism and the pervasive evangelical belief in human perfectibility.[2]

The nineteenth-century reform movement to establish asylums such as the Texas State Lunatic Asylum grew out of this great optimism—the belief that under ideal conditions mental illness could be cured. In Texas, the asylum movement began with the authorization of the State Lunatic Asylum in 1856, and in many ways the history of this institution represented the history of national mental health care in microcosm. Certainly, asylums in other southern states, including the Alabama Insane Hospital, which, like Texas State Lunatic Asylum, opened in 1861, followed the same path from "cult of curability" to custodial institution.[3] Similarly, South Carolina's asylums "were influenced by avant-garde ideas of moral treatment and therapeutic optimism. The South Carolina Lunatic Asylum was intended to be a curative, not simply a custodial institution."[4]

From the beginning, the Texas State Lunatic Asylum followed national trends. After an extensive examination of other mental institutions, the Texas State Lunatic Asylum's first superintendent, J. C. Perry, recommended the adoption of architectural plans for the asylum developed by Thomas Kirkbride, the author of a leading text on insanity.[5] These plans mandated a central structure with wings on either side. The central portion of the Texas asylum was completed in 1861, and two wings were added in 1865.[6] Kirkbride designed asylums to provide a stress-free environment where individuals could regain their mental health away from the demands of work and family. Thus, the asylum's very architecture supposedly contributed to the restoration of sanity. At Austin, Texas, as at so many other places, elements of Kirkbride's social and architectural design for curing insanity through asylum lasted for more than a century.

Not only did the new optimism about the nature of mental illness and the possibility of curing it facilitate the growth of the asylum movement, but also the creation of the asylum itself influenced thinking about mental illness and its treatment. Historian Mary Ann Jimenez wrote, "The concept of madness became a widely available symbolic construction to explain a broad number of unacceptable and disturbing behaviors. In the same way, the creation of an institution specifically for the mad clearly influenced the perception of madness and the ideas of what should be done about it."[7] Thus, the emerging belief in the curability of insanity led to the creation of asylums to provide the best setting for its treatment, and the existence of the asylum led to the expectation that most people manifesting signs of insanity should be housed there. In time the earlier belief in curability faded, but the expectation remained that the asylum was the appropriate site for care of the insane. Other factors that contributed to the growth of asylums included the need to provide care for the aging poor—a role that almshouses could no longer fill as the numbers of indigent elderly increased.[8]

The Texas State Lunatic Asylum opened its doors in 1861 with the expectation of curing Texans afflicted with mental illness and sending them back to their communities. As time passed, however, various forces operated to turn the asylum into a permanent home where many patients lived out their entire lives. Frequently, asylum staff and their families also became permanent residents, and many had family connections to the asylum extending back several generations. Together, patients, staff, and their families created a complex society that endured for decades.

As overcrowding and underfunding caused most asylums, later called "mental hospitals," to assume a mainly custodial role, the belief that sufferers of mental illness would be cured waned. Nevertheless, most continued to regard mental institutions as appropriate sites for treatment of mental illness until the middle of the twentieth century. At that time, critics began to argue that such institutions did not work and could not be made to work. In recent years, this negative viewpoint, which culminated in massive "deinstitutionalization" of tens of thousands of persons from mental hospitals across the country, has dominated the perception of these institutions.

Certainly, many aspects of life in the asylum merited reform. However, accounts of this life are not uniformly negative. Participants in a multifaceted social organization, such as a mental hospital, experience different realities depending upon their roles in the institution. Consequently, the accounts of employees' children who grew up on the hospital grounds, or those of former residents of the back wards, or of the hospital's superintendent all contribute to our understanding of the complex culture of the place. As did the blind men touching the elephant in the old parable, the various memorists simply had hold of different parts of the same complicated animal.

Throughout its history, many found it difficult to be objective about the asylum. In addition to differing perspectives, a desire to change the status quo often colored the accounts of asylum residents and observers. Former mental patients' accounts, such as Clifford Beers's memoir, *A Mind That Found Itself,* and Mary Jane Ward's novel, *The Snake Pit,* a fictionalized version of her life in a New York mental hospital, focused on aspects of institutional life needing reform and frequently succeeded in galvanizing public and governmental opinion to that end. Similarly, reform writings of the 1940s, such as Albert Deutsch's *Shame of the States* and Edith Stern's "Our Ailing Mental Hospitals," succeeded in directing public opinion to the need for change in state mental institutions and ultimately in legislation creating community mental health centers.[9] The National Mental Health Act passed in 1946 paved the way for reform of mental health care.

The reform movement gained momentum in Texas as well. At the request of Governor Allan Shivers, journalists Bill Brammer, Bert Kruger Smith, and others visited the state's mental institutions during the early

1950s and wrote about the sometimes dreadful conditions they encountered. Their efforts resulted first in greater state funding for the hospitals and later in a shift to a community-based care system and the deinstitutionalization of thousands of Texans.

Likewise, sociological analyses of mental institutions, such as Erving Goffman's *Asylums*, based on his fieldwork at an asylum in Washington, D.C., and Ivan Belknap's *Human Problems of a State Mental Hospital*, which dealt with the Austin State Hospital (ASH), also adopted unfavorable perspectives. However, as Belknap himself admitted, this perspective was far from the whole story. He wrote: "The negative tone of this report has resulted from the fact that I have taken as a point of departure the persistence of certain major problems in state hospitals' social organization. Another selection of materials might have given a more cheerful or constructive picture of Southern State Hospital [ASH]."[10]

As Belknap noted, other interpretations were possible. Reformers' focus on the problems faced by mental institutions in providing adequate care for patients and the difficulty in curing mental illness created the climate in which change could occur. But these reformers' writings did not tell the full story about the experience of life in a mental hospital and in some instances may even have distorted it.

Changing professional beliefs also colored views of the asylum. During the 142 years since the establishment of Texas' first asylum for the care of the mentally ill, the legal, medical, economic, bureaucratic, sociological, and psychological aspects of the treatment of mental illness all have changed, some of them several times. In truth, the very definition of mental illness changes with each new edition of the *Diagnostic and Statistical Manual* of the American Psychiatric Association; old conditions, such as epilepsy, disappear from the list of mental illnesses, while new ones, such as passive-aggressive personality disorder, are added.

As Mary Ann Jimenez has noted, in some ways our present system of treatment for the mentally ill shares more with colonial America than with the asylum movement of the nineteenth century, which brought the great public mental hospitals into being.[11] Like early Americans, we accept more freedom of movement for the mentally ill and see less need to "institutionalize" them away. Colonial Americans viewed insanity as God's will, which no human had the ability or the right to change. As long as the insane did not harm themselves or others, they were tolerated and provided for by their families and their communities. Of course, then as now, economics played a role in mental health care, with communities and families often readily agreeing for the state to assume responsibility for the care of the insane.

By the mid-1990s, however, the emphasis on community mental health care and outpatient treatment, or deinstitutionalization, had nearly emptied the halls of the state hospitals. Former patients had been discharged and persons who would have been admitted in the past were "deflected" to community centers. As Leona Bachrach noted, the concept of deinstitutionalization is multifaceted, consisting not only of depopulation of mental hospitals but also deflection and decentralization of care.[12] Under this policy, the inpatient population at ASH shrank to about three hundred, down from a maximum of over three thousand in the early 1960s. Most medical services were "outsourced," and few mental patients strolled on the institution's grounds or ate in the dining halls. For all practical purposes, the centralized, residential, state mental hospital, as created through the asylum movement, had disappeared.

By 1990, the historical evidence about the asylum's century-old experiment in mental health care in Texas resided chiefly in terse medical records, the repetitive annual reports of superintendents, and the fragile memories of those who had resided or worked there. Increasingly, the story of the rise and fall of the asylum is of more than historical interest, and the accounts of former patients and staff should be heard. The long debate about how to care for the mentally ill still seems far from resolved. Just as the asylum did not always succeed in treating mental illness, neither has the community mental health care system that replaced it enjoyed universal success. At the national level, some have even termed it "the shame of the streets."[13]

Critics look at the large percentage of the homeless who suffer from substance abuse and/or mental illness and point to the political and economic complexities of managed care programs, which often leave the most seriously and chronically ill underserved, and to the increased incarceration of the mentally ill in jails or prisons ill-equipped to care for them. Meanwhile, the number of state hospital beds for the mentally ill continues to decline.[14]

As in other areas where social problems are both complex and intractable, trends in mental health care have tended to cycle back and forth between extremes, and some observers now see the pendulum swinging back toward greater centralization. It seems important, therefore, to review the asylum and record not only the failures of the institution but also its successes.

The reexamination of the asylum has already begun,[15] but the task presents daunting obstacles. State hospitals such as the Texas State Lunatic Asylum were complex and deceptive institutions where the "formal structure" of rules, regulations, and chain of command often did not closely correspond to the day-to-day experiences of patients and staff. While critics have noted that mental institutions were characterized by great imbalances of power, as in any complex society, the daily interactions between asylum members, including patients and various levels of the institution's hierarchy, did not always follow rigid status distinctions. As historian Gerald Grob commented regarding life in asylums, "Inarticulate and lower-class groups exercise agency; hegemonic control by elite is rarely complete or absolute."[16] And even Erving Goffman, whose critical account of the "total institution" greatly influenced thinking about mental institutions, wrote at length about patient "underlife" at the institutions he observed—traditions of outlaw behavior whereby inmates asserted personal autonomy in defiance of institutional controls. In fact, Goffman noted that patient underlife, as well as that practiced by lower-level staff, sometimes turned out to be the most meaningful reality of the place. At Austin State Hospital, for example, sociologist Ivan Belknap discovered that at ward level an informal league of attendants and minimally impaired patients made most of the decisions that determined the day-to-day realities of the actual experience of hospital life.[17]

Many former residents and employees recalled the Austin State Hospital as "our little town," and, as in any community of several thousand, life brought joy and satisfaction as well as heartbreak and misery. For about a third of those admitted, the asylum experience succeeded, and they were discharged as cured. In addition, certain vocational rehabilitation programs succeeded in teaching skills that resulted in jobs and independence for some. For others, those more severely or permanently afflicted, the protected environment allowed them to live out their lives with almost normal functioning that would have been impossible in the complex society outside the institution. Former California mental patient Priscilla Allen explained to the California Select Committee on Proposed Phasing Out of Hospital Services in 1973: "For many of these individuals the community [outside] was a threat to their very existence. In a hospital setting, on the other hand, patients are able to participate in a scaled-down, less threatening semi-community. They 'go to the bank' (the trust office), eat in a restaurant (the canteen), attend 'town meetings' where it is possible to exchange ideas with the administrators of the hospital, go to the post office, attend dances, attend various churches, and hold jobs."[18]

Other asylum residents for whom there was only scant hope of improvement—the senile and the brain damaged—sometimes benefited from the custodial care provided by the institution. Certainly, by the 1940s state hospitals needed reform, but reviewing only the reformers' writing leaves an incomplete portrait of life in the mental institution, which for some patients fulfilled its early promise of asylum.

As elsewhere in the United States, the ultimate downfall of the Texas asylum stemmed from administrators' inability to limit the population to those thought to benefit most from the asylum experience (the newly disturbed), from a chronic lack of funding, and, at the end, from changing professional approaches to defining and treating mental illness. Under-staffed, underfunded, and overpopulated, the asylum became a holding area for a wide variety of ill and disabled persons. And once it devolved into a custodial institution, critics could offer valid arguments that the asylum's very social organization impeded patients' improvement and that the only solution was to shift to community-based mental health care.

# ~ CHAPTER 2 ~

# Origins

## *"In a Beautiful Grove of Live Oaks"*

The Texas Constitution of 1845 formally committed the new state to provide hospital treatment for insane Texans unable to afford it for themselves. However, it was 1856 before Governor Elisha Pease signed a bill passed by the Sixth Texas Legislature to establish the Texas State Lunatic Asylum in Austin.[1] The term "lunatic asylum," commonly used to designate such institutions, reflected the prevailing view that the moon ("luna" in Latin) influenced the mind and caused madness. Thus, mental illness became lunacy and those afflicted, lunatics. This notion has now been thoroughly discredited by research, but at the time, lunacy was the customary term for mental illness.[2]

Prior to the construction of the state's first asylum, mentally ill Texans had been maintained at home or, if dangerous, incarcerated in local jails. Unlike many states, Texas had few almshouses for paupers. As David Rothman pointed out, it was the inability of the mentally ill to support themselves, rather than any distinctive trait of insanity, that drew the attention of local authorities. He wrote, "The lunatic came to public attention not as someone afflicted with delusions or fears, but as someone suffering from poverty." Before the beginning of the asylum movement, most of the mentally ill mingled freely with the rest of society. In Massachusetts, wrote Mary Ann Jimenez, "The insane were as a rule not confined but were largely left alone to live out their lives with little interference."[3] Only if dangerous or uncontrollable were they placed in an institution. Similarly, in Texas the mentally ill had much freedom of movement, and many of them spent their days wandering the streets.

At first, many, but certainly not all of the state's mentally ill, were housed at the Texas State Lunatic Asylum. In Austin, as elsewhere, some of the mentally ill continued to roam the streets. Local attorney George Shelley recalled that in the 1890s an old man called Damos "wandered the streets of the city from morning until night, and perhaps then also."[4] Shelley concluded that the man "was doubtless demented" but commented that the local citizenry regarded him more as an object of pity and charity rather than someone who needed to be sent to the asylum. Perhaps Damos had no family to commit him, and as long as he did not run afoul of the law, he maintained his freedom. Certainly, most of the admissions to the State Lunatic Asylum were initiated by family members or the local sheriffs. Few involved voluntary commitment.[5]

Most Texans were well aware of the option of committing their loved ones to the asylum. For over sixty years, until the name was officially changed to the Austin State Hospital in 1925, the letters "SLA" boldly marked the institution's property. Before this change, a person's name and SLA were sufficient to ensure delivery of a penny postcard from anywhere in the state.

In fact, many local residents continued to refer to the institution as "the insane asylum" or simply "the asylum" long after the name changed. Formal terminology for mental institutions had shifted shortly after Texas opened its second facility at Terrell in July 1885. The North Texas Lunatic Asylum became the North Texas Hospital for the Insane in 1887. However, it was not until 1924 that a state-wide study recommended similar name changes for all Texas's asylums.[6]

The term "asylum" had important implications for the treatment of mental illness since it implied a place of safety away from the cares and responsibilities of everyday life. In the United States and elsewhere, the asylum movement advocated reforms for more humane treatment of the mentally ill, using compassion in place of the physical abuse of jails, poor houses, and life on the streets. This movement stressed that the chaos of mental illness could be controlled by the imposition of order and routine on the patient's life in calm and pleasant surroundings. And it asserted that, if treated early enough, insanity could be cured.

Mid–nineteenth century Texas physicians knew of the reforms and sought to establish an asylum based on these ideals for the treatment of mental illness. The first order of business was to select an appropriate construction site. In 1851, the Association of Medical Superintendents of American Institutions for the Insane (the forerunner of the American Psychiatric Association) had adopted a set of twenty-six standards regarding the location and construction of asylums, and in 1857 Dr. J. C. Perry, an Austin physician who became the Texas asylum's first superintendent, appointed to oversee the asylum's planning and construction, appended these to his first annual report to Governor Pease. Standard One stated, "Every hospital for the insane should be in the country, not within less than two miles of a large town, and easily accessible at all seasons."[7] The country environment would provide quietude and removal from the stress of urban living, while proximity to town would ensure ease of provisioning and access for visitors.

According to Standard Two, "No hospital for the insane, however limited its capacity, should have less than fifty acres of land devoted to gardens and pleasure gardens for its patients. At least one hundred acres should be possessed by every State Hospital, or other institution, for two hundred patients, to which number these propositions apply, unless otherwise mentioned."[8]

Governor Pease appointed three commissioners—Samuel Bogart of Collin County, E. T. Branch of Liberty County, and C. R. Johns of Hays County—to locate a site close to Austin that met these requirements and further stipulated that the land not cost more than five dollars per acre.[9] Early in 1857, the state purchased 380 acres of land, located two miles north of the capitol building from William Fields of Galveston for the sum of twenty-five hundred dollars. The Tonkawa, Lipan Apache, and Comanche, who had formerly camped at the site, moved west shortly after construction of the new asylum began, although a few remained in the vicinity and hired themselves out as day laborers to help dig the steam tunnels.[10]

Superintendent Perry described the asylum's location in his initial report to Governor Pease: "The grounds have been surveyed and enclosed with a substantial cedar fence. The two-thirds of the tract, now covered with post-oaks and underbrush, afford the area usually reserved for pleasure grounds and for ornamental purposes. The sandy absorbent nature of the soil peculiarly adapts it to these uses, and should insure the salubrity of the site; while the natural growth properly trimmed, will give cheerfulness to the view, and yield grateful protection from the sun."[11]

Superintendent Dr. Beriah Graham, a graduate of Transylvania and St. Louis Medical College, prefaced his 1869 report to Governor Pease with a portrait of the site. "The institution is situated upon a slight elevation, about two and a half miles north of Austin city; upon the south and surrounding it, is a beautiful grove of live oaks, and west is a range of mountains covered with evergreen, while north and east of it stretches the broad prairie."[12] Forty-five years later, Superintendent John Preston embellished this description in the "Prosperity Edition" of the local paper: "There is a chain of hills which makes a beautiful purplish background for the intervening fields in various shades of green and gold."[13]

*Dr. Beriah Graham served as superintendent of the State
Lunatic Asylum twice in the 1860s. Courtesy ASH*

The idea that a beautiful location could have curative power derived from
the new moral treatment for insanity, which emphasized kindness instead
of coercion and a daily routine incorporating social contact, exercise, and
productive labor. Walking in a pleasure garden provided both exercise and
social contact, and in general the ordered life of an asylum facilitated moral
treatment.

This approach to the treatment of mental illness contrasted sharply with
older approaches, which were based on the theory of demonic possession
and had included flogging or immersion in cold water in an attempt to make
the body undesirable to the demon. Even after most people no longer accepted demonic possession as a cause of mental illness, the notion of mas-

tering madness by aggressive tactics persisted, and treatments involving the use of powerful purgatives, starvation, leeching, and physical restraints continued.[14] British asylums used less restraint, a circumstance that Dr. Isaac Ray, superintendent of the Maine Insane Asylum, attributed to the "different style of manners existing in European society."[15] Although committed to the new moral treatment, early superintendents at the Texas asylum continued to resort to some of the older methods of restraint and punishment. Restraint chairs, iron handcuffs, locked boxes, cold showers, plunge baths, and other holdovers from the days of belief in demonic possession were not abolished until 1871, after Dr. T. F. Weiselberg became superintendent. To accommodate violent inmates, Weiselberg added a room padded with cotton and lined with sailcloth.[16]

Reformers believing in moral treatment asserted that mental illness could be cured in a humanely run asylum. In fact, some early reports indicated that moral treatment enjoyed incredible success. At Worcester State Hospital in Massachusetts, for example, the discharge rate reported for recently diagnosed patients was 71 percent.[17] However, some contemporary authorities questioned the method for calculating recovery rates. Dr. Pliny Earle, in a paper delivered to the New England Psychological Society in 1876, noted that statistics for the Friends' Asylum at Frankford, Pennsylvania, indicated an average of more than three recoveries to each person, and one person had recovered fifteen times. By Earle's reckoning, the actual recovery rate at Worcester for 1871–75 was only 29.75 percent.[18] It is unclear if these data apply only to recently diagnosed persons.

Doctors agreed that certain conditions had to be met to optimize the possibility of cure. First, the diagnosis of mental illness and the onset of treatment needed to occur quickly. Most believed that the majority of cures were accomplished during the first year. Superintendent Perry and many of his successors attested to the need for prompt treatment. "For want of timely attention," Perry wrote in 1857, "many a useful mind will sink into hopeless imbecility." Second, the treatment of mental illness needed to occur in an asylum. Perry continued, "For it is well ascertained that a far greater proportion of insane recover in Asylums, where every means of treatment is provided than at home, where the original exciting causes and associations continue."[19]

By the mid–nineteenth century, reformers firmly believed that the architectural designs of asylums strongly affected the rates of cure. Dr. Isaac Ray toured the great asylums of Europe and reported, "Probably no better style can be used for the construction of hospitals for the insane, than the

Tudor-Gothic, or the style used for domestic purposes in the time of Elizabeth." He admired the variety of form and size of doors and windows, which allowed for the regulation of air and light, as well as its "comparatively trifling expense."[20]

So popular was the "linear plan" devised by Dr. Thomas Kirkbride of Pennsylvania that it became known as the American plan for mental institutions. In deciding on the specifications for the Texas State Lunatic Asylum, Superintendent Perry consulted several national experts in the field including Dr. Kirkbride, whose "moral architecture," or linear plan, was ultimately adopted for the new asylum. Perry's report of 1857 noted:

> All standard American and European authorities have been consulted. In matters where my personal experience was at fault, advice has been attained from more experienced members of the Speciality; to whom our warmest thanks are due for the interest they have manifested in the success of the enterprise—for their hospitality and polite attentions—for their promptness to afford every facility for examining their buildings and readiness to point out deficit, and the means by which they are to be avoided.[21]

The difficulties inherent in mid–nineteenth-century travel illustrate Perry's commitment to securing the best plans for the asylum. Since the railroad did not reach Austin until 1872, Perry's travels included a stagecoach ride to the port of Galveston and then, if visiting East Coast asylums, a journey on a sailing ship; to view midwestern destinations, he traveled by packet boat across to New Orleans in order to connect with a steamboat headed up the Mississippi.

The Kirkbride plan addressed not only the mental health of patients but also their physical health, comfort, and safety. A major consideration for the site was the availability of water. According to Standard Three, endorsed by the Association of Medical Superintendents of American Institutions for the Insane (AMSAII), of which Kirkbride was perhaps the most influential member, "Means should be provided to raise ten thousand gallons of water daily to reservoirs that will supply the highest part of the building." Doubtless one of the attractions of the Texas asylum site was the presence of ample water. As Perry described, "The spring has not failed during the recent unprecedented drouth; and from indications it is thought that other sources can be opened near, and that water can be procured by wells at little depth, on other parts of the grounds, so as to afford a more plentiful supply if it should ever be required."[22] This prediction proved accurate, and later several artesian wells were dug on the property, including one whose sulphurous water was unfit to drink but which later supplied the asylum's natatorium, one of the first indoor swimming pools in Texas. The institution's autonomous water system proved especially fortunate in April 1900, when Austin's MacDonald Dam on the Colorado River broke, leaving the city without a public water supply.[23]

Properly maintained asylums needed copious water, not only for drinking and cleaning but also for steam heating (viewed as the safest means of warming an asylum) and for the water closets, a recent innovation in sanitation. Like any new technology, the early water closets had their problems. In 1866, five years after the opening of the asylum, Superintendent Beriah Graham reported:

> The water closets were, and still are also in a very defective state; the sewers are entirely too small, and there are no pipes to convey the water necessary to clean the waste pipes; it is therefore necessary to carry all the water required for this purpose by hand, in buckets, thereby causing much additional labor. Unless the utmost precaution is constantly paid to the cleansing of these pipes the liquid contents will gradually ooze through the floor and ceiling, causing great injury and inconvenience.[24]

Similarly, successive superintendents detailed difficulties with the pipes. Both Superintendent D. R. Wallace's report for 1878 and Dr. L. J. Graham's report for 1882 noted continuing problems with toilets and sewer lines. In 1882, for example, Graham wrote, "The pipes from the water-closets frequently become obstructed, filling up with filth, giving out offensive gasses, and thus increasing the danger of sickness and death." Apparently, builders of the Austin asylum had failed to fully implement Kirkbride's 1854 admonitions that water closets should be constructed of sturdy materials, be simply arranged, and have a "strong downward ventilation connected with them."[25]

Like sanitation, adequate ventilation presented a major concern for asylum designers at a time when several diseases were thought to result from "bad air." The Kirkbride plan stipulated, "A complete system of forced ventilation, in connection with the heating is indispensable to give purity to the air of a hospital for the insane, and no expense that is required to effect this object thoroughly can be deemed either misplaced or injudicious." Superintendent Perry fully agreed, noting that "Without proper natural and forced ventilation, dysentery and typhoid fever, the peculiar diseases of this country, and the scourges of hospitals and asylums everywhere, would soon make ours an opprobrium to the State."[26]

To ensure adequate ventilation, the design for the State Lunatic Asylum incorporated wide hallways, high ceilings, and large windows and transoms. Builders installed a system of flues in the corridor walls that connected with all the rooms and allowed for the "escape of air rendered foul by respiration or otherwise."[27]

More than northern institutions, the Austin asylum relied on good ventilation for cooling in the summer. To this end, builders included a second system of flues to introduce "cold air impelled by the fan, when necessary."[28] The use of local limestone for building construction resulted in a cheap, strong structure that offered some protection against the area's torrid summer heat.

Another advantage of the limestone lay in its being fireproof. Kirkbride had insisted that all asylums "be constructed of stone or brick, have slate or metallic roofs, and as far as possible be made secure from accidents by fire." The threat of fire dictated that asylum stairways be constructed of iron, stone, or other nonflammable material and that gas lighting be used instead of candles or other sources of open flames. In fact, Perry noted in 1857 that one of the advantages of steam heat was that steam worked better than water for extinguishing fires; it had recently allowed the wings of the New York State Asylum to be saved while the central portion of the building burned.[29]

Reformers believed that besides its importance for patients' safety and comfort, the design of the asylum provided direct therapeutic benefit. Hence, designers of the State Lunatic Asylum took care to locate buildings to ensure attractive views of natural settings. However, while the Texas State Lunatic Asylum offered pleasant vistas of stately live oaks and inviting pathways, the main building afforded a clear view of the patients' cemetery until the mid-1880s, when Superintendent A. N. Denton moved it well north of the asylum.[30]

Improvements of the Austin asylum grounds began under the administration of Dr. W. W. Reeves in 1891 and culminated with the creation of six hundred yards of gravelled drives and a chain of "artistic" lakes and lily ponds on the site of a former dump south of the main building.[31] Arthur James Seiders, superintendent of Grounds in the 1890s, supervised the creation of the new landscape. His daughter Myrtle Cuthbertson recalled: "There were many beautiful oak trees on the property but very little had

*The lawn in front of the women's dormitory offered a pleasant place to visit.*
*Pica 04375. Courtesy AHC*

been done to improve the landscape. The southeast corner, an area of about two acres, was practically a swamp; there were some small springs originating a little further north making more or less a gully running down to the southeast corner." Using patient labor, Seiders excavated this natural drainage, planting Bermuda grass on the berms created with the excess soil. The chain of lakes began with a lily pond ornamented with water lilies so large they could support the weight of a six-year-old child.[32] In time, smaller lakes flowed southeasterly into a much larger lake, approximately two hundred yards long by fifty feet wide, lying "like a huge mirror in the southern extremity of the park." Decorative bridges of native cedar in a latticework design linked the smaller lakes into a chain. The lake's beauty inspired Superintendent Preston to write, "[the] rustic bridges, odd shrubbery and smooth patches of lawn enclosed by tall grasses and vine-covered trees all give it the effect of a Japanese garden, and its tiny islands and smooth grassy banks fringed with willows and shrubs make it a most inviting spot. . . . In early spring the gentle slopes about it are sprinkled with bluebonnets, rain lilies and other Texas wild flowers, which rival in beauty the formal flower beds near the buildings."[33]

Not only did the patients benefit from being "marched out around the lakes and then allowed to sit for an hour or so under the oak trees," but the townspeople of Austin soon enjoyed the new landscape as well.[34] The asylum grounds became a preferred destination for Sunday afternoon carriage drives out from town. The resortlike setting continued across the road from the asylum at the new suburb of Hyde Park, which boasted another lake and a large wooden dance pavilion.

Courting couples especially enjoyed visiting the asylum grounds, and many local children liked to relate that their mothers and fathers had met at the State Lunatic Asylum. Driving around the well-kept gravel roads, walking the paths, or even rowing out to one of the islands in the lake provided an afternoon's pleasure. Many visitors brought along a camera for a "kodaking" party, taking photographs of friends enjoying themselves and being photographed in turn.

At the time, the permeable boundaries of the asylum encouraged intermingling of townspeople and those residents of the asylum who were well enough to walk on the grounds. Public opinion of the asylum, as reflected in local newspapers, was quite favorable, and asylum officials had little reason to fear negative public reaction.

Emphasizing the therapeutic benefit of the attractive settings, Kirkbride stated that each patient's room was to have a window, and while pleasure gardens (and asylum perimeters) could be fenced, the fences were never to be "unpleasantly visible from the building."[35] Because of Kirkbride's belief in the importance of pleasant vistas, he stipulated that patients never be housed underground. Additionally, rooms for single patients must never be less than eight feet by ten feet and the ceilings never less than twelve feet high. He recommended that the wooden floors slope toward the door to allow ease of cleaning. Similarly, walls were to be of the hardest plaster to allow scrubbing. He wrote that each ward "should have in it a parlor, a corridor, single lodging rooms for patients, an associated dormitory, communicating with a chamber for two attendants; two clothes rooms, a bath room, a water closet, a dining room, a dumb waiter, and a speaking tube, leading to the kitchen or other central part of the building."[36]

The asylum's ward system required segregation not only by sex but also by type and severity of illness. Kirkbride thought there should be sixteen wards, eight for each sex, to accommodate a maximum patient population of two hundred. However, seven years after the Texas asylum opened, Superintendent Beriah Graham reported that only one quarter of the buildings in the original plan had been completed. He wrote, "These present buildings cannot afford accommodation for more than 60 to 70 patients

*Courting couples of the 1890s frequently visited the grounds of the asylum,
landscaped by Arthur James Seiders. Pica 06687. Courtesy AHC*

including a detached building. This constitutes one ward in which we keep
ten male patients; there is one ward for males in the main building and
two for females." He noted that this shortage of space prevented classification "in a manner to promote comfort and recovery." He also lamented
the poor accommodations for the asylum's three black patients, who were
housed in the basement of the main building.[37]

Mid–nineteenth-century classification of mental patients emphasized
practicalities and distinguished the "quiet" from the "noisy insane" and the
"clean" from the "filthy insane." Kirkbride recommended placing the noisy
or filthy insane on the first floor at the ends of the wings and the "better"
patients on the top floor near the center to separate them as much as possible.[38] The problem was noise. Describing two nineteenth-century New
York asylums, Ellen Dwyer commented: "Patients could be forced to retire by mid-evening, but not to sleep. Screams, noisy songs and loud ob-
scenities filled the night air, despite vocal complaints from quieter patients."
Similarly, the table manners of some patients were less than fastidious. "A

common sort of dinner companion, declared one Utica patient, was the hungry man with 'long, lank lantern-jaws' who gobbled all the food in sight. After finishing, he blew his nose between 'splashy digits[,] strangers to pocket handkerchiefs' and then used his fork to pick his teeth."[39]

Early superintendents took pains to convince the relatives of the "better class" of patients that the ward system would prevent their kin from associating with the lower sort of insane. In the nineteenth-century South, segregation in the wards also extended to race. Although there was nothing in the legislation to prevent admission of black patients to the asylum, Dr. Perry noted in his 1857 report that, as a matter of practicality, "Until the building is extended, or some suitable out-building erected, (as the plan adopted contemplates), the admission of blacks and idiots will be attended with considerable inconvenience and annoyance. We could not separate the negroes from the whites, and anything like a close association must be productive of general complaint."[40]

Certainly, violent inmates had to be isolated from others. Even reformers such as Dr. Weiselberg, who wanted to rid the asylum of all forms of restraint, recognized this need. During his superintendency he repaired a jaillike structure at the Austin asylum known as "the Cross Place, a build-

*Children enjoyed playing on the grounds of the asylum, especially rowing to one of the small islands in the lake. Pica 06685. Courtesy AHC*

*The men's ward contained the high ceilings and hard plaster walls recommended by Dr. Thomas Kirkbride, designer of "the linear plan" for mental institutions of the nineteenth century. Courtesy AHC*

ing where 12 or more violent patients were kept." In 1879, Superintendent M. E. Saunders enlarged the Cross Place to house sixty more patients.[41]

For moral treatment to work effectively, Kirkbride thought ward size needed to be limited to twelve to fifteen patients and to exclude those with incurable disorders, such as mental retardation or senility. As Perry stated, "The first object of a Lunatic Asylum is the *cure* of the insane; but there will not be room in ours for the curables, much less for idiots, who are incurable; and who, by their intractability, filthy habits and evil example, will interfere with the enforcement of proper discipline, and derange the order and *morale* of the whole establishment."[42]

To determine the number of Texans who might qualify for residence in the new asylum, Perry cited the 1850 U.S. Census data, which indicated that there were precisely 141 insane persons in Texas. Taking into account the population growth during the next seven years, he projected that in 1857 insane Texans would number 352. However, Perry believed that these numbers were inaccurate due to the common confounding of mental illness and retardation. To get a more accurate estimate of the population of "curable" insane, he consulted all county officials and many doctors across the state and received information from 79 counties of the 126 surveyed. While noting the problem of missing data, he concluded from the information in hand that there were 88 idiots and 145 insane persons in the responding counties.[43] To keep the numbers of admissions within optimal limits, a quota system was imposed, restricting each of the state's thirty senatorial districts to two patients each.[44]

As the construction of the Texas asylum continued, local newspapers reported on its progress. "This building is going up gradually and substantially," the *State Gazette* noted. "The building contractors appear to be doing their duty. Capt. Glasscock has left for the North to procure necessary iron and other material for this edifice."[45]

By March 1861, workers completed the first section of the building, much to the satisfaction of an Austin reporter, who enthused, "It was our pleasure to examine the magnificent building from cellar to garret, and we must confess we view it as far superior edifice of the kind that we ever saw." The State Lunatic Asylum officially opened on March 11, 1861, with twelve patients. Budgetary constraints later prevented completion of the original plan, and by the time that funds again became available, opinions had changed; the cottage plan for asylum buildings had gained popularity and replaced the monolithical notions of Kirkbride.[46]

In spite of Dr. Perry's insistence on the need for speedy treatment and the priority of treating the curable, patient records from the period indicate that several of the very first patients had long-standing symptoms of mental illness. One man, for instance, had been diagnosed two years previously with chronic mania caused by "disappointed pride." Frederica Schmidt, admitted on July 6, 1861, and possibly the asylum's first female patient, suffered chronic dementia for twenty-one years. Schmidt's condition failed to improve under moral treatment, and when she died at the asylum twenty-five years later a physician, Dr. J. T. Wilson, wrote a poem commemorating the woman who had arrived:

> *Beneath the burning rays of a memorable July sun,*
> *In that well remembered year of 1861,*
> *She came with glaring eyes, and wild disheveled hair,*
> *With shout and shriek, she essayed a maddening air;*
> *To bide within these walls no one could know how long,*
> *To mingle with the desolate, to join the madman's song;*
> *Full five and twenty years, long, weary, changing years.*

Patient records from the 1860s noted various causes for commitment, including an eighteen-year-old man admitted on September 1, 1862, who had been diagnosed with acute mania caused by masturbation; another man with acute mania caused by disappointment in love; and a thirty-seven-year-old minister's wife with melancholia caused by deranged menstruation. Asked at the close of the Civil War if the war had influenced the number and causes of cases of insanity, Superintendent Graham responded: "In reply I would briefly say that the most distinguished writers upon these subjects agree that mental disorders receive a marked impetus from the cause above alluded to. Thousands of persons have been driven from their homes in poverty and distress; family ties have been rudely sundered; domestic afflictions of every kind have been suffered; what causes let me ask, more potent than these to drive the mind from a normal condition?"[47] In truth, during the 1860s many of the causes listed for the State Lunatic Asylum's patients' insanity were "the war," "fright from soldiers," and "marauding soldiers."

While acknowledging the role of the environment, most professionals concerned with mental health in the nineteenth century believed that a physical disorder of the brain contributed to insanity. As Superintendent J. A. Corley stated in his report of 1870, "On all hands it is admitted that the manifestations of mind take place through the nervous system; and that its derangements are the result of nervous disease, amenable to the same method of investigation as other nervous diseases." And while the precipitating cause might be "religious excitement, solitary habit, bad health, general dissipation and excessive venery, syphilis, epilepsy, uterine trouble, change of scene, irregular habits," or twenty other categories listed in Superintendent D. R. Wallace's annual report for 1878, and, while the symptoms might be alleviated by treatment with opium, morphine, hyoscyamin, chloral hydrate, or other sedatives, most experts of the time agreed that the best chance to cure insanity was through moral treatment.[48]

In addition to a calm, pleasant environment, moral treatment required the establishment of a precise routine to regulate patients' lives. At the Pennsylvania hospital where Thomas Kirkbride was superintendent, patients rose promptly at 5:00 A.M., received their medicines at 6:00, and ate breakfast at 6:30. After an 8:00 A.M. physical examination, they turned to work or some other form of exercise. At 12:30 P.M. they ate their main meal and then resumed work; at 6:00 P.M. they had "tea"; by 9:30 P.M. they went to bed.[49]

The routine at the Texas State Lunatic Asylum closely resembled that of other state asylums in the 1860s. According to the *By-laws, Rules and Regulations for the Government of the Texas State Lunatic Asylum* published in 1861:

"The morning bell shall be rung at half past four o'clock A.M. in May, June, July, and August. At five o'clock A.M. in March, April, September, and October and Half past five o'clock A.M. in November, December, January and February. Breakfast must always be placed on the table within two hours after the ringing of the morning bell. Dinner will be served at 12 M. and Tea at six P.M." As soon as the morning bell rang, attendants began their duties, seeing that each patient was "thoroughly washed, hair combed, clothes brushed and cleaned if necessary; collars, wristbands &c buttoned and all parts of dress properly adjusted, boots and shoes cleaned and the latter tied and in short that all parts of the patient's dress are neat and in good repair."[50]

Moral treatment also stipulated that the patient's day be filled with healthy activity. However, while male patients might report to work in the gardens for the day, the opportunity for healthy activities at the Texas asylum were limited. Dr. Beriah Graham, who served as superintendent twice in one decade, noted in his 1866 report to Governor J. W. Throckmorton that:

> Some additional facilities for the amusement of the patients should at least be added. Such useful employments as are calculated to exercise, and develop at once, the mental and physical powers, are of the highest advantage to the insane. Our vegetable and flower gardens afford us the only occupation of this kind. Amusements and entertainments exert a most happy influence upon the insane, causing them for a time to forget their melancholy thoughts and harassing emotions. Anything which can fix the attention of the mind, to the exclusion of morbid ideas, may be a means of its restoration to health.[51]

Many who worked with the mentally ill believed that they benefitted from productive work. In her book *Masters of Madness,* historian Constance M. McGovern noted: "Doctors believed that it not only diverted the mind and exercised the body but also instilled a sense of discipline and accomplishment. Thus Friends' Asylum required the male patients to work for three to four hours on the asylum farm each day and the women to participate in the household chores. Gardening, the sawing of wood, carpentry, and the making of embroidery, sewing, knitting and work in the laundry room for women." Kirkbride went so far as to recommend plain interior decoration of the wards, since "Monotony of the parlors and halls would lead patients to regard work as a welcome diversion, a privilege and not a punishment."[52]

British hospitals provided additional incentives. Dr. Isaac Ray, following his 1846 tour of the major asylums in Europe, reported:

> In many of the foreign asylums, the patients receive a certain proportion of the proceeds of their labor, and in Great Britain, it is an almost, if not universal practice, to give those who labor an extra allowance of beer and tobacco, and this is a sufficient inducement to bring out most of those who are able to labor. I have no doubt that something of this kind would greatly increase the amount of labor in our institutions, but it is too abhorrent to the severe simplicity of our national tastes, to be thought of at present.[53]

Not incidentally, requiring patients to work also reduced the cost of running the asylum. As Dr. Graham noted, "Our garden has, and still continues to supply us with an abundant amount of vegetables, for the use of the entire house, winter and summer, not having been under the necessity of purchasing a dollar's worth, we have sold an amount sufficient to furnish us with seed Irish potatoes, and such other seed as were needed, and we have still a small balance of the garden fund on hand."[54]

While it clearly pleased Graham to report the financial benefits from the asylum's gardens, the portion of his report dealing with personnel noted some problems. He stated: "During the past year, trying difficulties have environed us. The change in our labor system [the abolition of slavery] which has so affected the industrial interests of the South, has fallen with peculiar weight upon our Institution. I have found it very hard to obtain reliable labor, either black or white."[55]

Part of Graham's difficulty in filling positions may have related to the strict regulations applied to those employed by the asylum, as outlined in the 1861 bylaws. Virtually all personnel were required to live on the grounds, making possible the statement: "The *entire time* of attendants and assistants belongs to the Asylum. This rule applies equally to every officer and employee of every grade who accepts service in the institution."[56] Bachelors resided in the basement, which also housed the laundry and the kitchen, while "maiden ladies" slept on the third floor.[57]

Duties of attendants included dispensing medications, reporting the conduct and habits of patients to the physician, seeing that patients were comfortable, preventing improper conduct (such as fighting or lying on the floor or ground), soothing those who were irritated, cheering the melancholy, and "to instruct, interest and amuse them by talking or reading to them."[58] In addition, attendants were to set good examples for proper behavior by dressing neatly, never wearing hats indoors, avoiding obscene, vulgar, or profane language, abstaining from tobacco (especially smoking), and avoiding distilled spirits or intoxicating liquor.

Some male attendants broke the latter rule. Mary Pinckney related the story of her husband's grandmother, Mathilda Jarl, a young immigrant from Sweden in the 1870s, who took a job cleaning employees' quarters at the asylum. Since several of the young attendants had asked her out, and since she was determined never to marry a drunkard, she always searched each potential beau's quarters for a hidden liquor bottle. More than once Jarl found one, and she never accepted invitations from any of the men who kept whiskey.[59]

The bylaws listed several reasons for immediate dismissal. First and foremost, "Violent hands are never to be laid upon a patient under any provocation." If a patient became violent the attendant was to call for assistance so that the patient could be restrained without excessive force. Furthermore, "any attendant or any other employee receiving a present or gratuity from any patient or receiving any thing of value of any kind whatever shall be immediately dismissed from the service of the Asylum."

The bylaws even stipulated appropriate conduct between employees in the institution. "Treat each other with uniform politeness, be civil, cordial and frank," it advised. "Maintain at all times a quiet and cheerful deportment as befits your employment, cultivate a high sense of moral obligation and an humble self-denying spirit, seek to be useful in your sphere and maintain your puristic truth, sobriety, truthfulness and honesty."[60] Small wonder, then, that Dr. Graham had difficulty filling these positions or keeping experienced personnel.

One of Graham's successors, Dr. D. R. Wallace, perhaps in an attempt to improve employee morale, praised those few attendants who had served for three years or longer in his annual report for 1878: "Mr. Conrad Mantele, head of excited ward, in service with short intermission, seven years; Mr. J. F. Brannon, in charge of epileptic ward, three years. Mrs. Jennie Brannon, head of excited female ward, three years."[61] As a morale booster, the strategy perhaps worked for Mrs. Brannon, who sixteen years later could be found on the asylum staff listed as "matron."

Desperate for ward workers, another of Graham's successors even hired a patient to work as charge attendant in the black female ward. This woman had been admitted as a patient in 1870 but by February 1, 1881, was also identified as a staff member. Her record noted that "she exercises very good judgment and care of the Negro female lunatics and has them under good control." Unfortunately, after breaking her leg she could not continue in the role, relapsed, and "has become very crazy and is full of delusions."[62]

The hiring of patients and former patients could be fraught with peril, as Superintendent W. W. Reeves discovered. He had hired former patient Henry Purnell as storekeeper and then fired him from that position. On December 29, 1891, Purnell purchased a double-barreled shotgun in downtown Austin, rode the electric streetcar out to the asylum, and killed Reeves as he descended the front steps of the main building. Photographers who had set up their cameras to take pictures of the building attempted to get Purnell to give them the gun, but he refused to do so. He also declined to explain his actions, simply stating that he had his reasons. Purnell then rode the electric streetcar back downtown and turned himself in to the sheriff.[63]

Not surprisingly, Superintendent F. S. White, who succeeded Reeves, refused to readmit Purnell to the asylum. Local physician Dr. James Coleman recalled, "After eight months in the County jail the murderer went on a hunger strike and was removed to the City-County Hospital where he vowed that he would kill Governor James S. Hogg. At this point Governor Hogg demanded that the murderer be readmitted to the State Lunatic Asylum and his demands were met."[64]

Although Dr. Reeves was the only superintendent to lose his life in the line of duty, the job in general was not an easy one. Appointed by the governor, the superintendent's term of office expired every two years along with the governor's. During the asylum's eventful first decade, which encompassed the chaos of the Civil War and the occupation by military government following the South's defeat, five men served as superintendent: Dr. J. C. Perry, Dr. C. G. Keenan, Dr. B. Graham, Dr. J. M. Steiner, and Dr. W. P. Beall. However, the superintendency actually changed hands eight times during this period, since Keenan served twice and Graham three times under different governors. During the asylum's first twenty years the average term of office for superintendents spanned less than two years.

At the time, Texas governors appointed the asylum's superintendents who served only until the next governor was elected. Eight men served as governor of Texas from 1857 until 1870, when Edmond Davis became the first governor in thirteen years to succeed himself. Illustrating the turmoil of the time period, Davis refused to leave office after his defeat by Richard Coke in 1873, claiming the election law under which he lost was unconstitutional. Only when President Grant refused to send federal troops to Austin did Davis step down.[65] Shortly thereafter, Davis's successor, Gov-

ernor Coke, appointed his personal physician, Dr. D. R. Wallace, a graduate of New York Medical College, as superintendent, which caused a local
reporter to complain:

> Coke appoints only Waco men; he has Waco on the brain. A gentleman
> offers an explanation of part of the appointments. He says Coke could
> not be censored for appointing Dr. Wallace of Waco, who had never
> visited a lunatic asylum, as Superintendent of the Lunatic Asylum of this
> state because Dr. Wallace has been his Excellency's family physician for
> years and must have sufficient experience as his physician, at least so far
> as moral insanity is concerned.[66]

New governors sometimes attempted to discredit their predecessor and
his appointees by calling for investigations of the asylum or other eleemosynary institutions. Following Governor Coke's resignation, Governor
Richard B. Hubbard (1876–79) commissioned Dr. Turner, an expert from
New South Wales, Australia, to inspect the State Lunatic Asylum. Turner
found that "corridors were disgustingly filthy, walls were cracked, ceilings
were falling down, and furnishings were in fragments." Dr. Wallace weath-
ered Dr. Turner's criticisms, however, and remained superintendent of the
asylum until 1879. In 1875, the Texas legislature tried to stop the appointment of physicians with no background in mental illness by passing a law
that required superintendents of the State Lunatic Asylum to have a minimum of two years' experience in the treatment of the insane, but Governor David B. Culberson vetoed the bill.[67]

The asylum's board of managers consisted of five men also appointed
by the governor for two year terms. They supervised all operations and
expenditures, set wages for employees, and approved or disapproved the
superintendent's decisions regarding the hiring of personnel and the discharging of both patients and employees.[68] They visited the asylum each
month and prepared an annual report to the governor. At least one member of the board, Rev. Dr. R. K. Smoot, who served in the 1870s, found
these duties too onerous, explaining in his letter of resignation to Governor Ross that he needed "to relieve himself of the cares and vexations of
official position, in which there is heavy responsibility and slight remunera-
tion."[69]

The board of managers and the superintendent sometimes disagreed
about the management of the asylum. Dr. Beriah Graham disagreed with
his board, who considered religious services ill advised for mental patients,

and tried to get support for such services from the Association for Medical Superintendents of American Institutions for the Insane at its annual meeting in 1869. He offered the following resolution: "Resolved, that in the opinion of the Association, a judicious system of religious worship introduced and practiced in an Insane Hospital may prove in many cases a remedial, or at least an ameliorative agent, and need not necessarily be injurious in any way." Although a few of the members agreed with him, discussion revealed that the resolution probably would not carry, and it was relegated to a committee for further study. Dr. Workman of the Provincial Lunatic Asylum of Toronto commented, "If the Governors of the Texas Asylum are so peculiar as to repudiate Divine worship, I think they would not be inclined to listen to what we might say."[70]

In a more serious conflict with his board, Dr. J. S. Dorsett, a physician from Bonham, Texas, who served as superintendent from 1887 until 1891, was censured during his first week in office for discharging a patient and for throwing a spittoon at a male nurse. Dr. James Coleman recalled:

> The board of Managers voted four to one for Dr. Dorsett to resign but he refused to submit a resignation and it was ruled that he could be removed only by a unanimous vote. Dorsett now appeared before the Board with a list of employees that he wished discharged. After some delay the Board voted three to two to sustain the discharge of six of these employees, whereupon the minority resigned. Dr. Dorsett functioned well as an administrator at times but often behaved in a bizarre manner. One dissident even believed him more suitable as a patient than as a responsible officer.[71]

Not only did superintendents have to maintain good relations with their boards, they also had to negotiate the treacherous waters of state politics to create conditions that would make moral treatment possible, namely, limiting the number of patients and restricting admission to those who had been ill for less than one year. However, from the very beginning powerful forces operated against such restrictions. Counties wanted to shift to the state the responsibility (and in many instances the financial burden) of caring for persons who could not support themselves. Besides the insane, such persons included retardates, alcoholics, and the senile. Similarly, many families created political pressure through their legislative representatives in trying to force the admission of relatives who fell into one or more of these categories.

By Dr. Beriah Graham's report of 1869, the patient population of the asylum had grown to seventy, "which is as many as we are able to accommodate by associating some of them in small rooms." Graham also noted that most of the patients were in poor physical health upon admission to the asylum, and that before moral treatment could succeed patients' physical needs had to be addressed. He viewed excess as the usual cause of insanity: excessive use of alcohol, opiates, tobacco, and "prolonged physical and mental exertion, accompanied with continued loss of sleep; excessive grief, anger, anxiety, fear, and great revulsions of feeling of any kind."[72]

In addition to the calming effect of the asylum's simple routine on insanity caused by excess, Superintendent Graham regarded music as an excellent technique of moral treatment. Describing frequent vocal and instrumental concerts for the patients, Graham noted in his report of 1866 that "Musical entertainments perhaps contribute as much to the gratification and improvement of many cases of insanity as any other means which can be resorted to."[73] Staff encouraged interested patients to participate in the music-making and dancing, and music often became part of other celebrations, such as the annual Fourth of July festivities. Besides the fireworks display and the picnic of sandwiches, cake, lemonade, watermelon, peaches, and ice cream, there was "some tripping of the light fantastic toe on the grass to the music of the accordion," followed by the singing of patriotic songs such as "Hail Columbia." To close the evening, "all with badges of red white and blue disappeared into the house, and the evening ended with good music in the parlor by the crazy people."[74]

Asylum staff also regarded good food as part of the moral treatment program, and the institution strove to furnish its own provisions. Superintendent Graham stated, "Vegetables are among the best articles of diet, and of these our garden, which is mostly cultivated by the inmates of the institution, furnishes an abundant supply." Later in the report he recorded that the asylum had dried 700 pounds of peaches and preserved 350 pounds more for winter use. He also estimated that the sweet potato crop would exceed 500 bushels. In addition, the farm had produced ten tons of oats, three tons of hay, about six tons of fodder, and 450 bushels of corn to feed the asylum's horses, mules, hogs, and cattle. All institutional livestock had to have an identifying mark, and the asylum's herd of milk cows displayed a "little straight line on the hip" since "a jersey cow looks badly with a big brand and everybody knows our brand such as it is."[75]

Superintendent Wallace's report for 1875 gave an even more complete account of the vegetables and fruit produced by the asylum, noting copious quantities of asparagus, beets, beans, cucumbers, figs, grapes, lettuce, leeks, melons, onions, pears, Irish potatoes, plums, peas, radishes, squashes, strawberries, and turnips.[76]

Not only did the asylum produce most of its own food, but by the 1890s it was also self-sufficient in many other ways: operating its own power plant, water system, laundry, carpenter shop, barber shop, dairy, sewing room and tailor shop, ice factory, infirmaries, cemetery, and even a bowling alley.[77] In this respect it strongly resembled the Willard Asylum in New York, which Ellen Dwyer compared to a "thrifty and prosperous New England settlement, having its own fire station, hotel, cemetery and even a small local train system."[78]

Patients fulfilled moral treatment's requirement of physical exercise not only by cultivating the garden but also by clearing the undergrowth on the asylum grounds. Graham described the "beautiful walk or drive of nearly a mile through our grounds, within a dense grove of live oaks" that the patients and attendants had constructed that year. They also had constructed two fenced "airing courts." Improving the landscape allowed patients to be outside for six to eight hours every day, which alleviated some of the overcrowding that already had begun to afflict the asylum.[79]

Graham's successor, Dr. J. A. Corley, agreed with Graham that insanity could be cured if treated quickly. However, he noted in his 1870 report: "But why attempt to impress the public with the urgent necessity of early treatment unless the asylum accommodations shall keep pace with the wants of the rapidly increasing population? The new building opened for reception of patients in August is already about full to its utmost capacity." Corley then attempted to shame the legislature with information about the accommodations for the insane in other states, observing that "Our sister State of California, though younger than Texas, has provided accommodations for over one thousand of her insane. Tennessee, with little, if any more numerous population, in addition to her present Asylum, capable of accommodating five hundred inmates, at the last meeting of the legislature, took steps for the immediate establishment of two others."[80]

In spite of such pleas, increases in the population of the Texas asylum continued to outpace its capacity. Although new wings were added to the asylum in the 1870s, inadequate funding prevented a strict adherence to the original Kirkbride plan, forcing the construction of significantly smaller wings than planned.[81]

By the time of Dr. Wallace's 1875 report, the asylum housed 152 patients, an increase of twenty-five from the last term. The report also indicated that

*The women's infirmary reflected Victorian decorating preferences of the 1890s, with wicker furniture and potted plants. Courtesy ASH*

increasing numbers of patients considered incurable—the senile and the retarded—were being admitted to the asylum. Wallace summarized:

Admitted since [the previous report], 90; total number cared for, 217. Of these there have been discharged, restored 33; improved, 19; incurable, 2; escaped, 2; died 9; remaining on hand Sept. 30, 1875, 152. Died 5 males and 4 females—one was of mere old age, the subject being over 90, two of gangrene of lungs; also quite aged, one being over 70 and the other about 60. One a little idiot girl, of corrosive poisoning, having accidently got hold of some concentrated lye in the bathroom.[82]

Death of patients always greatly concerned asylum administrators, and the ratio of deaths to total number of patients often exceeded the one from 1875. For example, Dr. L. J. Graham's annual report for 1882 noted that fifty-nine of the asylum's 509 patients had died in the previous year, "34 from nervous diseases peculiar to insanity; ten from bowel diseases, which were complicated with diseases of the brain and nervous system with great nervous prostration; and the other fifteen from various acute and chronic diseases." Graham blamed the large number on the "extreme and unusual heat of the past summer and the crowded condition of the ill-ventilated wards." Crowded living conditions increased the danger of infectious disease, and during the administration of Dr. B. M. Worsham during the late 1890s, there were serious outbreaks of typhoid fever, measles, mumps, smallpox, and Beri Beri.[83]

In spite of the hazards associated with extremely crowded conditions, pressures to admit additional patients intensified over time, and superintendents turned people away at their political peril. Superintendent Wallace defensively noted in his 1878 report that "No little care has been exercised and pains taken to get at the facts in each case, to give the benefits of the institution to the most deserving." However, "Some offense may have been given in discriminating too closely in this direction."[84]

Similarly, Superintendent F. S. White reported in 1893 that "The one thing kept prominently in view is, that this is a hospital for the treatment of the insane, rather than a home for the accommodation of the incurables. On account of the pursuance of this policy, dissatisfaction has often been manifested by some county authorities who desired to unload on the asylum all their chronic insane."[85]

By the time of White's report, however, it had become clear that limiting the number and the type of patients to those most likely to benefit from moral treatment was impossible, and some had even begun to doubt that the Kirkbride asylum was beneficial. Was the crowded institution itself contributing to mental illness? White's report for 1894 sounded a note of concern:

> Our asylum methods are in many instances wrong and misleading; their tendency is often to make lunatics rather than to cure them. In the commodious, magnificent, well kept and beautiful parks of all modern asylums will be seen hundreds of lunatics sitting day in and day out in idleness and misery, watched by attendants who take little interest in them further than to be very careful that no one makes his escape. The monotony of such a life is something terrible. Cases that are kept locked up in magnificent edifices, who become chronic by gazing day after day at snow-white walls and polished floors.

White advocated the "cottage plan" for asylum buildings and argued for putting the patients to work. "If there is a class in the world that needs stimulating, moving, jostling and stirring up, it certainly is the chronic insane. By these means cures may be effected in cases that would otherwise go down into oblivion and draw out a miserable living death, dead to themselves, dead to the world, and dead to their friends and loved ones."[86]

Despite all complaints, the population of the State Lunatic Asylum grew ever larger as the years passed. By 1896 the number of patients had increased to 696 and Superintendent Worsham lamented, "There is a growing tendency on the part of the people to place all classes of persons who are, either from old age or congenital defect, of feeble mind, in an insane asylum to the great detriment of the insane, whose habits and conditions necessary for their care are in no way suited to be associated on wards with this class of people."[87]

In truth, by the time of Worsham's report of 1897 the battle had been lost. While elements of moral treatment remained, the Texas State Lunatic Asylum had become primarily a custodial institution, and it would remain so for fully three-quarters of a century.

# CHAPTER 3

# Superintendents and Professional Staff

## *"Their Own Fiefdom"*

The Civil War and Reconstruction, which brought almost constant change in the Texas governorship, resulted in many early superintendents who served two years or less. Following these turbulent first decades, the stabilization of Texas politics after the end of Reconstruction in 1874 greatly increased the likelihood of governors winning reelection and asylum superintendents remaining in place. However, even after the political situation normalized, the average length of service for superintendents remained less than three years until Dr. B. M. Worsham held the job for thirteen years between 1896 and 1909. While no longer automatically replaced when new governors took office, superintendents continued to be appointed for two year terms—subject to removal for misbehavior—until the state legislature passed a law giving them indefinite terms of appointment in 1943.[1] Following Dr. Worsham, the next superintendent, Dr. John Preston, held office for sixteen years. Preston, a graduate of The University of Virginia and Bellevue Hospital Medical College, lamented the role politics had played in the short careers of his predecessors: "It is a melancholy fact that for many years—as manifested by the frequent changes of superintendents—the Asylum was a part of the political spoils of the party in power. No superintendent was able, no matter how efficiently he performed his duties, to hold his place longer than the Governor who appointed him."[2]

Governors also chose each mental institution's five-member board of managers for two-year terms until 1913, when members began to serve overlapping six-year terms, perhaps appointed by three different governors. Further reducing the governor's power, in 1919, after a long battle, the State

Conference of Charities and Corrections finally succeeded in lobbying for a board of control. In spite of a 1915 study by Dr. Thomas W. Salmon of the National Committee for Mental Hygiene, which deplored conditions in Texas asylums and jails and urged the creation of a central authority, the legislation had failed to pass in three prior attempts.[3]

Under the earlier board of managers system, most governors expected to be able to dictate asylum policy as they chose. For example, Governor Coke sternly reprimanded Superintendent Wallace (1874–79) for failing to hire as an attendant a woman Coke had sent to the asylum.[4] Certainly, survival in the job required excellent political skills, and several superintendents became active in state or local politics. Some held local office, and former superintendent Dr. Beriah Graham served as state treasurer in 1872.

Although some superintendents had much longer tenures than others and exercised greater influence on the life of the asylum, all superintendents experienced the same frustrations of the job. Newly arrived superintendents soon discovered that they were expected to supervise all the asylum's operations, from the most trivial to the momentous, and to deal effectively with the sometimes quarreling constituencies inside and outside the precincts of the asylum, including patients and their relatives, medical personnel and other staff, the state legislature, and interested members of the general public. Consequently, while a superintendent had to have a medical degree and some training in psychiatry, success as head of the asylum depended far more on political and administrative skills than on medical ability. Superintendents essentially functioned as hospital administrators, and even the name of the parent organization of the American Psychiatric Association, the Association of Medical Superintendents of American Institutions for the Insane, emphasized this aspect of the role.

Although the Texas asylum's bylaws of 1861 placed onerous responsibilities on the superintendent, many of the administrative duties of the incumbent were not discussed in that document, which emphasized the responsibilities of patient care. These bylaws specified that superintendents must either visit each patient daily or learn of his or her condition; must personally supervise patients' medical, moral and "dietic [sic] treatment"; and must keep a complete history of each patient, including treatment and results. While early superintendents may have complied with many of these duties, the sparseness of medical records for the period—often less than one third of a page for several decades of care—indicates considerably less than complete histories for each patient. The bylaws also required superintendents to determine how many attendants to hire, as well as their duties and wages; to answer or "cause to be answered" all communications regarding the asylum; and to prepare an annual report to the governor of Texas detailing the status of patients and all fiscal matters related to the asylum.[5]

Most superintendents used these annual reports to lobby the legislature for additional funds, and some proved especially eloquent in this regard. For example, Dr. J. A. Corley informed the legislators in 1870 that: "Not a female in the institution has a single sleeping gown, and a very large majority not even a decent outside garment. This, gentlemen, should not be the case in Texas."[6]

Such pleas did not necessarily succeed in eliciting more funds from the legislature, as Superintendent Wallace (1874–79) discovered. At the 1875 meeting of the AMSAII he complained to his fellow professionals:

> Knowing that even legislators are not any too well informed upon this subject, at the close of last year, in my report, I went somewhat into the minutiae of the subject, and by the aid of figures prepared by Dr. Jarvis and others, demonstrated, as I thought, that it is no less economy than humanity for the State, to provide accommodations, ample for every insane person in her borders. The report was sent to every member of our Legislature. This body assembling, upon meeting the individual members, they were loud in their praise of the exhibit I had made. The report was a credit to the State, said many, so excellent, said one large minded senator, I had my wife to read it . . . well, to make a long story short, after so much outside sympathy and encouragement, when these same men set about embodying their views in legislative enactment, by some unaccountable *psychological abnormality*, they did not give me a cent!

Wallace then promised his "everlasting gratitude" to anyone who "could enlighten my ignorance concerning the subtle influences that control legislative action."[7]

While many of the Texas superintendents attended the annual meeting of the AMSAII, none rose to leadership, participating instead in various organizational activities. In 1876, David R. Wallace served on a committee to audit the treasurer's report, and in 1885 A. N. Denton drafted a resolution to honor a deceased colleague.[8] Their typically short tenure doubtless hindered advancement within their professional organization. Most who left the asylum returned to private practice and resigned from the association.

As outlined in the *By-Laws, Rules and Regulations* of 1861, the duties of the superintendent included the "general superintendence of the Buildings and Grounds—the charge of the patients—the expenditures of the Institution, and the direction and control of all persons therein subject to the regulation of the Board of Managers."[9] The bylaws also stipulated that the superintendent be married and live on the asylum grounds. For the first twenty-six years of the asylum's existence, until the construction of a superintendent's residence, the superintendent and his family occupied an apartment in the main building.

The mental hospital of the turn of the century resembled a small town, with the resident superintendent serving as mayor, city manager, chief of police, and judge. Observers sometimes likened the role of superintendent to that of a medieval lord.[10] Former director of Rehabilitative Services Joe Pearce explained: "The superintendents were really the feudal lords. This was their own little fiefdom. They were very paternalistic. They saw the whole hospital, not only the patients but also the employees, as theirs."[11]

Most hospital employees apparently accepted this situation. Pearce noted: "Most of the superintendents were benevolent. Many employees who worked under this type of environment look back fondly on those days with a warm regard for Dr. So and So." An anonymous female attendant, who began work in 1912, agreed, writing, "Our Superintendent, Dr. James [*sic*] Preston, a very stately old gentleman, was very strict, but loved by us all [as were] his assistant Dr. [J. W.] Bradfield, and the three other doctors, Dr. Wilhite, Dr. Brownlee and Dr. Shaw."[12]

After Dr. Preston's lengthy administration, politics again played a key role in the appointment of his successors, as a 1927 letter from Rusk attorney B. B. Perkins to chair of the Board of Control R. B. Walthall indicated. Perkins wrote:

Since I was in Austin and talked with you about Dr. Standifer and Dr. Thomas, I have investigated the matter considerably, and have reached the conclusion that Dr. Standifer is the proper man for this place, if a change is to be made. I desire to say further that *we* do not believe Dr. Card is the proper man to be sent here, and, if he is sent here, we, of course, understand fully that it will be done with the approval and at the solicitation of Mr. W. T. Norman, who spent last Friday conferring with him at Palestine, and also at the request of Mr. Michael Campbell, and Hon. Barry Miller of Dallas. We presume these Gentlemen will not need our co-operation and if they send him here, we shall, of course, not burden them with our solicitude for the welfare of their protegee.[13]

Dr. Standifer became superintendent of Austin State Hospital in 1927 and served until 1943. Being located in the state capital resulted in high visibility and constant legislative oversight, and Standifer and his wife entertained legislators frequently. His son Charles Jr. recalled: "Dad would call from the office at noon and say Senator so-and-so is coming for dinner tonight. We had a cook and a helper and Mother'd get busy and get a meal on the table that night."[14] To help set these recurrent political tables, Standifer received a liberal food allowance of five hundred dollars a month in addition to his salary of six hundred dollars. If the costs of entertaining exceeded the food allowance, he paid for it out of his own pocket and kept careful records for potential enquiries. Similarly, to avoid any criticism of misuse of state funds, Standifer sent Charles Jr. to Dallas for minor surgery rather than use the hospital facilities on the grounds.

The Standifers always attended the governor's inaugural ball, proceeds of which helped defray campaign costs, since as daughter Margaret told, "They dunned us for it whether we went or not." However, since Texas became essentially a one-party state following Reconstruction, later superintendents managed to avoid some of the heavy-handed partisan politics characteristic of other states. Recalling his experiences as a physician in seven East Coast and midwestern mental hospitals, John Grimes wrote in his memoir: "The first thing I had to do when I took a job at a state hospital was to go to the capital to meet the Senator. I was expected to join the current administration's political club whose dues were two per cent of my monthly salary. I was also expected to vote the party line."[15]

In addition to political acumen, several of the men with long tenure in the Texas superintendency had military or law enforcement experience. Dr. Preston, born and educated in Virginia, came to Texas in the early 1870s and served as a Texas Ranger until his discharge in 1875. Part of his duties as a Ranger included fighting Indians in Montague County.[16] Dr. Standifer served in an army medical corps unit during World War I. Both men ran the hospital on a military model with a strict hierarchical arrangement of personnel.

The military social structure of the asylum persisted until the mid-1950s. Writing in 1956, sociologist Ivan Belknap noted in his book about the Austin State Hospital:

> In its overall structure, the clinical system closely resembled a military command system; so closely, in fact, that a previous superintendent of 20 years ago used military terminology in communicating with his staff,

and punishment and privilege systems corresponding almost exactly to those of American infantry organization. As he translated the system into military terminology, the line between levels II [supervisory] and III [attendants] was equivalent to the line between commissioned and enlisted personnel."[17]

Joe Pearce confirmed Belknap's observation of a military-style caste system:

There was a definite pecking order. The laundry and kitchen were the lowest levels and the yard crew. Then the attendants. Then the professional and the office staff. Then the doctors. Then the superintendent. Within the caste system that evolved under this type of system, if you worked in the laundry you associated only with other laundry employees. If you worked in the kitchen, you associated with other kitchen employees. You associated with the levels of your type of employee. This was very strictly adhered to. You didn't cross the lines.[18]

Such caste restrictions extended to courtship among employees. Pearce recalled: "If a single male employee wished to court a single young female employee, he approached the superintendent with a request to begin courting her." If the couple occupied the same caste level and if the superintendent approved, the couple could associate socially, and if the relationship developed they might request the superintendent's permission to wed. Permission depended in part on the availability of housing, since both spouses had to continue living on the asylum grounds. Occasionally, the superintendent disapproved of the marriage and refused permission. One woman recalled that Superintendent Preston had discouraged her from marrying because he felt she was too young and did not know her own mind. She married anyway, and the union lasted sixty-eight years until her husband's death.[19]

Other military-like practices occurred in the daily operation of the hospital. Bells and, later, whistles signalled meal times and shift changes. Like drill sergeants supervising military trainees, attendants sometimes marched patients around the grounds for exercise or to attend the movie. Employees had to have passes to leave the grounds and were locked out if they returned after curfew. Asylum staff took the curfew seriously, and once a new gate guard refused to allow Superintendent Aloysius T. Hanretta, whom he did not recognize, to enter the grounds after curfew. After arguing with the guard for several minutes, Hanretta simply "backed up his big Buick and crashed through the gate."[20]

Like boot camp recruits, patients normally could not leave the premises, though they might be allowed to go home on "furlough" before being eligible for discharge from the hospital. Patients might even be "stationed" away from the hospital, as in the case of some men who lived and worked at the State School Farm Colony and the State Hog Farm.[21]

In addition to attending to the daily operations of the hospital, superintendents responded to numerous requests for information from national groups, state officials, and the general public regarding their institution. A sample of Superintendent Preston's correspondence revealed just how many requests he received. For example, John Hayes of the California Board of Charities and Corrections solicited any Texas law permitting sterilization of inmates of insane asylums. John I. Bernstein of the Hebrew Sheltering and Immigrant Society of America in New York asked for information regarding the number of Jewish patients in Texas. The National Committee for Mental Hygiene requested copies of all forms and reports as well as regular updates on personnel. A. P. Herring, chairman of the American Medico-Psychological Association, solicited information to be used in an exhibit on diversional occupation at their next convention, noting: "if we do not hear from you, we will naturally imply that your institution is not doing much in the way of Diversional Occupation, consequently you will be in the RED STAR CLASS."[22]

The public at large also had many troublesome questions regarding mental illness, as a 1919 letter from H. W. Davis of Denton, Texas, illustrated: "Will you please tell me what percent of the women inmates of the asylum are farmers' wives? Also, why in your opinion more farmers' wives than any other class?"[23]

Local officials proved even more relentless in their requests for information—sometimes quite unwilling to take "no" for an answer. Ernest Winkler of the Texas Library and Historical Commission wrote: "I fear the report that you have no library may be erroneous. Will you give a brief statement of the reading facilities your patients enjoy?"[24]

Predictably, much of the superintendent's most pressing correspondence pertained to the legislative and budgetary processes. R. V. Nichols, chairman of the Senate's finance committee, wrote on January 16, 1917:

I am instructed by Hon. C. B. Hudspeth Chairman of the Senate Finance Committee to notify you that work will be started in the preparation of drafting the appropriation bills soon. The committee has before it your estimates furnished the Comptroller for the two fiscal years ending August 31, 1919, and it is now the desire of this committee to know whether or not you contemplate making any changes in your budget? Two years ago we had considerable trouble in regard to changes being made after the bill had been prepared.

Similarly, L. W. Saterwhite, chairman of the Appropriations Committee of the House of Representatives, brusquely demanded, "Will you please inform me by return mail with reference to your facilities for caring for more inmates than you now have in your institution."[25]

State officials also offered purchasing advice. A letter of March 30, 1916, from State Purchasing Agent George Leavy, informed Dr. Preston that the price of fuel oil was too high and asked what grade of coal he would like to use instead.[26]

Another large block of the superintendent's correspondence involved requests from family and friends of patients regarding information about their loved ones' physical and mental health. Superintendent Hanretta estimated that his office of five stenographers mailed twenty-five hundred to three thousand letters of this sort every month for a patient population of 3,819.[27]

Still another of the superintendent's many duties involved overseeing the complex operations of the institution's physical plant. Hanretta described the hospital's power and light plant, operated by L. G. Sloan and a team of "machinists, pump adjusters, firemen, electricians, ice-plant operators, plumbers, steamfitters, welders, ice-plant and other utility service that might be required in the upkeep of a 'Town' of more than 3,500 population."[28] In addition to the power and light plant, the superintendent directed the hospital's utilities department, which handled carpentry and related chores, supervised pest control around the kitchens, and passed judgment on every detail of landscaping, farm operations, and asylum grounds.

A particularly vexing problem, rodent control, troubled successive generations of superintendents. "Sewer rats, the big kind," had plagued the asylum for many decades. A report to the 48th Texas Legislature admitted that "thousands of dollars of feed and food are being destroyed by rats." Furthermore, the rodents were brazen. Employee Bess Greene recalled seeing what she thought were loaves of bread cooling on racks on a porch behind the bakery and being appalled when the loaves turned out to be enormous rats, taking their ease. Similarly, Joe Pearce once watched a rat nonchalantly make his way along one of the rafters in a dining hall as patients ate below.[29]

At times rats even intruded into the superintendent's residence, as one superintendent's daughter recalled: "We had rats in the house. Mother called A&M and they told her to put poison in sacks and to tie the top closed. The rats would be curious and would gnaw in to get the poison. It worked."[30]

Sometimes boys' shooting skills were enlisted to control the pests. Adults organized formal rat hunts for the boys, who dispatched the rodents with their pellet guns.[31] The fear of rabies occasionally prompted similar hunts for the feral cats living in large numbers on the asylum grounds (and somehow coexisting with the rats). Because of the nearby Pasteur Institute, the only rabies-treatment center in the state, everyone who lived at the asylum became very aware of the danger of rabies from animal bites and the painful shots that were the bite victim's only hope of survival. The Pasteur Institute had been constructed on the asylum grounds in 1904, and by 1928, when it moved downtown, it had treated tens of thousands of patients from across Texas.[32]

Keeping the asylum lakes stocked with fish was yet another duty that befell the superintendent. At the request of Superintendent Preston in 1914, area congressman J. O. Buchanon wrote that he had arranged that fish for restocking the lakes be sent from government hatcheries at San Marcos. Later correspondence with H. H. Smith, commissioner of the Department of Commerce, Bureau of Fisheries, informed Preston that "it is believed the waters you desire to stock are suited to the cultivation of BLACK BASS and the assignment thereon has been made accordingly." The black bass arrived at the asylum on April 15, 1915.[33]

In truth, early or late in the history of the Texas asylum, no detail seemed too insignificant to require the attention of the superintendent. Staff minutes for November 28, 1958, recorded that business manager "Williams asked Dr. Hoerster if he would like to pick out the colors of the tile flooring on the second floor of the Administration Building. Dr. Hoerster said to get them to match as close as possible to our present flooring."[34]

The superintendent also had to arbitrate conflicts among personnel. Parking privileges, as well as many other things, could spark conflict, as staff minutes for June 2, 1961, recorded. Dr. Miller mentioned the roads, especially

*Dr. Bohls, a physician at the state hospital, chatted with Floyd Huff, a technician who prepared slides for the detection of rabies at the Pasteur Institute, located on the grounds of the asylum, ca. 1927. Courtesy ASH*

that area from 45th Street where you turn off to the doctors' residences. He stated that the chaplain's wife usually comes driving around that area and cuts short at the corner to where there is a great gap between the road and the hedge at Dr. de Chenar's residence and, that before long the whole thing will collapse and probably cause an accident. He wants a concrete bib. He also suggested cutting off a part of Dr. Bolding's yard and evening it up, as "it is almost impossible for anyone to park a car outside of my residence due to lack of space."[35]

In the early years, the superintendent also served as the chief fiscal officer of the hospital, juggling budget constraints with the hospital's needs, which sometimes resulted in "job obfuscation." Belknap noted: "Administrative records in the hospital are often deliberately deceptive, since historically the superintendents have had to smuggle necessary jobs into the hospital under other classifications than those needed."[36]

The superintendent accounted to the legislature for the hospital's efficient and economical operation, and the annual reports clearly reflected this responsibility. Superintendent Worsham, for example, reported to Governor Culbertson in 1898 that the per capita cost of maintenance of inmates for the previous year was $140.83. As did later superintendents, Worsham

*The Administration Building added a classical portico in 1904. C00743.*
*Courtesy AHC*

oversaw the operation of many cottage industries, such as a sewing room, a knitting room, and a shoe shop, designed to keep costs low. In 1901 he reported that the asylum hauled its own coal and most other supplies. A half century later, the per capita cost had risen only to $216.13 compared to the national average of $300.63.[37] Superintendents repeatedly pointed to economy of operation as an indicator of their success. Critics, however, commonly faulted the superintendents for failing to maintain "good business practices."[38]

The 1917 report of the Legislative Committee to Investigate State Departments and Institutions stressed the possibility of pilferage by employees and cheating by those who did business with the asylum, since institutional bookkeeping was minimal. Similarly, the report on fiscal administration authorized by the Board for Texas State Hospitals and Special Schools noted: "When the hospital board was created in 1949 there was no formal system of accounting in operation in the hospital system. The principal business officers at the institutions were storekeeper-accountants, most of whom were not trained in accounting. The position of business manager did not exist." Even after the creation of the business manager position in the early 1950s, confusion over duties remained due to conflicting laws, and the report observed, "This statutory confusion makes it necessary for each individual superintendent–business manager team to work out its relationship and distribution of duties."[39] Officially, the superintendent held the ultimate authority on fiscal matters but sometimes chose to delegate this authority to the business manager.

On paper at least, the creation of the job of business manager appeared to ease the superintendent's burdens in administering the hospital. At a minimum, this position should have reduced the number of people reporting directly to the superintendent. The 1931 report of the Joint Legislative Committee on Organization and Economy had found that "the outline of the organization reveals some of its weaknesses but none is more glaring than the number of persons who are responsible only and directly to the superintendent. There are 19 sub-executives."[40] However, twenty-three years later, the investigation commissioned by the Board for Texas State Hospitals and Special Schools and conducted by the Texas Research League investigating the organizational structure and personnel administration of state mental institutions estimated that up to 90 percent of the superintendents' time was still "spent on non-medical often minor administrative details." This report attributed the short tenure of most superintendents, who served an average of only 1.4 years, to "pressure from local officials, relatives of patients and from the community; ever increasing numbers of patients with few trained employees, over-crowded facilities, and insufficient control."[41]

Superintendents found one perennial problem: Employee pilferage was almost impossible to control despite concerted attempts to apprehend violators. Superintendent Standifer's son Charles recalled that his father "worked seven days a week and on Sunday would go around the grounds to see what was going on. He caught several people stealing and going out the gate with meat and things like that. He would call the supervisor and tell him what was happening and they'd go catch them." After a while, Standifer's employees felt themselves under his constant scrutiny. Ethel Brack recalled: "You could go to Hyde Park Drug to get a Coke. Before you left, Dr. Standifer would be there."[42]

Nonetheless, much pilferage continued at ASH. For example, stealing from the kitchen had become so accepted that Food Service employees referred to it as "totin' privileges." Kitchen employees were not particularly cautious about their activities. State Auditor C. H. Cavness wrote in 1948:

"Several instances which proved to be misappropriation of foodstuffs were observed by our representative, quantities of such being loaded into automobiles not owned by the state (some into a taxi-cab). Employees were seen taking canned goods, meat and other merchandise through the gates of the hospital."[43]

Stemming the plague of pilferage required curious rules. For example, Superintendent Hoerster required that women employees not carry purses larger than eight inches, since he felt larger ones would allow them to carry off supplies. Lolita Roberson recalled, "Many times Dr. Sam Hoerster would be there waiting when we got off at 11, waiting to see if we were coming out early or whatever." Hoerster became so obsessed with the problem of pilferage that he even issued a memo forbidding the gathering of windfall pecans on the hospital grounds. Anyone caught pocketing pecans had his or her pay docked by ten dollars for three consecutive months.[44]

Employees often stole bed linen, since the only mark on each piece was a small "SLA" near the hem of the sheet. Rehemming the sheet obliterated all traces of ownership. Staff simply signed a form that the sheet had been damaged and discarded, and there was no check system. Employees also frequently stole towels, and a staff meeting of August 11, 1958, sought possible solutions to the problem. Hoerster suggested that each patient be issued one towel per week and be made responsible for it. Persons incapable of caring for their own towels could be helped by those who could.[45]

In addition to handling the many details of the hospital's day-to-day operation, superintendents personally dealt with the inevitable crises that arose, including fires, epidemics, escapes by dangerous inmates, patients' deaths, and a variety of scandals. From the asylum's beginning, superintendents at the state asylum worried about the threat of fire. Several mental hospitals in other states had suffered the loss of many lives due to fires, and in its history the Texas State Lunatic Asylum experienced several serious conflagrations. On January 24, 1875, the *Austin Daily Democratic Statesman* reported, "one year ago Christmas the Lunatic Asylum caught on fire and came within an ace of burning down, and on last Monday it caught on fire again and it was with the greatest difficulty that the flames were extinguished." The article concluded with a call for a legislative investigation, a common journalistic admonition for the state asylum.[46]

In 1882, a dormitory housing forty-six men burned to the ground. Fortunately, all patients were saved. Lightning caused a fire in 1892, and "the fire department was notified by horse and rider since the lightning had knocked out the asylum's telephone." Some fires originated from flames associated with the everyday operation of the hospital. The asylum's laundry, worth thirty-three thousand dollars, burned on December 15, 1916, presumably when a fire got out of control in the drying room.[47]

The fear of fire had not diminished by the 1950s. During his first week as superintendent in March 1955, Dr. Sam Hoerster "marked some sections of the hospital grounds off limits to employee parking" so that emergency vehicles, including fire trucks, might have easy access to the buildings. Being forced to park farther away angered employees, and so many of them complained to their state legislator that he launched a brief investigation into the matter. However, a huge fire on December 18, 1958, vindicated Superintendent Hoerster's decision regarding parking. The *Austin American* reported: "A few days ago at the peak of evening traffic on Guadalupe and Lamar, two of Austin's busiest traffic arteries, ugly flames swept through the 50,000 square foot building housing the hospital's central kitchen, dining hall, recreation hall and basement store room."[48] The article attributed the successful evacuation of patients and lack of injury to Hoerster's foresight in providing access for the emergency vehicles.

Nurse Tisha Kinnard, who discovered the blaze, described: "I looked back and saw smoke while making night rounds. I ran back to the switchboard to call in the alarm. Police, fire, Red Cross all came out. We worked straight through till the next day evacuating patients. We moved about nine hundred patients from surrounding buildings."[49]

Austin State Hospital's 1958 fire apparently had ignited from a smoldering cigarette. There had been much staff discussion regarding the danger, since in this era of free cigarettes for patients, smoking in bed caused frequent fires. Executive staff meeting minutes for September 19, 1958, reported "more than one fire every single week, or an average of two per week." Administrators had even considered posting "No Smoking Unless Properly Supervised" signs but decided against it. As Dr. Lara remarked, "Many patients were too disturbed to understand the meaning of the signs."[50]

While none of the hospital's several fires hurt anyone, a gas explosion in the late 1930s caused serious injuries. Former employee Otto Schultz recalled: "One of the patients smelled gas, and two others went to see. The attendant and the patient sniffed out down to the manhole, and it led down to a wide tunnel, and all the utilities ran through there. Another patient went with them and didn't think of the seriousness of the gas. The attendant on the surface started to close the manhole and just as he did the explosion took place. It blew the manhole cover back at him and he burned from here to here on up very badly. The two patients ran out."[51]

While accidents such as the gas explosion could not be anticipated, at the height of the cold war during the 1950s the hospital planned for the contingency of nuclear war and readied an emergency plan. This plan included issuing every patient a laminated identification card.[52]

The death of a patient always constituted a crisis with which the superintendent had to deal, and such events were all too common. Superintendents' annual reports carefully enumerated and explained any patient death occurring during the previous year. For example, Superintendent B. M. Worsham's annual report for 1897 noted: "There was one homicide. Two patients occupied the same room. The stronger of the two believing his room-mate (a harmless dement) to be the devil, proceeded to take his life by choking him. The night watchman attracted by the noise, dragged him from his hapless victim, but too late." Dr. Worsham's report for 1902 explained: "In June there was a severe epidemic of typhoid fever, 35 cases in all, 12 patients, and one death. The source of the infection was thought to be the water supply. Germs blew into the reservoir which was left uncovered to cool the 100 degree artesian water before pumping it into the standpipe."[53]

Sixteen years later, the widespread influenza epidemic of 1918 struck the crowded hospital with terrible effect, and so many attendants fell ill or left their posts in fear that patients had to assume responsibility for running the wards. Some recalled the situation as reminiscent of historical accounts of the black death of the Middle Ages, when bodies were stacked outside each morning to be carried off in the wagon.[54]

In addition to deaths from exhaustion from various agitative forms of insanity, paresis, and two homicides, Dr. Worsham's report for 1904 listed "two suicides, one woman hung herself with bedclothing. A man broke into the case on his ward where razors were kept, and securing one cut his throat from ear to ear. He received immediate attention and it is believed he would have recovered had he not been in such an excited condition and so determined to defeat every object to save him."[55]

Prevention of suicide proved very difficult, since patients constantly devised ingenious methods to kill themselves, such as by jumping head first down stairwells or diving off lavatories. As each new suicide technique succeeded, superintendents instituted policies designed to prevent others from committing suicide in that way. For example, a memo from Superintendent Hoerster to all employees dated December 1, 1957, directed: "Marking ink is to be kept under lock and key and clearly marked poison. The danger of toxic effects of these inks makes this order necessary." Executive staff minutes from November 5, 1958, recorded that a patient had used a spoon to

*Unidentified nurses posted a "For Sale" sign on the front gate of the asylum, 1918.*
*Courtesy ASH*

cut his wrists, and "Dr. Hoerster commented that attendants should pick up the silver ware while patients are still seated in order to make sure that all silverware has been collected before patients leave the dining room."[56]

In their reports, superintendents often attributed patients' deaths to natural causes, to the effects of preexisting conditions, or to advanced age. Clearly, any death raised the possibility of negligence or actual complicity on the part of hospital personnel, which the superintendent had to address. Superintendents seized upon any explanation that exonerated the hospital from blame. Similarly, other agencies that had had contact with the deceased likewise tried to eschew responsibility for the death. On one occasion a Houston deputy sheriff tried to convince a hospital physician, Dr. Hannis, that the woman he had transported to Austin had been alive upon entering the grounds of the state hospital, claiming, "She walked to that bench herself." Dr. Hannis replied, "I don't see how. She's got rigor mortis."[57]

With so many deaths to deal with, asylum staff followed a routine for mortuary procedures. After a patient died, the attendant on duty transported the body to the morgue, located in the basement of the hospital building.

As former attendant Jim Cooper recalled, "When one died you had to clean them up, take the tubes out, and take the mattress over to the place to clean it up." Cooper, a student at the University of Texas, once missed a final exam following a patient's death. His professor allowed him to retake the exam saying, "You couldn't possibly have made up a story like that."[58]

Normally, the physician on duty completed the death certificate. The lack of complete data on these certificates troubled W. A. Davis, the state registrar of vital statistics, and in 1917 Davis twice wrote to Superintendent Preston complaining about items left blank on the certificates.[59] Sometimes the doctor on duty at the time of death and the pathologist disagreed about the cause of death. Discussing this issue in a staff meeting in 1958, Superintendent Hoerster decided that the pathologist should sign the death certificate when he disagreed with the physician on duty.[60]

Upon a patient's death, the hospital notified the family, if any, requesting instruction regarding the handling of the body. Sometimes the family responded immediately; a telegram sent to Superintendent Preston from Luke Word of Hempstead requested, "Send the body at our expense first train." Often, however, the family failed to respond, and the body was then buried in a plain wooden coffin at the asylum cemetery, located several blocks north. Supervisors had the responsibility for seeing that the "remains are prepared in a becoming manner for burial." Patients usually had charge of digging the grave and transporting the deceased to the cemetery at Austin State Hospital, although at another Texas mental hospital grave digging had become a permanent duty of the recreational therapist.[61]

For its short trip to the cemetery, the simple wooden casket rode in a horse-drawn wagon through the streets of the neighborhood adjacent to Hyde Park. Erna Wisian Leigh recalled seeing caskets slide off the back of the wagon as the careless driver attempted to take the corner by her home at too great a speed. However, "They'd just get down and load it up again and off they'd go."[62]

In the complexities of the mental institution, with its thousands of patients, occasional errors occurred, as in the case of "Alfred," whose family upon notification of his death requested that the body be returned to Houston. However, upon its arrival the family failed to recognize the deceased. A letter dated January 8, 1926, from undertaker F. M. Fairchild to Superintendent J. G. Springer declared, "All of [Alfred]'s relatives declared at first sight, the man was not their kinsman, but finally were convinced that a mistake by the Hospital at Austin would be impossible and he had been changed by death."[63]

Faith in the asylum's infallibility proved misplaced, however, since Springer later acknowledged that the hospital had indeed made a mistake and that Alfred "is here and in fairly good health for one of his age." He enclosed a check for $159.62 "to cover the expenses of shipping and internment of 'Mack,'" the man mistaken for Alfred.[64]

Institutional births created almost as many problems for superintendents as institutional deaths, and they might be even more embarrassing. Whenever possible, the hospital tried to establish that patients had been pregnant upon admission. To avoid the stigma of listing Austin State Hospital as the place of birth on the birth certificate, staff members routinely transported patients in labor to a local hospital for the delivery. As former ASH employee Don Howell commented: "Sometimes we would break all kinds of records to see that they got to Brackenridge. We were told that it just would not happen that a baby would be born on the state hospital grounds, and it didn't."[65]

In addition to dealing with periodic crises and handling daily administrative details, superintendents' success in recruiting and supervising medical personnel had great importance to the efficient functioning of the institution. Superintendents often had difficulty hiring well-qualified assistant physicians, as a legislative committee on organization and economy reported in 1931:

> The salary schedule of assistant physicians is from $150 to $183.33 a month with full maintenance, one room only being allowed as quarters regardless of the size of family. This, together with the fact that there are no particularly attractive higher posts in the State service to which they might aspire, necessarily limits the applicants to those who, due to professional, physical, or temperamental infirmities, cannot make a living elsewhere or who are merely looking for a "stop-gap" pending some more attractive offer.[66]

Some of the personnel at ASH were even less charitable in their assessments of the assistant physicians. Social worker Ruth Howard commented: "We had doctors from other countries. Their personalities were such they could never be in private practice. There were [also] a few good old boys who had been in practice in rural areas and their practices had dwindled away. They were not psychiatrists, just family practitioners, but at least they were nice."[67]

Serious shortages of qualified physicians meant that sometimes the hospital employed doctors who were not licensed to practice in Texas as "medical technicians." In 1963, 48 of the 207 individuals performing the duties of physicians in the Texas state hospitals had no medical license.[68]

State hospitals also attracted a few unscrupulous doctors, those who had lost—or nearly lost—their licenses for malpractice, and even an occasional imposter. One such doctor frequently prescribed lethal levels of drugs, which fortunately the nurses almost always caught in time to reduce the dosage.[69]

Alcoholism among physicians could be a problem as well. Ruth Howard stated: "There was one [doctor] who was an alcoholic, and he would come on his rounds when he had had too much to drink. Everybody looked the other way." And one superintendent, who continually complained to the governor about his woefully inadequate budget, nevertheless found the funds to purchase two and one-half gallons of whiskey and five gallons each of port and sherry each week.[70]

Other staff members widely recounted doctors' eccentricities. One germ-conscious doctor carried a bottle of rubbing alcohol with him at all times to cleanse his hands. As Howard Brack described, "His hands looked like a scaly lizard." Brack identified another doctor as a "pistol," commenting that one index finger was shorter than the other from pushing the button on the shock box so often. Another asylum physician, Dr. Ramsdell, liked to joke with the staff that a certain patient "smells like a schizophrenic to me."[71] On rare occasions, eccentricity verged over into actual mental illness, as another staff member recalled: "One doctor was as psychotic as any patient. He was tall and thin and always wore a pith helmet and rubber raincoat and a mask. He was scared of electroshock therapy and always wore a mask when he gave it. He would sit in his office and hallucinate and talk. He would take three steps forward and one step back as he walked across the grounds, but he could do a perfect workup on new patients. However, he would never give a diagnosis of schizophrenia."[72]

Sometimes the hospital knowingly employed physicians who had been mentally ill themselves. Staff minutes for March 16, 1959, indicated: "Dr. Lara reported that Dr. _____ called him Saturday and informed him that she was returning to Wichita Falls. The reason she gave for leaving was that she was ill and felt she should return home now as she felt that she should see her own physician." Superintendent Hoerster then asked Dr. Lara for his impression of that doctor and her work, and Dr. Lara replied: "She is quite set in her ways and not able to follow instructions and procedures. Her readings of tracings is adequate enough, but she gets quite upset about disagreements contrary to her readings." Dr. Hoerster then explained that the doctor had been a patient at two other state hospitals, where she had worked as a lab technician.[73]

Some staff believed that one superintendent had become unbalanced himself. Tales of his eccentric behavior included yelling at birds to quiet them, illegally arming the hospital's night watchmen with guns, and firing employees for walking on the grass or other minimal infractions.

Superintendents justified hiring physicians who had been treated for mental illness as setting an example for other employers. If the state hospital denied jobs to doctors who were former mental patients, who else could be expected to hire them? In truth, the state hospital had such a shortage of physicians that superintendents welcomed virtually any who applied for a position, including four female physicians who served before 1930. Like their male colleagues, they tended to stay less than a year.[74]

Attracting and retaining competent physicians challenged the skills of superintendents, and some did this better than others. A report on Texas mental institutions by the U.S. Public Health Service in 1943 commended Superintendent Standifer for his success in the recruitment of physicians, noting that, "The superintendent has persuaded several men who otherwise might have been quite justified in cutting down their activities and enjoying the leisure to which years of steady service in the community has entitled them to come into the organization and carry some responsibilities at least for the duration of the war."[75]

One of these elderly physicians, Dr. Spencer, had graduated from medical school in 1898. Some thought that the beliefs of Spencer's wife, a Christian Scientist, had "rubbed off" on the doctor, since the only remedies he prescribed were aspirin and salt water.[76]

Like other well-qualified physicians identified in the 1931 report as taking positions at the state hospitals as "stop-gaps," Dr. Elbert Leggett had planned to remain only three months and then to accept an internship at Scott and White Hospital in Temple. Circumstances intervened, however, and the day Leggett had planned to leave he contracted polio. The only doctor on duty that night, he developed a headache and flulike symptoms. He told the switchboard he was going to the home of his wife's parents and could be reached there in case of an emergency. The emergency turned out to be his own, however, and by the time Dr. Leggett had recovered enough from the polio to leave the hospital, he was in a wheelchair and incapable of making rounds at Scott and White. He rejoiced when Dr. Bolding, the assistant superintendent, asked him to come back to work at the state hospital. Ramps were installed and a patient was assigned to wheel him around until he "graduated to crutches." He commented, "I was surprised at how much I enjoyed working there," and remained on the staff until his retirement in 1981.[77]

Whatever their hopes or expectations for practicing psychiatry, the physicians soon found that they spent most of their time looking after patients' physical health. Dr. Margaret Sedberry recalled: "There was little psychotherapy due to most of the patients being psychotic. Later there were a few neurotics and some psychotherapy was done. I started out thinking I could cure schizophrenia, but now I think most of it is organic or genetic."[78]

The ratio of doctors to patients was always a problem. A 1950 survey of mental institutions in Texas by the National Institute of Mental Health reported that the Austin State Hospital had only nine physicians, and that two of these, Superintendent Hanretta and Assistant Superintendent Bolding, functioned as administrative rather than clinical staff. The nine physicians served a patient population of 3,198, a caseload of approximately 457 patients per doctor. Overall, Texas had fewer than one-fifth of the number of physicians recommended for mental institutions by the American Psychiatric Association at that time.[79]

One method for alleviating this shortage involved hiring consulting physicians from the community. Dr. James Lassiter came to Austin in 1951 and joined the Austin Anesthesiology Group, serving as a consulting anesthesiologist for the state hospital. Lassiter found that the mentally ill generally withstood surgery very well. One patient had been operated on for a peptic ulcer at 6:00 P.M., then woke up about eight o'clock and "got out of bed and beat up the patient in the bed next to him." Another patient

> was a little lady about 65 or 70 years old. I put her to sleep. We did not have a recovery room in those days and we'd wake them up in the operating room for a couple of minutes and then take them back to their regular room. After putting her back to bed, I went down to the nurses' station and was writing up the final part of the operation on her chart. I heard steps and looked up, and here was this patient walking down the hall, and I said, "Where are you going?" And she said, "I'm going to wee."[80]

Physicians often found it difficult to get a complete medical history from their mental patients. As Dr. Will VanWisse noted, "Usually the patient withheld information because he did not expect to be understood by other people or he tended to misrepresent his symptoms." Dr. Leggett likened practice in the asylum to veterinary medicine, saying that in neither circumstance could your patients tell you what was wrong with them. Illustrating this dilemma, one doctor reported his "humiliation" at spending days trying to quiet an agitated patient before finding the man's abscessed tooth.[81]

State hospital physicians had other difficulties besides their extremely heavy caseloads. Dr. Sedberry reported great frustration in dealing with the political hierarchy and the variety of administrative duties that made huge demands on her time. Belknap's research bore her out, since he estimated that ASH physicians spent up to 60 percent of their time with "paperwork and correspondence, record reading and analysis, organizational and medical staff meetings, assisting in surgery or other hospital duty of a non-psychiatric sort, conferring with auxiliary medical personnel, carrying special responsibilities during the rotating officer-of-the-day period for receiving service and conferring and working with other physicians and the superintendent on the chronic problems of recruiting, training, and firing personnel."[82]

In conversations with Belknap, state hospital physicians identified the major reasons for the high turnover rate. Eighty percent left within three years—as one doctor noted—because "[i]t is almost impossible to practice psychiatry in this institution." Other reasons mentioned included the inability to conduct research, low prestige of psychiatrists practicing on the wards, low pay, and unpleasant and depressing working conditions.[83]

Not all doctors at the hospital agreed with these critics. Those who stayed believed in their profession, enjoyed working directly with the mentally ill, and, in general, "did the best we could for as long as we could."[84]

In the early days, very few trained nurses worked at the asylum. Typically, attendants filled this role, dispensing medications, giving shots, and assisting the physicians. Nurse Ida Lou Bruce, who began work at Austin State Hospital in 1931, enjoyed working directly with patients, recalling, "There was this one guy. You'd give him a shot and he'd write you a check for one hundred thousand dollars."[85]

By the mid-1950s, when Lillian Eidelbach became director of Nursing Services, only eight nurses worked the day shift for three thousand patients. She commented: "I could see how much we were needed and all the things we could do." She believed her nurses loved the job because they had a lot of authority and were given considerable responsibility for medical decisions. She stated, "Their morale was high and they felt respected." Nurse Penny Marks affirmed, "My proudest moment was when Dr. Hoerster gave me my set of keys."[86]

In contrast, social services staff had decidedly lower morale, believing themselves poorly paid and housed, and poorly treated in comparison to some business office personnel and craft employees such as the electricians. This dissatisfaction was evidenced by a median length of service of only 1.3 years between 1927–50.[87]

Superintendent A. T. Hanretta described the duties of sociologist Velma Stigler and junior sociologists Angelien Cobble and Emma Lee Massey. "In our state hospital, the Sociologist and her [assistants] have many many duties. She carries a gracious authority as to the policy of this Department among her co-workers, assigning duties, individually advising in cases and problems, consulting Physicians relative to their respective patients' work, conferring with outside social agencies, when the last mentioned are interested."[88] However, in spite of Hanretta's assessment of their "many many duties," social services staff chaffed at their limited authority. Ruth Howard recalled: "The main thing we did was social histories, and we did extensive social histories for each patient. We'd interview the patients and the families if they were with them. They did not recognize the ability of social work to help patients, so the position was sort of boring for me."[89]

Social workers who stepped over these boundaries might be chastised severely, as in the case of the person who "encouraged patients about the possibility of going home." After the ward attendant complained to the doctor that the social worker was agitating his patients, the physician told the social worker to "keep her psychiatric opinions to herself."[90]

Similarly, the duties of the first clinical psychologists at the state hospital were limited to administering psychological tests; they did not include participation as members of the patient-treatment teams. As Belknap explained, "In 1950 the division of psychology was new, headed by a full-time Ph.D. who left rather quickly since he was not paid what had been promised nor allowed to do research and it was likely that clerical, administrative duties would increase."[91]

Belknap reported a much lower turnover rate and higher rate of job satisfaction among business personnel than medical personnel. Business staff's turnover rate was only about 1 percent a year compared to the physicians' rate of almost 30 percent. Such statistics indicated the remarkable degree to which formal organizational structure at Austin State Hospital differed from the actual structure. As Belknap noted: "The informal relationships between the attendants, the clerical personnel and certain employees in the business system were among the most important in the hospital. The employees involved in this system were invariably the oldest in point of service in the hospital. Their uninterrupted tenure and experience made them reliable informants on what could and could not be done in the hospital." The superintendent and others used them as an informal advisory staff. While their official position on organizational charts might be quite low, in actuality their seniority and knowledge about the hospital gave them enormous power. On one occasion, a lab technician cursed an older attendant, who was late getting a patient to him for a blood test. Bypassing the formal chain of command, the irate attendant went directly to the superintendent to complain.[92]

Confronted with these remarkable discrepancies between formal and informal power relationships at the state hospital, the superintendents' dilemma was clear. They possessed the official authority to run the hospital according to modern psychiatric practices, but attempts to do so meant changing traditional routines and the habits of the older employees, which this group successfully resisted. Although attendants rarely challenged authority directly, they consistently managed to adjust "the requirements of psychiatric treatment with the requirements of daily patient management."[93]

A new superintendent grappling with lack of funding and ever-expanding patient populations soon confronted the realities of running the asylum. Superintendents, like the governors who appointed them, came and went; meanwhile, life on the grounds and in the wards remained much the same throughout the decades. From the nineteenth century on, overcrowding and limited resources meant that attendants had to enlist the help of less disturbed patients in running the wards and in handling other patients. Thus, assignment to wards depended not only on a patient's diagnosis but also on the needs of the attendants to have some "good" patients on each ward. While superintendents might exercise enormous authority over many other aspects of the asylum's operation, any attempt to change the ward system met with passive resistance from the attendants and failed utterly.

Attendants, especially "clan" members who had a hereditary relationship to the hospital dating back several generations and who often had several relatives employed there, had a clear view of their value to the institution. As one stated: "This place would go to pieces if it weren't for the attendants. But we never get any credit or recognition. That bunch in the front office sit around on their ___ 's all day and read reports and write letters and diagnose the cases at long range, but we're the boys who have to handle the problems."[94]

# ⌁ CHAPTER 4 ⌁

# Attendants

## *"The Boys who Handle the Problems"*

Initially, the morning bell called attendants to their posts an hour before the sun began to lighten the eastern horizon, and they remained on duty until the asylum officially closed at 9:30 P.M. Even after retiring for the night, they had to cope with any emergencies that arose, their only assistance being a night watchman, who responded to the signal of a kerosene lantern hung outside a dormitory window. The successful operation of the asylum depended directly on attendants' skillful performance of their duties, especially this round-the-clock supervision of patients. As a result, the asylum claimed virtually all of its attendants' time, strictly limiting any hours off duty.

In her recollections of working at the asylum in 1913, an anonymous attendant reported: "I got one Sunday off each month. Other Sundays I worked until the ward was cleaned up and then got off about 9 AM and had to be back in time to serve supper."[1] Attendants could not leave the grounds without a pass, and anyone returning after the curfew faced dismissal.

Asylum rules also demanded that attendants wear uniforms. The same attendant wrote: "My first day of work was December 12, 1912. Our uniforms were grayish blue chambray, long sleeves, high neck, open and buttoned down the back to the bottom of the placket. They had three rows of white braid on the skirt, on cuffs, collar and belt. We wore these white aprons with bib and straps over the shoulder. We also had to wear black shoes."[2]

Uniform styles changed over time. When Bess McCord started work in 1930, the uniforms for female attendants had blue and white stripes. She remembered: "The laundry did them for us, and you could stand them up and get in them. We had gathered white shirt collars and cuffs and we had to have a cap on at all times. We had cotton hose at twenty-five cents a pair

*Women attendants wore nurses' uniforms in the 1940s. Courtesy ASH*

and nurses' oxfords. You did not go to work without a cap or hose on."[3] Still later, female attendants dressed in white nurses' uniforms, and male attendants wore white pants, white long-sleeved shirts, and black bow ties. As late as the 1950s, deviation from the dress code could result in a severe reprimand or even dismissal, as one attendant caught rolling up his shirt sleeves on the way to his car discovered.

In addition to working long hours (and being ever on call), level III, or nonprofessional, staff received low salaries. An employment application dated June 8, 1915, stated that attendants were paid from fifteen to twenty-five dollars per month and were "promoted on merit." In 1913 the new attendant's check totaled only fifteen dollars, but her salary increased to twenty-five dollars after she took over C North, a very violent ward.[4]

By the early 1930s, salaries had risen to thirty dollars per month, a good wage during the Great Depression. As one attendant stated: "You got thirty dollars a month plus room, board, laundry, and your doctor. That was a good salary back in those days."[5] However, unlike earlier attendants, who were paid in gold coins, depression-era employees often received warrants instead of money. Otto Schultz explained: "The state of Texas was running in the red and pay was issued in warrants. But on each payday there was seated near the pay window a man with very much money who cashed the warrants at a discount." Another former employee added: "A ward attendant set up a loan shark operation and made fantastic money. That's when employees were paid in state warrants, and the state warrant companies would discount them for a certain percent, but he would cash them for a fee."[6]

In the early 1950s the number of working hours required per week diminished, but "attendants did not understand why clerical personnel could work only forty hours per week and they had to work forty-four to forty-eight hours per week." By this time employee benefits also had improved, with workers receiving twelve days of paid sick leave per year. When ill, employees had to notify the hospital at least one hour before their shift began. The regulations stated, "Sick leave papers must be filled out in triplicate, and turned in to the Supervisor's office within three days after the return to duty."[7] In spite of these strict guidelines, employees sometimes abused sick leave. For example, supervisory staff noticed the frequency with which University of Texas students fell ill before major examinations. College students had to provide a doctor's certificate even if they missed only one day, but a local doctor readily produced these for a fee of $1.50 or $2.00 without even seeing the patients.[8]

As noted, asylum employees' benefits customarily included the "emoluments" of room, board, laundry, and medical care. Assigned by an employee's rank, living quarters were generally minimal, with single men occupying the basement in the Administration Building. Though spartan, Otto Schultz's room on the east end of the basement met his needs, since it positioned him strategically close to the streetcar line. Similarly, attendant Wendell Worley enjoyed his basement room and even arranged a private telephone line. He remembered: "They had the old system of a switchboard with one ring for one person and two rings for another. If it had four rings it was for me. Then I got greedy and wired in a private line and the phone company caught it and made me take it out."[9]

By the 1930s married couples received more spacious accommodations, two- or three-room apartments or, for top-level personnel and physicians, separate houses located on the perimeter of the hospital grounds. Physicians' families lived on the north side and other families along the west and south borders. Dr. Elbert Leggett recalled that he and his family occupied a newly constructed house that was quite nice. Similarly, the family of male supervisor R. I. Worley found their home on the south side of the grounds small but adequate.[10] Lower-ranking personnel had more complaints. Those who had rooms over the laundry recalled almost unbearable heat in the summer, made tolerable only by a fan blowing over a dishpan containing a block of ice.

As did most of the families that lived on the grounds, the family of R. I. Worley often employed patients in their homes. Mary Worley Hopkins recalled: "Back then, if they [the patients] had some job, they could get outside. Mother was very compassionate and loving and would find something for them to do." One patient, George, cooked for them on Sundays, and another worked on their automobiles. "Our playmates were inmates," Hopkins commented. "They would play hopscotch with you or anything." Another favored patient, "Tiny," always watched after the youngest Worley children.[11]

When both parents worked, patients frequently provided child care. Ethel Brack, who worked first in Food Service and then in the hospital's dental office, returned to work when her first son was about a year old. She commented, "We hired a patient as baby-sitter. She may have been a schizophrenic, but she was fairly normal."[12]

Of all the children who grew up on the asylum grounds, those in the superintendent's family enjoyed the most privileges. Charles Standifer's father became superintendent in 1927 when Charles Jr. was ten years old and his sister Margaret was six. Charles recalled, "I could walk anywhere on the grounds except the wards and be given cookies or candy or something else. The cook kept a chocolate cake all the time, and I loved it."[13]

Like other asylum children, Charles accepted patient behavior as a normal part of his world, no matter how bizarre that behavior might be. He recalled, "One patient would pick up dirt and pile it over here and move it over there. I never did pay too much attention to that. Now I realize that it was a symptom of mental disorder, but I was just used to it."[14]

Sometimes the children formed special friendships with individual patients such as "Redbeard," who took a proprietary interest in the lakes on the asylum grounds. Redbeard cleaned the lakes by throwing out a rake tied to a rope and dragging it through the water to remove the waterweed. He often built a fire to warm himself as he cleaned the lakes or fished, and children walking across the grounds to school took advantage of his fire before continuing on their way. Sometimes he exchanged the fish he caught for chewing tobacco, which neighborhood children, the Basey brothers, acquired from their father's store.[15]

Children listened with interest to the stories some patients told about being an admiral in the Russian navy, or Joan of Arc, or the nation's first president. Mary Worley Hopkins remembered: "George Washington was in the first building on the right as you came in the gate, and he would sit out on a little porch, and he always liked us because we called him 'Mr. President,' and he thought he really was the president, but we knew he was not but we acted like he was, and every Christmas he gave us silver dollars and for our family he ordered crates of grapefruit and oranges and apples and sent it to our house."[16]

For children, experiences of growing up on the asylum grounds resembled those of their counterparts in any small town of the time. Local reporter Mary Jimperieff wrote that the eighteen hundred inmates of the State Lunatic Asylum "live the life of a quiet country village. They have picture shows, the victrolas, all their actual needs supplied, bowling alley, a dance hall and on Sunday there is church. The institution is equipped with a laundry, steam plant, ice plant, blacksmith shop, dairy, carpenter shop, [and] barber shop." Similarly, Charles Stanford, whose father directed landscaping, recalled: "The state hospital was like a little town, had the hospital, a shoe shop, a library. Our home was nice and the environment was good. We could play. Mother was a worrywart, but she didn't worry about us playing since it was fenced in. It was just our little town."[17]

In spite of the general contentment of long-term employees and their families with life at the state hospital, some new employees evaluated their circumstances quite differently. The combination of low salaries and poor conditions resulted in an especially high turnover rate for new attendants. Unlike the clan members long accustomed to hospital conditions, these new employees often left rapidly. During 1951–52, for example, about 80 percent of the ward attendants quit. "Every day for the first month I was going to quit," Lolita Roberson recalled. "I would come home and I would be in tears. I'd say, 'I'm not going back.' Every morning I'd say, 'It'll probably be better today.'"[18] Like many of those who stayed, Roberson had a relative working at the hospital, a sister who had told her about the job.

Recruitment of attendants could be difficult. At one time, Assistant Superintendent Bolding even carried application forms around in his vest pocket so that he could sign up likely candidates on the spot.[19] In general, the public perceived the working conditions at the hospital much less positively than people who worked there, and Roberson reported a certain stigma attached to being an employee. She explained: "You learned to simply say that you worked for the state. The stigma was that that was probably the only job you could get because the pay was so low and the conditions so bad." Moreover, the public had an exaggerated fear of violent patients. While employees agreed that patients could become violent on occasion, they did not see the threat of violence as a great problem. Supervisor of Nursing Lillian Eidelbach did not fear violent patients. She recalled: "I was attacked by a patient who was paranoid and thought I had stolen her husband. One of my favorite patients, who had been a school teacher, pulled her off and said, 'Don't you hurt my nurse.'"[20]

Similarly, Otto Schultz, who worked with patients on the asylum concrete gang while a student at the University of Texas in the early 1930s, wrote: "We knew the hazards involved in the work with the patients, and we saw incidents that reminded us that vigilance was necessary in our work. But we formed lasting friendships with several of the blacks in our gang and that was pleasant. We felt that if a patient lost control suddenly, others would come to our aid."[21]

Perhaps anticipation of physical struggles with patients caused the criteria for employment as an attendant to include height and weight guidelines. An employment application form dated 1915 listed the following physical requirements: "Good physical health and temperate habits. Women must not be less than 19 or over 40 years of age, and men not less than 21 and not over 40 years of age. Women must be at least 5'4" in height and men 5'7". Applicants must not be over 20% above the average weight, proportional to height; and not less than 15% below."[22] For a woman of five feet, four inches tall, the acceptable weight range was 115 to 165. Later, psychological tests helped screen potential applicants. The Texas Research League stated: "Placement of employees is determined by IQ. Laundry workers must have an IQ of 85 or better and hydrotherapists must have an IQ of 95 or better. No other criteria are used such as experience or aptitude."[23] Several later employees remembered drawing a house, a tree, and a person when they applied—the House-Tree-Person Projective Technique. These drawings supposedly reflected the person's attitude toward home, their role in life, and interpersonal relations.[24] Lolita Roberson recalled that one person giving the tests in the 1960s commonly advised applicants never to work longer than five years in psychiatric nursing since after that "you were likely to convert over and become a patient."[25]

Because of their firsthand knowledge of working conditions at the state hospital, long-term employees made excellent recruiters for the institution. Sue Pearce, who held a variety of jobs at the hospital, remembered: "The state hospital was not generally known as a good place to work [in the 1950s]. It was not considered safe, but the people who were working there would tell their relatives and have them come out there so they could see that you would not be killed by walking on the grounds. I went to work there because I had a great aunt who worked there. She talked me into applying for a job."[26]

Sometimes inside information provided just the right incentive for an individual. Willie Crow's mother, who worked at the asylum in 1917 before she married, told Willie about the gallon cans of pineapple stored in the pantry. This impressed the young girl, since her family had only a little pineapple at Christmas as a special treat. The abundance of institutional pineapple helped Willie decide to work at the hospital.[27]

The Report of the Joint Legislative Committee summed up the clan system at the state hospital. "A very large number of the employes have been there several years, have intermarried and really know no other home. This results in a tolerance of working and living conditions and of wage rates that would otherwise be impossible." Twenty-five years later, Belknap's study also identified a group of "core families with a hereditary relation to the hospital, whose members in each generation, having grown up in the hospital campus, found it natural to work there." These employees tended to be very loyal and typically had long years of service. Former employee Verna Lee Ferguson Tedford affirmed, "My father worked there, first in the TB ward and later in the garden, and my mother was in Food Service as a cook." Together, her parents put in sixty-six years of service. Verna Lee grew up on the grounds of the hospital and loved the place. However, her parents wanted her to get an education and objected to her working at the hospital. They told her, "You're not going to pick with the chickens," but working at the state hospital was all she wanted to do.[28]

At one time during the 1950s, approximately thirty-five members of one family worked at the hospital. Doubtless well aware of the degree to which familial relations affected day-to-day functioning of the institution, Superintendent L. P. Ristine (1953–55) went so far as to make a chart to help in understanding the complex family relationships.[29] The clan system characterized many large asylums and became even more pronounced at mental hospitals in smaller communities. Dr. Margaret Sedberry recalled of Rusk State Hospital: "The only other industry was the tomatoes. So many people wanted to work at the hospital. Even more than at ASH you had whole families working there."[30]

While the clan members were loyal and stable workers, problems could be associated with them. "A lot of people had relatives who worked here, so if you gossiped about someone you had to be real careful because they might be related," one third-generation employee explained. Lillian

Eidelbach affirmed, "If you started having trouble over here, you discovered that one of the relatives over there would cause trouble for you, too."[31]

Belknap estimated that the clan system had originated as early as the 1870s. Certainly, there were no restraints on hiring family members in the late-nineteenth and early-twentieth centuries. Myrtle Seiders Cuthbertson's mother Eva Cozby came to Austin around 1890 to work as an attendant with her cousin, previously a matron at an asylum in Little Rock, after the cousin accepted a better job at the Texas State Lunatic Asylum. Lewis Brownlow's parents met while working at the hospital about 1908, and, following his father's untimely death, Lewis welcomed his aunts Cora and Lillian White who joined his mother there.[32] Being related by blood or marriage to at least one other employee was more the norm than the exception.

While these extended family relationships created solidarity among employees, they had the side effect of creating an informal organizational structure very different from the formal structure. Even low-level employees could wield considerable power since they often had long tenure, detailed "institutional memory" of the hospital's working arrangements, or were related to someone who did. Belknap wrote:

> The main function of the informal organization on the wards for the attendant is to set up a system which permits him to adjust personally the requirements of psychiatric treatment, as represented by the hospital's formal classification on the one hand, with the requirements of daily patient management on the other. This adjustment involves a definite organization of interpersonal relations between the attendant and his fellow attendants, between the attendants and the members of the two upper administrative levels, and between the attendants and the patients. The system includes patterns of expected behavior and ideas for the attendants in relation to patients and to the upper-level professionals in the hospital. These patterns are justified by an ideology centering around the attendant's functions in the hospital, and the entire system is held together with considerable solidarity, or in-group feeling, against patients and the professionals, who are out-groups. The system is a complete social organization, with an ideology and a tradition at least seventy years old. It can be considered as a type of culture in the hospital, with its own functionaries, legends, and justifications.[33]

After observing an attempt by hospital administrators to reorganize the hospital and to establish a more rigidly-adhered-to chain of command that placed more authority in the hands of the upper-level personnel, Belknap noted: "At the end of about a year of our observation, the informal organization of the attendant staff was reestablishing itself through a system of direct and indirect channels. The attendant supervisors bypassed the director of nursing service by going directly to the superintendent when a policy was causing trouble in the attendant system, or when they wished to initiate action."[34]

The Texas Research League report on organizational structure and personnel administration viewed this situation very negatively: "Informal and highly personal power centers of control exist at the secondary supervisory levels because of frequent changes in the top administration in many institutions. Small personal empires grow and flourish, breeding unhealthy jealousies, discrimination against individual employees, and the malpractice of nepotism."[35] The report did not, however, suggest an alternative solution for recruiting and keeping personnel.

Students attending the University of Texas represented another major group of level III employees, one very distinct from the clan members. Since they could arrange their courses for mornings and their work for afternoons or evenings, these jobs suited their schedules ideally and in many cases were considered plums to be dispensed as political favors. Otto Schultz's arrival at the hospital typified many. He recalled: "When I came to Austin in 1933 with one hundred dollars in my pocket, I looked all around and that was the depression. But the man who was still superintendent at the orphanage [where Schultz grew up] called up the pastor of the Presbyterian church here and he called Senator Pearl, and from there it was nothing. They called me to go out and see Mr. Sneed, and I was assigned to working with the concrete gang." Long-term employee Joe Pearce confirmed: "All these legislators had friends or relatives attending UT, and they wanted to get them jobs at ASH. They would say, 'Now give him a good job over there, not one where he has to work with a lot of crazy people.'"[36]

Sometimes these patronage positions fell into the more extreme category of "must hire—can't fire." In at least one instance at an asylum in Georgia, the person hired under these circumstances proved to be abusive toward patients, which normally meant immediate dismissal, but due to his political connections he could not be fired.[37] The worry that attendants might take advantage of their power over patients remained a perennial concern, and the institution had very strict guidelines concerning attendants' behaviors. A description of employees' duties written about 1900 noted: "Patients should be soothed and calmed when irritated, encouraged and cheered when melancholy. Never pushed, collared or rudely handled. To induce them to move gentle persuasive measures will generally prevail. When these fail report to the superintendent or one of the assistant physicians. Violent hands are never to be laid upon a patient under any provocation."[38] Similarly, the 1911 *By-laws, Rules and Regulations* of the asylum stated: "Attendants are to treat the patients with respect and attention [and] under all circumstances be firm, kind and considerate. Never address a patient rudely, by nickname, Christian name, or surname, but always politely as 'Mr.' 'Mrs.' or 'Miss'. . . . Attendants shall understand at all times that kindness toward the patients is demanded, and under no circumstances will they be excused for cruelty or abuse of the patients. They must not restrain or lock patients in their room without the authority of the Physician or Supervisor and report at once to the General Office."[39]

However, rumors of staff abuse of patients continued to circulate. During the legislative investigation of 1917, the committee chair asked Dr. Wooten Dudley Lightfoot, the first assistant physician, "Did you ever find any difficulty with the patients in the handling of them?" Lightfoot responded: "Now and then but very little. Much less than I would have imagined. I have only had one patient jump on me since I am out there." The questioner pursued the issue. "Do you ever find it necessary in handling patients to be a little bit rough with them?" Lightfoot replied, "I do not personally and we try to keep the attendants from doing so. This is not as easy to do as you might imagine. We have to watch the attendants pretty closely. They get rough after they stay there a while. We do not keep attendants when they get rough. We let them go right away." Similarly, Clifford Beers in his book, *A Mind that Found Itself,* described the tendency for attendants to become rough after they had been on the job for a while. One attendant told Beers: "When I came here, if someone had told me I would be guilty of striking patients I would have called him crazy himself, but now I take delight in punching the hell out of them."[40]

The natural tendency when attacked is to fight back. Some of the attendants had trouble handling violent patients in nonviolent ways, and a few developed a real taste for combat. As former attendant Phillip Otting told, "They liked to hire attendants that had some physical build to them. One of my friends liked to fight and told me about this one black guy who was a troublemaker, and this guy said, 'Okay, come on Buster,' and took him into a back room, and they had a fist fight and called it quits after a while."[41]

Actions of this sort could mean immediate dismissal, as an employee directive entitled *Conduct Subject to Dismissal* asserted. "Abuses, mistreatment or mishandling of patients; by threats, pulling hair, or striking the patient, etc." were not to be tolerated, and supervisors of attendants caught abusing patients were directed to fire them immediately. Wendell Worley recalled that his father, R. I. Worley, "would fire them on the spot and point out to them that they were not really suited for this line of work, and that it takes a certain type of individual to deal with patients." Few of the men fired in this manner ever expressed any resentment. One later told Wendell, "I walked out of your dad's office thinking that he had done me a favor by firing me."[42]

Other reasons for discharge included "borrowing money or taking personal belongings from patients; stealing, misuse, or destruction of State property; use of alcohol or drugs on duty or before reporting for duty; absence from duty without permission; offensive language or conduct; inefficiency, lack of interest, inability to perform duties and refusal to cooperate; sleeping on duty; gambling with the patients; and failure to abide by New Policies put into effect."[43]

The possibility of attendants stealing belongings from patients always concerned supervisors. As Mary Manoque testified in 1917 regarding her duties as supervisor of the white female wards, a position that she had held since 1885, "I have supervision of all of the white patients and their clothing and see that they are properly cared for and everything kept clean and see that the patients get the benefit of the private clothing." Both Manoque and J. C. Flowers, the male supervisor, admitted that they could have stolen if they had wanted to.[44]

Most new employees found the first day on the job to be the most difficult. Veteran attendants contributed to this, since they often encouraged initiation tours of the hospital morgue and a visit to Dr. Coleman de Chenar's collection of "pickled" brains, an important pathology collection for which both Harvard University and the University of Texas later vied. The University of Texas won, housing the two hundred specimens in its neuropathology museum.[45] Like many pathologists, Dr. de Chenar did not like to have untrained people watch as he performed autopsies. Dee Turner recalled, "He told them if they fainted they would be left where they lay."[46]

In an ancient practical joke for new medical personnel, first-day employees often were sent to the lab to pick up two fallopian tubes. Nurse Ida Lou Bruce responded to one such request with more teasing of the new staff member. "There are only two in this room," Bruce said, "and I'll be damned if you're going to get mine." New employees also might be mistaken for patients. One was told, "'Go on in, honey, and take your clothes off and take a shower?' She thought maybe all got it [similar treatment]. Then he said, 'Now go take a nap.' She knew it was wrong then."[47]

Experienced employees also played pranks on each other. Howard Brack recalled: "Old Man Welch was the night watchman. Old [L. G.] Sloan was the night engineer, and he'd put on a raincoat and pull his hat down and get to where Welch could see him and run. Welch would wave his flashlight around and chase him." Brack also told about the jokes men played on other men in their quarters. "There was no air conditioning. In the laundry building we slept out on the porch on these iron beds with springs. You were always getting short-sheeted, or you didn't know what would be in your bed." John Supak told how practical joker Greg Traho, who worked in Heating, Ventilation and Cooling, once threw his cap over the edge of the roof of the five-story hospital, cried, "I can't handle this any more!" and then jumped off. Supak ran over to the edge. Leaning over, he saw Traho on a ledge a few feet below, laughing. Another time, Traho hid on one of the trays in the morgue and waited for Supak to come in to check the temperature. Then he raised up under the sheet and said, "It's about time you got here, I'm getting cold."[48]

Sometimes employees involved patients in their practical jokes. Howard Brack told: "We'd send Doc McGraw [a patient] out to call Dr. Howard an SOB. Doc would say, 'Howard, you old son of a bitch.' Dr. Howard would call and send Doc up to Three [the most disturbed ward]. John [the attendant in charge of the ward] would get him back after a few days because he was a good worker."[49]

Very occasionally, these practical jokes had serious consequences, and Brack regretted his role in one of them. "You'd give Doc McGraw a nickel and tell him to kiss somebody, and he would. So I gave him a nickel and told him to kiss [male supervisor R. I.] Worley. The floor was soapy. It had just been mopped, and Worley slipped and broke his leg trying to get away. I felt bad about that."[50]

In the early days new employees received little training, but by the 1940s limited attendant-training programs existed. One instructional outline, dated October 1948, covered such topics as prevention of mental illness, sterilization, and personnel practices. However, the preponderance of the material, as in years past, dealt with appropriate conduct and included twenty-three rules for interaction with patients. Besides the usual admonitions, new guidelines included, "Don't tell patients' history to other patients; no smoking when over patient directly; and be able to meet changing needs without tension."[51]

Another training manual from about this time outlined the topics to be covered during the ten-hour training, which included:

*The role of the attendant and relation to his co-workers*
*The historical development of state institutions*
*Personnel practices*
*General hospital procedures*
*Principles of body mechanics*
*Application of good body mechanics*
*Psychiatric problem of seclusion and restraint*
*How to meet emergency situations*
*Emergency situation involving risk of patient's life*
*Summary and Review*[52]

Beginning in the early 1950s, a two-year Psychiatric Nurse Technician Program operated in conjunction with Blinn Junior College in Brenham, allowing attendants to improve their medical skills while on the job. In spite of these training efforts, a 1954 report by the Texas Research League indicated that a perceived lack of adequate training continued to be a major area of dissatisfaction among attendants, creating "a feeling of insecurity in doing their jobs."[53]

The 1950s manual advised against giving new employees a complete tour of the hospital during orientation since "[such] a procedure is hazardous for the individual unfamiliar with the mental hospital. Frightening features, such as the problems of suicide and assault, are called to his attention. The size of the hospital and the confusion of seeing so many sick patients is, indeed, often an overwhelming experience."[54] Instead, it advised placing new employees on the admitting ward where they would see a variety of patients and could gain self-confidence in working with them. By the early 1960s, most new employees were sent to the medical unit first and then dispersed out to the grounds.[55]

Others favored exactly the opposite approach, however. Ethel Brack noted that Dr. Bolding had always assigned new employees to the "drag ward" for elderly, mostly wheelchair-bound patients on the assumption that if they lasted there, they would last anywhere.[56]

The 1931 Report of the Joint Legislative Committee on Organization and Economy noted that there were three levels of attendants: the "charge attendant," who was in charge of individual wards; the attendant who is subordinate to the charge attendant; and, at the lowest level, the "back-hall probationer." An anonymous attendant from the San Antonio State Hospital described his reaction to one such back ward: "As you turn the key in the door of a locked 'Chronic Ward' and take a good look at the patients, approximately 125 men, you get a sick feeling in your stomach. How could any man fall so low, and why? Unshaven, barefoot, lying on the floor completely dejected or the ones that continually pace up and down. Some never speak a word—and some talk much too loud to no one in particular."[57]

Many employees avoided the wards for the most disturbed or violent patients. Raymond Habbit recalled one maintenance worker who greatly feared the violent wards. Once, while this man's crew painted in one of these wards, a patient placed his hand on the worker's shoulder. He "wet his pants and never would go back."[58]

Fear of assault by patients on the disturbed wards was not unreasonable. Attendants learned never to walk down the halls alone at night and never to go into an open door. Staff violated these rules at their own risk. One University of Texas student unwisely opened a locked door one night, and the patient swung at him, breaking his jaw.[59] In another case, a new psychologist demanded that a patient be released from restraint, and the patient promptly "sprang up off the floor and knocked him down."[60] As one former employee explained, "Before psychotropic drugs you don't realize how violent some of the patients were. They would tear up the mattresses and empty the pot out in the hall and smear the feces on the wall."[61]

In manic states, patients could perform almost superhuman feats of strength. One former professional football player pulled an iron radiator from the wall. Seeing that, the attendants sprinted to the seclusion rooms and locked themselves in until the patient fell down exhausted.[62]

Not just the male patients became hyperaggressive. Attendant Lois Gainer recalled:

They had a maximum security for black ladies. My supervisor, Rena Cope, asked me to go to that ward. I was the only attendant for one hundred patients. The day shift had set up the medication and they showed me one good patient who knew everyone by name. I didn't have any problems, but one patient had a case knife which she had sharpened on the windowsill and honed to a razor-sharp edge on both sides. She carried it in her garter, and one day it fell out. I grabbed it. Ms. Cope sent a carryall to get it. Dr. Hoerster wanted to see it, and he got on them for not counting the knives.[63]

Joe Pearce recalled another incident with a manic patient:

Shortly after I went to work there, there was a local lady who would go into a manic episode and be wild as a March hare. She was very nice, very refined, except when she was in a manic state. The family called the local sheriff's deputies who were like Abbott and Costello, and they went out to pick her up. Cars started honking and people pointed. She had taken off all her clothes. One deputy started trying to get her to put them back on and she started fighting him. They got her out there and these two men were dragging this naked lady down the hall, trying to get her to admissions, and somebody said, "Pearce, help us hold her." And said, "Sit on her." So I tried to sit on her back and I thought, "Boy, what did I get myself into?" I missed the part of the job description that says how to sit on a naked lady.[64]

Even with constant vigilance and training for self protection, Lolita Roberson recalled, "You could not always be prepared. It was a scary place to work and I got beat by the best of them." Once a male patient attacked attendant Lois Gainer, breaking her leg. She had tried to calm him down but he kept repeating, "Ms. Gainer, you just don't understand." She commented, "I guess I didn't."[65]

Sometimes patients gave clues when they were about to have an episode. One nurse recalled: "We had one patient who had been in the lockup for many years, and she would start to sing. We had her there in the medical unit and they warned us that when she started to sing she would go wild."[66] Sometimes another patient would detect the signs of an impending outburst before the staff did and tell the attendant, "Old so-and-so is about to pitch a good one." With sufficient warning, the episode could often be avoided. Wendell Worley explained, "One of the warning signals for a patient was to get very nervous, excited, beginning to be a little bit violent, and you could tell just by looking at them that it was coming on and you could up their medication." Worley remembered one patient who occasionally looked him straight in the eye. The patient had told Worley that he saw snakes in Worley's eyes, so the attendant watched that patient very closely at such times.[67]

No matter what the provocation, attendants could not fight back. "We were taught not to hit them," one nurse told. "No matter what they were doing to you, you could not hit them. We had to devise methods how we wouldn't hurt them but so we could protect ourselves."[68]

Although attendants tried to ensure the physical safety of their charges, sometimes patients injured each other. Otto Schultz remembered: "This was told to me: Once a patient was talking to himself while he worked. He didn't know what he was saying, and the fellow behind him took a pick and hit him in the head. He thought the first guy was talking about him and he killed him." The lecture course for hospital attendants warned: "Many of the accidents on the male service are due to physical encounters between patients. Some patients have habits, such as the monotonous repetition of phrases, pushing patients around, etc. which are a source of great irritation to other patients and hence result in assaults."[69]

In addition to keeping patients from harming each other, attendants had to protect patients from harming themselves; each had to be considered as potentially suicidal. The outline of the lecture course for hospital attendants graphically illustrated the extent of the problem by listing the following means by which asylum patients had ended their lives:

Drowning in bathtub; cutting wrists and neck with eye glasses, watch crystals, safety razor blades, glassware, window panes; strangulation by belts, pajamas or bathrobe cords, neckties, towels and bed clothes; standing in high places such as the sink in the bathroom, window sills, beds and falling on head; use of scissors, occupational tools, knives, forks, spoons etc; tipping a chair over backwards; taking poison; drinking cleaning solutions; starvation; picking the body to obtain infection; biting and swallowing thermometers; knocking head against the wall; running head first through panes of glass; jumping off walls; and falling on head down the stairs.[70]

Early in the hospital's existence, patients often were physically restrained in handcuffs or straitjackets to prevent harm to themselves or to others. At one time there were shackles attached to the walls in the basement of the Administration Building. Later, sedative drugs usually replaced physical restraint. As Dr. Elbert Leggett explained, "Chloral hydrate is the same as the Mickey Finn; it works fast to calm somebody down."[71] Even after the advent of drugs, in special cases restraint continued, as in the case of the patient who killed an attendant with a towel roller and thereafter was kept perpetually handcuffed. Lolita Roberson affirmed: "Although drugs were widely used, we still used restraints, the vest restraint and the high wrist restraints. Straitjackets were not frequent and you had to have a specific order."[72]

Seriously disturbed patients sometimes were secluded, and Lois Gainer described the protocol for seclusion. "If you had to seclude a patient, you checked them every fifteen minutes and charted on them. They were always in the light." Other methods of control included placing "leather muffs" on the feet of kickers or extracting the teeth of biters.[73] The latter method had fallen into disuse by the 1950s, when written permission by the family was required for any dental extractions.

Prevention of escape was another crucial duty of attendants, but escapes commonly occurred. "Every morning we'd get a list of patients that were discharged and those who had escaped," Ruth Howard told, "and the list of those who had escaped was just about as long as the discharged."[74] Attendants were held responsible for escapes and could be fined or even fired for negligence in permitting them to occur.

Once again, the institutional bylaws offered precise guidelines to prevent escape. "When patients walk out with attendants they shall keep them together and avoid going near dangerous places such as rivers, wells, machinery &c and they must also avoid thick woods and other places favorable for elopement." Furthermore, attendants were liable for "the cost of capturing and returning" patients they had "through carelessness" allowed to escape. The asylum offered a bounty of five dollars for the return of escaped patients, which was charged to the negligent employee.[75]

In addition to the prevention of suicide or escape, training manuals identified cleanliness as "one of the first and most important lessons that should be studied and learned by Attendants." As outlined in the 1861 bylaws, attendants' duties included securing

the perfect and systematic cleanliness and neatness of the entire Asylum and its inmates. The floors, windows, tables, beds and bedding, basements, closets &c, are to be scrupulously cleaned every day so as to preserve a pure atmosphere. Chamber vessels are always to be removed and carefully cleaned as often as they are used and spittoons are to be cleaned every day. All dust flues and receptacles shall be emptied daily and all dressings or cloths saturated with oil and unfit to go into the rag room shall be immediately taken to the boiler house and burned.[76]

The attendants' duties regarding the personal hygiene of patients extended to the cleaning and trimming of toenails, which were to be cut every two weeks, and, "in the case of elderly ladies who have a tendency to grow hair on their face this hair should be removed either by clipping or shaving at least once a week. This will add greatly to the trimness of their appearance."[77]

Bess McCord recalled the ritual on bath day, which occurred once or twice each week during the 1930s. "We had a lady that worked in the bathroom, and she'd make up bath bundles. When we hollered 'Bath day' they all got in line. We had two patients on each side of the bathtub, and they'd bathe them. We had to have a lot of help, and they wanted to help." Some patients had their own routines for bathing, as Raymond Habbit recalled: "There was a patient on the violent ward who stayed in the bath until all the water had drained out, and nobody could get him out of the tub before." Not all patients enjoyed bath days, however. Howard Brack commented, "I worked on M12 where there were lots of senile patients. There was this one man who wore a black hat. He'd curse you. 'These young kids try to tell me to take a bath. I don't need one.' We'd finally get him to take a bath, but he wouldn't take off his hat."[78]

The geriatric wards especially required constant attention to maintain cleanliness. Many of the patients were incontinent, and their sheets often had to be changed several times a day. Lillian Eidelbach recalled many "excretia-careless" patients and commented, "I could see that working in the laundry was dirty work. The man in charge of the laundry complained that the attendants didn't clean off the sheets." Patients could also be careless about urination. Jo Jureka, who worked on a ward for older male patients, reported that "Some would even urinate during meals." She added, "No dignitaries ate with those patients."[79]

Other parts of the asylum had serious cleanliness problems. In the early days the floors of the dining hall were wooden, and food debris collected in the cracks between the boards, creating a stench impossible to completely eliminate. Even after a layer of concrete was laid over the floors, cracks formed and the smell returned. Otto Schultz remembered that he "did refloor some of the concrete that had become cracked and terribly smelly."[80]

This particular aspect helped to determine a ward's desirability as a work site and to place it within the pecking order of "good" and "bad" wards, as Ruth Howard explained: "The Alcoholic Ward was a good place to work. They were clean, whereas the senile patients were not clean. That was a real criterion—how the ward smelled."[81]

The lecture course for hospital attendants directly addressed the issue of patient incontinence, a major cause of malodorousness, stating: "The matter of bowel incontinence may be corrected by taking the patient to the toilet at the same times each day for ten or fifteen minutes. It may be necessary to do this three times a day. For urinary incontinence, take to the bathroom every two hours." Understandably, some patients objected to attempts to control the timing and duration of visits to the toilet. Howard Brack recalled: "My favorite patient would go to the bathroom and just sit on the commode, talking to Caesar or Napoleon. I went to get him and he said, 'Can't Jesus Christ even take a shit without some SOB coming in here?'"[82]

After attending to the hygiene of patients and escorting them to breakfast, attendants supervised the cleaning of the ward—a Sisyphean task and a big part of every workday. Attendants estimated that five of every eight hours were spent in housekeeping duties.[83] The training manual for new employees specified that mattresses and pillows should be aired daily and taken outdoors once a week. Sue Pearce recalled, "There was a big mattress rack in the back, and the patients would take the bedding out and air it in the sunshine."[84] When badly soiled, mattresses were remilled and recycled at the asylum. The Texas Research League reported:

The mattress shops sterilize and renovate mattresses but there is danger of cross-contamination from incoming dirty mattresses to sterilized mattresses due to lack of storage space. An undesirable condition for the final processing is created by the presence of the sterilization chamber and the gin for shredding and cleaning the cotton filler in the same room. The high temperature of the sterilization chamber produces unbearable heat and obnoxious odors. The gin creates dust and noise.[85]

As noted, the cleaning directives from about 1900 specified that the chamber vessels were to be cleaned after use and spittoons were be cleaned daily. The need for spittoons continued as late as 1959, as the executive staff minutes indicated: "Dr. Miller commented that he noticed patients on Ward 23 have tin cans under their beds which they use in lieu of regular cuspidors, and that Dr. Vega has ordered these cans removed. Dr. Miller went on to say that there are some patients who absolutely need these cans for spitting chewing tobacco etc."[86]

Soiled by splattered tobacco juice or whatever, floors had to be thoroughly cleaned every day. An attendant wrote of her experiences in 1912: "The floors were plank, no concrete, and were waxed and had a wide runner rug from one end of the hall to the other. The floors were polished each morning and were mopped." Similarly, the 1950 manual identified "Soap, water and elbow grease [as] the best cleansing agent," further noting that all mops were to be washed out and hung outdoors on racks after use. These detailed instructions on sanitation perhaps were necessary, since the Texas

Research League reported: "Daily cleaning of the ward buildings is usually performed by the patients under the guidance of ward attendants. Frequently, neither the attendants nor the patients understand the technical aspects of building maintenance or the proper cleaning compounds to be used."[87]

While patients performed most of the cleaning duties on both the male and female wards, sociologist Ivan Belknap found that distinct differences existed in the culture of the wards. Female wards tended to be run on a family model, with the attendant in a maternal role, in contrast to the male wards, which operated on a military model, with the attendant functioning as sergeant. Belknap wrote: "[Female attendants] could and did perform many housekeeping tasks with the patients. We almost never saw this on the male wards. If the pseudomaternal role, with its family connotations, is carried out skillfully, it can apparently achieve a much less irksome and more effective control of mental patients than the pseudomilitary system employed in the male wards."[88]

The male attendants doubtless thought they would lose authority if patients observed them performing the "women's work" of cleaning, Belknap surmised. Then, too, before racial integration of the wards during the late 1950s, white male attendants would not have felt they could clean up after African Americans without a serious loss of status.

The part of their job that many attendants most enjoyed involved social contact with patients. Lois Gainer recalled bingo games, sing-songs of hymns, and camp outs. She especially enjoyed one stormy night when the lights went out; she and several patients sat around a lantern and told stories about when they were young. Such conversations may have been part of a "remotivation" program in which attendants "carry on psychotherapy at the grass roots level by getting patients to participate in discussions" about such topics as "pets, plants, fish and cotton." The discussion of topics unrelated to their illness supposedly interested patients in things outside the hospital and thus improved their mental state. Superintendent C. R. Miller's annual report for 1966 recorded that 150 employees had completed training in remotivation therapy.[89]

Like Lois Gainer, many attendants enjoyed the companionship of patients, and some reported forming lasting friendships. Comparing the demographics of professional employees with those of attendants, Belknap found that in terms of educational background, age, and rural versus urban upbringing, the lower-level employees more closely resembled the patients than they did the professional staff. These similarities probably resulted in somewhat greater ease of communication between attendants and patients than between professional staff and patients. Erving Goffman noted that in the Washington, D.C., mental institution he studied, demographic similarities often overrode the status differences between mental patients and their attendants. He wrote, "Buddy relationships sometimes formed between patients and attendants, especially young males for whom the similarities of sex, age, and working class seemed to cut through the organizational distinctions."[90]

Similarly, in spite of their low salaries, low status, demanding and sometimes dangerous working conditions, many long-term attendants at Austin State Hospital reported enjoying their work with patients and expressed satisfaction in developing lasting friendships with them.

# CHAPTER 5

# The Patient's World: Admission and Treatment

## *"In the Bug House"*

Commitment to the asylum did not result from any one action, however bizarre. Families might seek to commit a relative who abused alcohol or drugs, who consistently failed to hold a job, wrote hot checks, or behaved in a promiscuous manner. Meanwhile, some people experiencing serious distortion of reality, such as Damos, who wandered the streets of Austin in the 1890s muttering to himself and asking for news of shipwrecks, managed to avoid commitment. Criteria for admission changed over time and were never absolute.

In the 1950s, an extensive study conducted by the Texas Research League at the request of the Board for Texas State Hospitals and Special Schools found that the increasing numbers of Texans being committed to mental institutions resulted from the state's urbanization. The report stated: "In towns the houses are smaller and the neighbors are closer. Pressures on families to commit mentally ill or geriatric family members increases. In the past many would have lived out their lives on the farm." Another demographic study of the incidence of mental disorders in Texas concluded that urban areas did have a higher incidence rate, or number of new cases, of psychoses than rural areas, with Houston having the highest incidence rate in the state.[1] As families moved from farms to the city, fewer were able or willing to care for mentally ill relatives.

Erving Goffman outlined the typical sequence of events that resulted in admission to a mental hospital. The admission process usually began with a complaint or series of complaints, often from close family. Goffman wrote, "A psychotic man is tolerated by his wife until she finds herself a boyfriend or by his adult children until they move from a house to an apartment, a rebellious adolescent daughter [until she] can no longer be managed at home."[2]

E. Gartly Jaco's study of mental illness in Texas also found that females exhibited a significantly higher incidence rate of psychoses than males.[3] However, populations at ASH did not consistently reflect this. Throughout much of its history, the hospital admitted more men than women. For example, in September 1878 there were 174 men and 101 women patients. During World War II and immediately afterward, women outnumbered men. By the mid 1960s, male admissions again exceeded those of females—3,021 men compared to 2,316 women in 1964.[4]

The Research League noted that Texas had three types of commitments: temporary commitment by a county judge, based on testimony by a physician, not to exceed ninety days; voluntary commitment for ninety days during which a sanity trial might occur in absentia; and indefinite commitment by a jury on the grounds of unsound mind and the need for restraint. For the latter type of commitment, both conditions had to be present for the jury to commit the person involuntarily to a mental institution. Ivan Belknap identified a fourth type of commitment: the five-day emergency admission, enforceable after two physicians signed a statement that a person was violently and dangerously insane. While doctors sometimes resented sharing authority for commitment and protested the absurdity of impaneling a jury to try a medical condition, the process usually combined legal and psychiatric judgments.[5]

Prior to admission to a mental institution, persons might be confined in county jails often ill-equipped to handle them. As the number of patients increased, mental hospitals frequently ran out of room, creating near desperation for some county law-enforcement officials. Typical correspondence to Dr. Preston, superintendent of the State Lunatic Asylum during the 1910s, included letters from sheriffs and others pleading for the admission of inmates from their counties.

Dr. Wilmer Allison described the situation in an article in the *Texas State Journal of Medicine*: "Asylum superintendents have been prevailed upon, begged, pleaded with, threatened and coerced by every known means, by private persons, lawyers, doctors, judges, preachers, legislators, in fact by any and all who wielded influence . . . " Illustrating this coercion, State Representative C. W. Bonner wrote to Dr. Preston in 1915:

I presume you remember me. Anyway, I write you to secure a place in the asylum for a party in Archer County, said party having been convicted of lunacy. My friend and constituent, County Judge Melugin, writes me that the parents are not able to take care of the hopeless lunatic and that the mother is down with nervous prostration besides the father is near a breakdown. It certainly is a pitiable case. Please do not turn down this; hold up decision if adverse until I can talk to you about the case. You know I will be down there at the call session and will see you at once.[6]

Sometimes the state hospital denied admission on the grounds that a patient's status as a resident of Texas was questionable. Mentally ill persons who had travelled from one state to another had to establish Texas residency before they could be admitted to Austin State Hospital. If they were not residents, they were returned to their home states. The Texas Research League noted, "The deportation officer is stationed in the central office and . . . is responsible for the return of nonresident patients to the state of their residence."[7]

The process also worked in reverse, and the hospital frequently received Texas residents deported from other states. Joe Pearce recalled: "[California mental health officials] would send two trains to the East Coast, one through the South and another that went through St. Louis. They'd fill them up and send telegrams ahead to say the patients were coming and for us to meet the train."[8]

When notified that the asylum had space for another patient, a county official typically lost no time in transporting an inmate there. Normally, the county sheriff or his deputy accompanied the person on the train to Austin and from the depot to the asylum, a distance of about three miles. In his memoirs about his law practice in Austin early in the century, George Elgin Shelley wrote:

> The officers were allowed the expense incurred in transporting the patients from the train to the institution, of $1.00 per capita. This mode of transportation had always been made by what was then called public hacks, drawn, of course, by horses. However, upon completion of the electric line railway from the depot to Hyde Park, such officers soon conceived and carried out the economical plan of transporting themselves and their charges to the Asylum by way of the new street railway.[9]

Since the fare for this mode of transportation was only five cents, the officials pocketed the difference.

*Director of Rehabilitation Services Joe C. Pearce relaxing in his office, 1963.
Courtesy ASH*

Understandably, the hack drivers became upset over this turn of events and protested to the city council, lobbying for a fine on persons who "transported upon street railways in the City of Austin, lunatics or other persons of unsound mind." City Attorney George Poindexter, called upon to issue an opinion as to the validity and enforcibility of the proposed ordinance, "rendered an opinion to the effect that he did not think such an ordinance could be enforced, because its effect would be to impose upon a street car motorman too great a burden of expert knowledge to discriminate between the officer and his charge as to who was, and was not, the lunatic, and any effort to solve this problem might result in consequences too doubtful to cast upon a motorman, whose experience could hardly qualify him for solving psychological problems of this nature."[10]

Sometimes jury members at a sanity trial felt hardly more qualified than the motorman to make decisions about a person's mental state.[11] Dr. Allison noted that the patient "is tried before a jury of his peers who know just about as much about mental disease as he does." Describing the sanity trial, Allison wrote, "He [the patient] is compelled to sit and listen to testimony given to prove that he is of unsound mind and that it is necessary for the welfare of himself and others that he be placed under restraint. . . . Just picture to yourself the infamous shame of it." The Texas Research League's study stressed the need to change the laws regarding the admission process, noting that Texas was the only state that still required a jury trial for commitment. The study found that jury trials sometimes resulted in "the commitment to mental hospitals of many patients who are not mentally ill including mental deficients, non-insane aged, alcoholics and psychopathic personalities."[12] The report recommended that the jury trial be made optional rather than mandatory, a situation that finally occurred in 1956 following a state election to approve a constitutional amendment to that effect.

Usually, sanity trials passed unnoticed, but that of Dr. Wendell Thrower in 1963 received wide publicity. A prestigious faculty member of the University of South Carolina Medical College, Thrower was considering relocating to Austin to practice thoracic surgery. Had he left South Carolina, he could have taken with him a $250,000 personal research grant—an amount more than 25 percent of the college's annual budget. While visiting Austin to reconnoiter his prospects, Thrower became agitated. The dean of the South Carolina Medical College, with whom Thrower had had several disagreements, suggested to Mrs. Thrower that she have Dr. Thrower committed to Austin State Hospital for ninety days' observation and treatment.

Thrower resisted and was then escorted to the hospital by Travis County Sheriff T. O. Lang. He immediately demanded a sanity trial. Thrower's defense, led by attorneys Percy Foreman and Paul Holt, attempted to prove that he was a victim of a conspiracy led by his colleagues in South Carolina, who wanted to have his grant money reassigned to the college. However, Thrower's wife and brothers, as well as potential Austin associates, testified that Thrower had shown signs of disturbance, "talking constantly and incessantly and doing trivial things with his hands—lighting his pipe and taking it apart."[13]

In light of the contradictory testimony, the jury reported itself deadlocked. After further deliberation, however, members announced that although Dr. Thrower was or had been insane, he did not require observation or treatment in a mental hospital. Since both conditions had to be met before involuntary commitment could occur, Thrower went free, triumphantly departing the courthouse in the "air conditioned automobile of a South Texas state senator."[14]

As in the Thrower case, family members often initiated commitment proceedings. Attendant Dee Turner recalled: "Most of my admissions were not voluntary, but by the families or neighbors—ninety-day commitment. Several women had written hot checks and their families got tired of covering the costs." Similarly, Wendell Worley, who worked on a senile ward, believed that many patients "weren't mentally ill, but placed there [by their families] to get rid of them." A 1963 article from the *Austin American* described the case of an elderly woman that had been released from the hospital to live with her daughter. Shortly afterward she was readmitted, since "the old lady had deliberately scorched her clothing; she refused to take baths; she stole articles from other members of the family and hoarded them."[15]

In some instances family members accused each other of being insane, and who was committed depended on who reached the sheriff first. Joe Pearce described one such situation:

> There was a childless couple up in a little Czech community. They spoke minimal English. She became psychotic and thought her husband was trying to kill her. The sheriff came out and arrested him and she signed him into the hospital. They [hospital personnel] knew there was nothing wrong with him and he told us about his wife's behavior. [However,] he was having the time of his life—off the farm and he got ice cream and to go to dances with all these pretty girls. [Finally] they got the judge to uncommit him and to commit her. He visited her every week in his Model-T Ford. She responded to Thorazine and was released after a couple of months.[16]

Similarly, Erving Goffman noted, "I have a record of a man who claims that he thought he was taking his wife to see the psychiatrist, not realizing until too late that his wife had made the arrangements." Sometimes family members deliberately participated in false commitments, as Pearce explained: "The wife would have a boyfriend and wanted to get the husband out of the way or the family wanted Granny's money. We could usually spot them. One local politico put one of his girlfriends out there. She was getting drunk and telling things they had done. He took her out there at two in the morning and got her into a ward, bypassed the admission process. The superintendent released her and the politician tried to pull strings and get her admitted, but it didn't work."[17]

Common practice in several states by the late 1800s, the jury trial for sanity originated to prevent scheming relatives from "railroading" persons into mental institutions.[18] One of the more famous cases of false commitment concerned an Illinois woman, Elizabeth Packard, who publicly disagreed with her Presbyterian-minister husband regarding the doctrine of man's total depravity. Rev. Theophilus Packard, who upheld the doctrine, contended that his wife's disagreement could only result from "the vagaries of a crazed brain" and so had her committed. In Illinois during the 1860s, a husband could commit his wife to a mental institution without benefit of a jury trial. After three years, the state asylum released Mrs. Packard to the care of her eldest son, who had turned twenty-one and could assume responsibility for her. She devoted the rest of her life to campaigning against the commitment laws for women, succeeding in changing the laws of Illinois and several other states. Mrs. Packard did comment, however, that her husband's behavior had altered her views on the total depravity of at least one man.[19]

Even when families acted in what they believed to be the best interests of a relative, conflict often arose over commitment. The family might simply tell the person that he or she was going to the hospital, omitting the term "mental." Marian King wrote of her sense of betrayal when another inmate in the New England asylum to which her father had taken her informed King: "You're in the bug house so you must be a nut."[20]

Most Texas commitments were involuntary. The National Institute of Mental Health's *Survey of the Mental Institutions in the State of Texas* reported that only 95 of 1,402 admissions were voluntary. However, the distinction between voluntary and involuntary commitment was crucial. A former patient at Austin State Hospital recalled: "My mother-in-law wanted to admit me to the hospital, but the social worker got in front at the admissions desk and said, '[the patient] is going to sign the papers.' I might not be where I am today if she hadn't done that."[21] Following her discharge from the hospital, which was facilitated by her voluntary status, this patient became a nurse.

Voluntary commitment might stem from the individual's perception that he or she needed therapy, as in the case of an Austin attorney who checked in periodically to receive a series of electroconvulsive shock treatments. Some patients had other motives for self-commitment, however. An article by local reporter Betty McNabb, discussing admissions to the hospital, noted: "Dr. Sedberry pointed out one patient's chart. 'This woman makes me furious, trying to use us. She does have mental problems—but she's back here again on a voluntary commitment because she has a flock of hot checks out.'" Similarly, Goffman reported that both patients and staff claimed that "some patients came into the hospital to avoid family and work responsibilities, to obtain free major medical and dental work, or to avoid a criminal charge." Psychologist Peter Cranford even reported one man who admitted himself to the Georgia State Hospital in Milledgeville as a means of avoiding the Mafia, who had "marked him for death."[22] If so, the tactic did not succeed, since a visitor claiming to be his father soon strangled him.

Ivan Belknap described the typical admission procedure at Austin State Hospital in the early 1950s. "Whether a patient goes to one admission ward or another depends upon sex and color and upon the current status of bed space in the wards. There are admission wards for the white males and females, and for the Negro males and females." Ruth Howard added: "Even the filing system was segregated. You had a card file on white males, a card file on white females, a card file on black males, and a card file on black females. If you needed to check on, say, Lee Smith, you had to look in four different files."[23]

The hospital had admitted a few blacks from its earliest days. Superintendent B. Graham's report of 1867 identified three of the sixty-nine inmates as "colored." Black patients were housed in the basement of the Main Building, away from the white patients, until a fire in the early 1890s necessitated their removal to separate buildings.[24] By 1909, two wards accommodated 150 blacks, and by 1953, 1,049 of the hospital's 2,947 patients were black. Throughout its history, the hospital admitted few Hispanics, who comprised only 5 percent of its population in 1970.[25] However, the Southwestern Lunatic Asylum, which opened in San Antonio in 1892, had a higher proportion of Hispanics.

Racial integration of the hospital began in 1958 and was completed in 1965. Superintendent C. R. Miller's annual report for that year noted, "These accomplishments were made so gradually and with so little comment that they have scarcely been noticed."[26]

Belknap observed that the hospital did not have a separate receiving unit or admission unit: "The patient is brought into the foyer of the main building by their relatives, friends, or by an officer of the county court. He is expected in the hospital, in the sense that the county judge has formally requested the Superintendent to receive him, and the Superintendent has agreed, usually by correspondence, but sometimes by telephone."[27]

The first step in the admissions process involved securing the patient's history. A 1919 protocol that had been adapted from Adolf Meyer of the Pathological Institute of New York detailed the need to obtain information concerning "character and disposition, peculiarities, hobbies, criminal record, tramp life, attacks of blues, irritability, variability of mood, etc." The mental examination required by this protocol included observations of the patient's general appearance and manner, adaptation to new surroundings, peculiarities of dress and personal cleanliness, facial expression, sleep, and stream of mental activity. Questions directed to the patient included "What is your name?"; "Your occupation?"; "Do you realize where you are?"; "What led to your coming here?"; "Are you sad?"; "Have you had any peculiar or any unpleasant experiences?"; and "Has anything strange happened?"[28]

The intake procedures covered physical as well as mental symptoms, as the lecture course for hospital attendants directed: "When a patient is admitted to the hospital he should receive prompt and understanding attention. Temperature, pulse and respiration should be taken immediately on admission." The manual instructed, "Take the temperature per rectum unless the patient is too disturbed in which case take by axilla—never take the temperature by mouth." The next step in admission was a bath in a tub of water between ninety-six and one hundred degrees, and the manual cautioned: "The patient may possibly never have been in a bath tub before, or never have seen a shower. Treat them gently and don't ridicule them." Following shampooing and drying the hair, the attendant should "fine comb the hair with larkspur." Afterward, the patient should be put to bed and given a glass of milk or Ovaltine.[29]

In the 1950s, the formal admission process began when the appropriate physician, the male or female supervising attendant, and the social worker all arrived. With the physical portion of the admission process finished, including X rays and complete laboratory work, "A mental examination is made by the attending physician as soon as the patient becomes mentally accessible and confident in his physician." Superintendent Hoerster noted that new admissions in the 1960s were seen by the staff within two days of arrival.[30]

Ruth Howard described an intake interview:

One day I was working on admissions and this young woman was brought in, and I said, "Why are you here?" And she said that she had killed her baby. A policeman was standing behind her and he shook his head "no." He said, "She didn't do that." About an hour later, I had another young woman, and the whole scenario repeated itself, but this time the policeman was not shaking his head. She really did do it. You couldn't tell the difference. They both had absolutely flat affect.[31]

Medical staff tested the patient's general knowledge by having him or her recite the alphabet, months, days of the week, the Lord's prayer, poetry, rivers of the East Coast, the five largest cities of the United States, and the wars of this century and their results. At least one patient objected to these questions:

> The staff would interview you and determine which unit you need to go on. So, the doctor asks the questions to the patient and other staff members could listen, and I became indignant. The doctor asked me to spell "animal" and "hospital." I did not want to spell those words because those words are easily learned in grade school. I told the doctor I was not crazy, and I was really uptight about being admitted to the hospital. She [the doctor] was very gentle and encouraging so I spelled those words and she thanked me for spelling them. I found out later that it only meant something if I didn't spell them.

Initially diagnosed as having schizophrenia, undifferentiated type, the patient's diagnosis was changed to simple depression following her discharge. She commented, "That was my biggest break. To get into nursing school I had to present my medical records. I think a diagnosis of depression would have been preferred over schizophrenia."[32]

A reporter for a local newspaper allowed to observe admission interviews recorded the following: "Only one patient seemed 'mad' and she was the most jovial of the group. She kept rolling her eyes slyly toward Dr. Hoerster and firing questions back at him. 'Do you shout at your church?' he asked her. 'I sure do. Don't you?'"[33]

In the staff meeting following the interview, each professional gave a report. The meeting culminated with a diagnosis and prognosis for the patient. Sometimes the extensive information taken by the social workers gave them an advantage in giving a prognosis for a particular patient. Ruth Howard recalled: "There was a man who was admitted and the doctor said he will never get out of here. And I said, 'I'll bet you a Coca-Cola that he does.' And he said, 'You're on.' Well, what I knew that he didn't know was that, although his wife had divorced him, she had taken him back, and as soon as he was better she would come get him."[34] The social worker knew that the man's ability to function outside the hospital depended on adequate family support.

The assessment process most commonly resulted in a diagnosis of schizophrenia. Belknap's data indicated that during the early 1950s, 40 percent of patients at Austin State Hospital were diagnosed as schizophrenic. Twenty years earlier, journalist Hugh Williamson had identified schizophrenia as the primary diagnosis at the hospital, noting, "Psychiatrists know that the immediate cause of schizophrenia is emotional stress, resulting from inability of the individual to fit into his environment. Victims are introverts who believing themselves unsuccessful in the battle with life, retire more and more into themselves and brood over their troubles."[35]

Commonly mistaken by the general public for multiple personality disorder, schizophrenia does not refer to "split personalities" but is characterized by delusional thinking, hallucinations, emotional blunting, and bizarre behavior. C. S. Yoakum's 1914 bulletin on Texas' care of the insane listed the following symptoms of insanity, which duplicate later criteria for a diagnosis of schizophrenia: "disorders of sensory experiences, of emotions, of ideas, and of actions." To illustrate incoherence, Yoakum quoted from a letter written by one of the patients in the Austin asylum. It read: "to March A Dew Bill to Editure of 1914, of Sarah, Democrat, Here of S.E.A of 14 years and Seven months. At Amarillo, texts, Raull, BAC Ces of my Head Word, Boston go. I have my tongue in my mouth to cast out my association with Hoo said, Boston, Massachusetts, United States after me."[36] Another patient suffering from delusions of grandeur told Yoakum that she was a queen and was ready for heaven, with "my wings nicely growing, till those persons [attendants] held me and cut them off." Few professionals disagreed about the prevalence of schizophrenia in mental institutions. A 1922 study noted that nationwide, nearly two-thirds of readmissions were because of manic depression and dementia praecox (schizophrenia).[37]

The severity of the schizophrenia symptoms precluded successful treatment through psychotherapy. Dr. Margaret Sedberry commented that very little psychotherapy was practiced at Austin State Hospital since most patients were psychotic. In his book *From Asylum to Community*, Gerald Grob affirmed that psychotherapy was not widely practiced in mental hospitals until after World War II. He cited a study by the Menniger Foundation, which found that psychoanalytic therapy could not be employed successfully with psychotics.[38]

In general, ward attendants did not view psychotherapy as helpful. Belknap reported, "The feeling tone of the attendants in this matter was one of tolerant pity for the doctor who was strictly 'psychiatric' (and of outstanding suspicion if he happened to be psychoanalytically oriented)."[39]

Because of overcrowding and a shortage of trained personnel and resources, therapy consisted mostly of "feeding and fanning." Keeping patients reasonably comfortable and well nourished was about all that could be done. Certainly, keeping patients cool in the Texas summer without air conditioning presented a major problem. Dr. Sedberry recalled: "In the days before air conditioning the geriatric patients suffered especially. I remember they ran water on the roof in an attempt to cool off the wards."[40] Sometimes the heat became so intense that cans of food exploded in the pantry.

Treatment options for schizophrenia before the mid-1950s were limited, although sedative drugs might be used, as Joe Pearce recalled: "Before tranquilizers we had paraldehyde. We would order it by the barrel. It smelled awful." An effective sedative, paraldehyde was widely used by hospital attendants, as Howard Brack reported: "One time, [another attendant] told me I'd have a quiet night. He'd lined them [the patients] all up and, except for the working patients, had given them a half cup of paraldehyde." In her book *The Snake Pit*, which detailed her experiences in a New York mental hospital, Mary Jane Ward aptly described the scent of paraldehyde as a "musky, fetid, straw smell."[41] Some of the alcoholics at Austin State Hospital became addicted to it, but when this happened the doctor would simply administer the drug intramuscularly in the buttocks, which usually cured the addiction.[42]

Overmedication of patients was a perennial problem. As early as 1874, one superintendent objected to the indiscriminate use of sedatives for patients at the asylum. Dr. D. R. Wallace reported to the annual meeting of the AMSAII in Nashville, "Upon taking charge of the asylum in Texas some months since, I found this agent [chloral hydrate] being used inordinately, I might say almost ad libitum, even by the attendants. The female night watch particularly, and I am quite sure there was in almost every case in which she was exhibiting it most freely, as shown by the morning reports, an aggravation of the symptoms, and in no single case an amelioration."[43]

Other common treatments for schizophrenia included hydrotherapy. A letter to Superintendent Preston from Dr. Rebekah B. Wright of Chicago, dated November 24, 1915, offered to train nurses in this form of therapy for fifty dollars per week, plus maintenance, laundry, and traveling expenses to and from Chicago. She wrote, "The nurses selected for this special instruction should include the man and woman at the head of the Hospital's nursing service and two men and two women attendants who, by their intelligence, tact, kindness, firmness and fidelity have proven themselves good mental nurses, and who are loyal to the superintendent."[44]

Preston apparently did not accept her offer, as his itemized expenses for the asylum for 1915–16 did not include payment to Dr. Wright. Nevertheless, hydrotherapy at the hospital became common. Lillian Eidelbach described the process. "We had continuous tubs and cold wet packs. Patients

loved them. They said it relaxed them so they could sleep."[45] A former patient in a New York mental hospital recalled her treatment: "A rubber sheet
was placed on the bed and I was stripped and bound in hot sheets that had
been run through steaming water. An ice cap was placed on top of my head
and I was strapped down by other sheets to keep my muscles quiet, and
covered with blankets to retain the heat." She found the process to be "not
unpleasant," and after an hour she was ready for sleep. She regarded the
cold pack, however, as punishment.[46]

Other forms of hydrotherapy included needle showers, continuous baths,
and enemas. Superintendent Hanretta described the hospital's hydrotherapy: "We have one completely equipped hydro-therapy unit affording
a wide variety of therapeutic baths and sprays—hot and cold packs, continual tubs and colonic irrigation." A training manual for new employees
explained: "Hydrotherapy which is a part of physical therapy is most important on a psychiatric service. The attendant can soon realize that it takes
the place of restraint and is more effective and humane. The continuous
tubs and packs quiet the patient instead of only rendering him helpless as
restraint does."[47]

While the prevalence of various diagnoses changed over time, mania
remained a common diagnosis for patients entering the Austin hospital.
Hospital records identify an eighteen-year-old male admitted in September 1862 as suffering from acute mania caused by masturbation. A woman
admitted in October 1869 received a diagnosis of chronic mania resulting
from disappointed pride. A notation in her record dated January 31, 1881,
states, "Has three or four annual attacks of excitement, becomes violent
noisy and destructive requiring restraints, passing off after a week or ten
days duration. She is left prostrated." Her treatment consisted of sedatives,
including potassium bromide, valerian, and chloral hydrate, "followed by
supportive measures such as tonics, stimulants and good diet such as eggs,
milk, rice, and beefsteak."[48]

Mania is characterized by an intense emotional state of excitement and
euphoria. Hugh Williamson's article for the *Austin Statesman* in 1937 noted
that "Manics are extroverts who attempt to do too much and work themselves into a state of nervous disorder, unable to eat or sleep." In the 1940s,
persons with this disorder might receive sleep therapy, which kept them
heavily sedated for weeks. One nurse remembered: "We had sleep therapy
in big cages for the manics. We'd wake them up for meals and bathe them
every day. This went on for a month. When they woke up they would be
better for a while, but the symptoms returned."[49]

By far the most famous of all treatments for mental illness, electroconvulsive shock, was employed extensively not only for schizophrenics but also for depressives and for anyone suicidal. The use of electricity to treat mental illness began soon after its discovery. A. W. Beveridge and E. B. Renvoize reported that by 1849, John Charles Bucknill applied electrical stimulation to the skin in the successful treatment of depressive patients. In 1873, the *American Journal of Insanity* quoted Dr. Moritz Benedickt of Vienna regarding the successful application of "electro-therapeutics" to the spine in the treatment of mental disorders whose origins were nutritional or circulatory. Low voltage current supposedly stimulated nerve cells, reducing enervation.[50] Robert Carson, James Butcher, and Susan Mineka noted that for several decades electrical stimulation to treat mental illness remained fairly widespread, but by the end of the nineteenth century "concern over its safe use resulted in a diminished application of electricity for treatment." However, medical staff used some form of electrical treatment at Austin State Hospital as early as 1902, when Dr. B. M. Worsham reported, "A first-class static electric apparatus has been put in during the last year and static electricity has been used in suitable cases with satisfactory results."[51]

The use of electrical stimulation greatly increased after the observation by doctors Ugo Cerletti and Lucio Bini in 1938 that animals lost consciousness after a current passed through their heads. They tried this method with mental patients and reported phenomenal success.[52] By the 1950s, electroconvulsive shock had almost completely replaced other forms of treatment that sought to induce convulsions, such as the harder-to-control insulin shock. A protocol for insulin shock dated November 14, 1957, noted that if the patient showed any signs of going in too deep, such as loss of reflexes, pinpoint pupils, slow heart rate, or depressed respiration, or if there were convulsive movements, the coma should be terminated immediately with 50 cubic centimeters of 50 percent glucose. Other convulsive treatments also had their drawbacks. Lillian Eidelbach recalled severe convulsions that led to broken bones with metrazol-induced comas.[53]

Dr. David Wade, psychiatrist and former commissioner of the Texas Department of Mental Health and Mental Retardation, surveyed the history of convulsive therapy:

There was electroshock—insulin shock, Metrazol shock, and electroshock. Now, Metrazol was the first convulsive treatment. It was an injectable liquid that had very good properties, and we didn't know at that time whether it was the Metrazol or the convulsion, but a couple of Italians,

Ugo Carletti and Lucio Bini, experimented with electrical stimulation of the central nervous system. In those days they kind of thought that electricity in and of itself had some curative power. Because, with Metrazol, the patient's first reaction was great fear, tremendous fear of the medication. It just engendered a sense of crisis, and so it was not real desirable. Three and four—rarely more than five—Metrazol convulsions were necessary to bring a depressed patient out of it. But we had to give a few more electroshock treatments than that, but with ECT there was no memory of the convulsion, and that was what was so horrifying to those people [treated with Metrazol]. They felt the convulsion.[54]

Also, the level of coma could be more easily controlled with electro-convulsive shock. Wendell Worley described the process.

With ECT the muscles would constrict and you had to hold them at the shoulder, the hips, and the elbows and use a tongue depressor to keep them from biting their tongues. It took four people to hold down the patients. They jerked violently and turned real blue and then would suddenly start breathing and go to sleep for about thirty minutes. I kept the records on ECT. I saw marvelous things. It looked inhumane, but it did marvelous things for the patient. Many times the patients did not have to return to the hospital after the ECT.[55]

Other employees agreed about the benefit of the treatment: "There was a lady in her thirties from an old Austin family and she would go into a manic state periodically. They got this gal in and it took five of us to hold her down. After ECT she was as nice as can be." However, Ivan Belknap noted that administration of ECT at the Texas hospital did not follow the most humane procedure: "The administration of shock on the ward is often carried out in full sight of a group of interested onlookers. The patient's convulsions often resemble those of an accident victim in death agony and are accompanied by choking gasps and at times by a foaming overflow of saliva from the mouth. The patient slowly recovers without memory of the occurrence, but he has served the others as a frightful spectacle of what may be done to them."[56] In later years, atropine dried up saliva and a muscle relaxant ensured that the patient would not break any bones.[57]

As Belknap also noted, the fear of electroshock might be used to control patient behavior. Attendants could use the threat of being placed on the shock list to keep patients in line, since doctors often followed their suggestions that certain patients could benefit from the treatment. Abuses might occur. One patient, who compulsively repeated the same boring story over and over, reputedly was placed on the list so that he would forget his oft-told story.[58] Another patient who had thrown scalding coffee on a pregnant kitchen worker received a series of shocks.[59]

Doctors varied in the frequency with which they prescribed electroshock. One became so prone to use it that patients called him "Ready Kilowatt." Howard Brack remembered that once a staff member complained so much about his health that another attendant told him: "'You need to get one of those shock treatments. That'll straighten you out.' So he asked Dr. ___, and he gave him one. He couldn't get out of bed the next day."[60]

Much rarer than electroconvulsive shock treatment, psychosurgical procedures such as the prefrontal lobotomy usually were employed only as a last resort for the most intractable cases. Attendant Lois Gainer recalled only one patient who received a lobotomy. She described: "She was so hostile and wild she couldn't be handled. We all cried about that. She was like a little child afterwards. Her spirit was broken." Portugese physician Antonio Moniz had developed the procedure in which the frontal lobes are severed from the rest of the brain. At first it attracted wide acclaim as a cure for mental illness. By the 1950s, however, many surgeons refused to perform the irreversible operation, since it often did not produce the desired results. Staff minutes for October 30, 1959, discussed the possibility of sending lobotomy patients to Galveston because consulting neurosurgeon Dr. Farris "declines to undertake this task." Fortunately, the advent of psychotropic drugs all but eliminated this type of surgery.[61]

By the mid-1950s, psychotropic drugs had become common, and an article in the *Austin Statesman* noted, "Amazing results claimed in use of two new drugs." Chlorpromazine and reserpine had been prescribed for 7 to 10 percent of the patients at ASH with such promising results that it was thought the need for shock treatment might be eliminated. Joe Pearce recalled: "In 1950 Thorazine came on the scene and was very effective. In 1955 we literally ordered barrels and barrels of Thorazine. Any time a patient opened his mouth, we popped a Thorazine into his mouth and it was a miracle drug. In just a few days patients would be transformed." However, some patients reacted to it by "turning purple or a little mauve colored," and with prolonged use it became obvious that there were more serious side effects to these miracle drugs, including tardive dyskinesia, or "stiff-man syndrome."[62] Nevertheless, the new drugs remained the most effective treatment for schizophrenia. Dr. Elbert Leggett remembered, "Thorazine and Compazine made all the difference in the world. The whole atmosphere of the hospital became calmer."[63]

In the early years of the twentieth century, before antibiotics effectively combatted venereal disease, a large percentage of mental patients suffered symptoms of tertiary syphilis. Gerald Grob wrote, "Between 1911 and 1920, for example, about twenty percent of all first admissions to New York State mental hospitals fell into this category." Similarly, Hugh Williamson reported in 1937 that "Paresis, caused by syphilis, is the third most prevalent form of insanity" at the Austin State Hospital. Prior to the discovery of antibiotics, injections of heavy metals commonly treated syphilis. Unfortunately, "massive doses of mercury and iodides of potassium often led to serious complications; loss of teeth, tongue fissures, and hemorrhaging of the bowel."[64]

These side effects and the general ineffectiveness of heavy metals as a treatment for syphilis caused many to welcome a new treatment, "fever therapy." Julius Wagner-Jauregg, an Austrian psychiatrist who received the Nobel prize in 1927, reported that neurosyphilitic patients often became less disturbed following typhoid fever.[65] Initially, doctors inoculated syphilitic patients with blood from patients with malaria or actually exposed them to mosquitoes that carried malaria. However, "You couldn't control it [the malaria], and some would die."[66]

Eventually, a machine safely induced the high body temperature needed to kill the syphilis spirochetes. Austin chiropractor Dr. Harvey Watkins received training in fever therapy from Dr. Beloit in Indianapolis and used the treatment for several years during the 1930s. Watkins recalled: "We had a machine which generated the heat and kept the temperature at 105 degrees. There were strips that came out of the machine that were put under the arms and so forth. The patient was wrapped in a blanket and a rubber sheet. A nurse had to sit there for an hour to check that the temperature did not get away from you."[67]

Austin State Hospital also administered this treatment. Howard Brack explained, "They had a heat box and used a mosquito treatment. The health department came out to do that." Lillian Eidelbach, who had worked in fever therapy in Denver, supervised the process of getting the patient's temperature up to 106.8 and holding it there for six hours.[68]

Fashions in patients' treatments came and went, but across the decades, life on the wards went on in much the same way. Patients' diagnostic categories primarily determined their assignments to wards. As Belknap described: "Senile patients, for example, usually go directly to a ward composed mainly of other senile patients. Patients with legal or criminal complications in their cases may go to a ward in which there are others of the same type." While the more disturbed patients were kept together according to their diagnosis, the less disturbed might be assigned to any ward. Practical matters determined many such assignments. As former ward attendant Phillip Otting explained: "It was hard to deal with a young schizophrenic if you had a geriatric losing his balance all over the place."[69]

However, practicality also demanded that each ward have some "good" patients who functioned well enough to help the attendants. "Patients are distributed throughout most of the wards without much homogeneity even in the institutional classification," Belknap observed. "Young persons are placed with senile persons, and wards which are predominantly made up of psychiatrically deteriorated mental patients frequently house a group of patients who are comparatively in much better condition." These "better" patients helped the attendants with housekeeping and control of unruly patients.[70]

In many ways, such patients became "assistant attendants," performing many of the same duties and in some cases actually working without supervision. Former employee Sue Pearce recalled: "Way back there, some of the patients were the night attendant. Sometimes they were the assistant day attendant."[71] In return, these patients received special privileges, such as sitting with attendants when they ate and freedom to leave the ward. With severe understaffing, it was perhaps inevitable that the less disturbed patients would assume such duties as helping with baths, seeing that other patients got in line for meals, making beds, and mopping the ward. Later, critics maintained that persons with such high levels of function should never have been institutionalized.

Occasionally, the hospital tacitly admitted the realities of ward life by hiring such experienced patients as attendants following their discharge. During the labor shortage of World War II and immediately afterward, several former patients became paid attendants. One reason was simple: "Nobody else wanted to work for $45 a month."[72]

At times the shift from patient to employee status made things complicated for state officials, as State Auditor Cavness's report for 1948 illustrated.

The manager of the enterprise (the little store on the grounds of ASH) during most of this period was ___. The records show that Mr. ___ was first a patient in the Austin State Hospital having been committed in 1938 and remaining as a patient until March 14, 1943, when (while on a

90 day furlough) he was employed and placed on the hospital payroll as a ward attendant; that on August 9, 1943 he received the restoration of his citizenship, having been officially discharged from the hospital on July 30, 1943. He was transferred to the management of "The Little Store" where he served until February 28, 1947. He re-entered the hospital as a patient on August 6, 1947 and was discharged on September 4, 1948. He was paid his salary from February 28 until April 7 while he was a patient.[73]

While state officials frowned on having current patients on the payroll, they happily endorsed unpaid patient labor. Many of the early superintendents' annual reports bragged about the economies achieved by using this method of staffing for most of the institution's essential functions. In the early years, many of the male patients had experience as farm laborers and easily assumed responsibility for the cultivation of the asylum's fruit and vegetable crops as well as the care of farm animals. According to Joe Pearce, as late as the 1950s "Patients were used when it was time to harvest. They'd give all the women sunbonnets and the men straw hats and they'd all go up there [to the farm immediately north of the hospital] early in the morning and harvest the crops."[74] Superintendents consistently justified patient labor in terms of its therapeutic value as well as its cost-saving efficiency. In his report for 1869, Dr. Beriah Graham wrote: "All the above improvements, except such as were compelled to be done by good mechanics, have been made by our attendants and patients, and has been a source of great benefit to the latter, by affording them healthful exercise, and breaking in upon the morbid train of ideas in which they are so constantly prone to indulge." Similarly, Superintendent Worsham reported to Governor Joseph D. Sayers in 1900: "Occupation is recognized as a measure of great value in the treatment of many of these unfortunates and has been considerably practiced during the past year."[75]

Attitudes and practices regarding the use of patient labor changed little over a century; work was good for patients and, besides, the asylum needed their help. While many of the patients were unskilled laborers, a few had skills vital to the operation of the hospital. As social worker Louis DeMoll recalled, "Many of the patients who had been there twenty to twenty-five years had vital skills—plumbing skills or carpentry skills. And they had become crucial to the operation of the hospital so that when we began working toward getting a job in town for the plumber, the person in charge of plumbing said, 'Who's going to fix the pipes?' He got agitated because

*Patients helped with the laundry and many other chores around the asylum, 1899.*
*Courtesy ASH*

he was losing his chief maintenance person, who was a patient."[76] Some of the female patients became equally indispensable to the operation of the hospital. Ethel Brack recalled of one woman, "Lugenia was a manic depressive, and in a manic state she was a *worker*."[77]

The quality of patient labor varied with the patient's level of disturbance. Attendants assigned patients to work crews. A former employee told: "The laundry would call the ward and say, 'I need three patients to help this morning,' and the attendant might send three that he wanted to get rid of for the day, or he might send some that were in good contact and would be able to work well." Many of these latter patients represented "institutional cures," a term used to describe those who functioned at a high level within the familiar confines of the institution. Some of these patients took great pride in their jobs. Ethel Brack remembered that the patients who worked with her in the kitchen often "relished their work. One man stirred the oatmeal in a large vat. He wouldn't let anyone else do it."[78]

Similarly, Otto Schultz recalled: "A man named Smith was in charge of the athletic boxes—croquet, etc. He told me that he had been at the hospital a third time and, 'I want to stay out here. I get home and all the things that I have responsibility for bother me. I'm free as a bird out here. I like it here. The other patients and employees all know me. I don't ever want to leave again.'"[79]

Not all of the staff found patient labor helpful. Maintenance worker Raymond Habbit told: "I had fifteen patients working for me. One stole my truck and stopped at the gate and laughed. Somebody else stole my scooter and my channel locks and sold them for a dollar and bought a bottle of wine and got drunk. They worked me harder than I worked them." Co-worker John Supak added: "I once saw a patient mowing with the blade up. He worked for an hour and didn't cut a single blade of grass." And Tony Garcia agreed that patient help generally left much to be desired: "You had to watch them so closely to see that they didn't get hurt."[80]

Some patients knew they could not perform certain jobs adequately in their impaired states. Mary Jane Ward recalled that she could not distin-

*The central kitchen, in which patients helped to prepare thousands of meals each day, burned in 1958. Courtesy ASH*

guish between wet mops and dry mops. She also flunked her job of sorting laundry.[81]

For patients, one of the major benefits of work was getting off the wards, since grounds privileges depended on having a job. A former patient described: "So the doctor said that in order for me to have ground privileges that I'd need to have a job. I'd never had a job except being a waitress in high school, but he said, 'No'; he wanted me to have a more responsible job, and he'd noticed on my application that I wanted to be a nurse, so he said to go to the Med-Surg Unit to wrap needles."[82]

For patients, getting off the wards, in addition to escaping the tedium of ward routine, meant escaping constant surveillance. Some of the trustees, the patients with grounds privileges, took advantage of this to climb the hospital fence and cross the street to visit the shops, perhaps to get a good haircut from Sid Rich's barbershop, to eat a hamburger at Crawford's or Big Boy Looney's, to purchase ice cream at Faulk and Eifler's Drug Store, or to shop at Winn's Variety Store.[83]

While a college student during the 1930s, Otto Schultz supervised the concrete gang, a group of unusually strong patients able to perform hard physical labor. Over time, a certain group solidarity developed, and Schultz recalled: "On the cold days when it was too cold to work, we might sit in the little house with those nine workers, me and another student, Bart Dillon, and play card games and things to kill time. That would get them out of the ward."[84]

Although staff members sometimes gave small presents as rewards, the working patients normally did not receive any money for their labor, being compensated through the special privileges and the status of interacting as near equals with staff. However, some of the duties performed by patients at ASH customarily netted small monetary rewards. The "hall boys" sat in rocking chairs in the administration building basement and, as Kay Fleet remembered, "If you wanted to send something over to medical records, they would take it and you'd give them a tip for spending money to go to the canteen." Similarly, Bess McCord recalled that patients would "do little things for the employees and we'd pay them. They'd wash and starch our uniforms if we didn't get them back from the laundry in time. Or, they'd make crocheted things and sell them to us, and if we had a good patient like that we'd see that they had money, even if it was just a nickel or a dime."[85] One patient, adept at painting, sold his artwork on Guadalupe Street just beyond the asylum fence, and another sold his carvings of horses.[86]

It was also customary to tip the patients who helped in the beauty shop.

Staff minutes for September 21, 1959, record that Dr. Hoerster said that he had heard about the tips "over the grapevine," and that he did not think patients getting permanents should have to tip other patients for the service.[87]

Erving Goffman identified ways patients at a Washington, D.C., hospital earned money: "Some patients lent money to others for high 25 per cent interest rates. They seemed to enjoy the social status it gave them as much as the income. Other patients earned money by giving good haircuts or ironing pants, etc."[88]

Occasionally a patient could earn a considerable amount of money. Joe Pearce described one such patient entrepreneur:

> We had a patient who came from the Schulenberg area. I guess about a second generation Czechoslovakian. They called him Adam Alphabet. He was over his psychotic episode but had become dependent on the hospital. He didn't have any other place to go. So to raise money for his cigarettes, and I'm sure he went out occasionally and got a few bottles of beer, Adam started washing cars for the employees. He was pretty good at this and washed it for twenty five cents or fifty cents, or for a monthly fee of one dollar or $1.50 he'd take care of the car. So finally he got the doctors' building parking lot, the yellow brick building over by Guadalupe. He staked squatter's rights to everyone who parked in the doctors' parking lot. He was so successful he started hiring other patients to wash for him. He moved on to other lots. After several years of this, with Thorazine and all, we started pushing Adam out, and he resisted leaving. He had a large amount of money in a downtown bank. We said, "Out you go." He went back to his home and opened up a little honky-tonk. Later he opened up a restaurant in Miami which was very successful.[89]

Another patient owned mechanic's tools and worked on employees' cars. Wendell Worley, who often observed him, learned various tricks of automobile repair from the man. While some patients opened bank accounts for their earnings, many simply buried their savings somewhere on the grounds in old Prince Albert tobacco cans.[90]

Rarely did a patient became so good at working the system that he or she caused trouble. Social worker Beth Covey recalled that one of her patients, a charming con artist who had made and lost three fortunes, managed to get a job in the University of Texas geology department while living at the hospital. He also managed to finance the purchase of a small airplane and generously offered trips to the hospital staff. Rumor had it that this same individual had tried to counterfeit money using the hospital's print shop.[91]

Eventually, formal vocational training became an integral part of a patient's therapy, and assignment to certain jobs depended on his or her diagnosis. Joe Pearce explained:

> If a patient had been an accountant and was exhibiting signs of guilt or depression, I might put the patient to work washing dishes in the kitchen. This might continue for several weeks. I'd get feedback from the supervisor and the ward attendant, and when they thought the patient was ready we might place him on a job in the accounting office, something clerical. This would help reestablish his profession and confidence— taking a shower everyday, dressing better, and so on, to reestablish a professional role. It worked. We could see improvement.[92]

A report by the Texas Research League further described the process: "The patient is referred to the rehabilitation worker by his doctor, or by an attendant or social worker with the doctor's approval. The patient's case history is then checked and a job assigned with the doctor's approval. After the patient begins working he is checked every two weeks to see what progress he is making. The occupational therapy must focus on therapy[,] not on the cash value of the product being created."[93]

Pearce also developed vocational training programs for patients designed to provide them with a means of making a living following discharge. This especially helped patients who "had been out of it for twenty years and weren't equipped to go back to the world, but who with the help of Thorazine had lost their psychotic symptoms." The superintendent's report for 1965–66 noted 369 patients who had been placed in gainful employment that year as a result of the program.[94]

Programs offered at ASH included vocational nursing, clerical skills, and beautician training. Beth Covey helped patients with grooming as well as social and clerical skills. Following this training, one patient was hired as a clerk at the Texas State Department of Human Resources and worked there until retirement.[95]

Bess McCord taught cosmetology in the hospital's vocational rehabilitation program. She recalled: "We had kids that gave their families problems and they put them with me, and they got their license, and a lot of

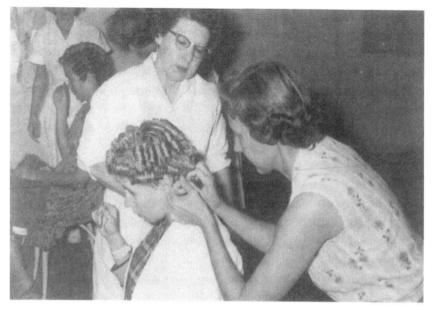

*Bess McCord directed the department of cosmetology, where patients were trained to become beauticians. Courtesy ASH*

them are working out in town now."[96] A former patient who participated in the vocational nursing program remembered that many graduates of the program got jobs in nursing homes for fifty cents an hour. Needing to earn a higher salary to support herself and her son, she enrolled in Brackenridge School of Nursing and became a registered nurse.[97]

Anticipating a shift in federal laws pertaining to patient labor, the hospital began issuing payment to a small percentage of patient workers on January 1, 1967, "with 110 patients authorized to receive a maximum of two dollars per week for work in the laundry, mattress factory, yard crew, trash, and garbage trucks."[98] Indeed, all unpaid labor by patients ended after 1973 when a U.S. district court ruled in *Souder* v. *Brennan* that patients in non-federal mental institutions had a right to compensation for work under the Fair Labor Standards Act. This ruling effectively outlawed unpaid patient labor. Wendell Worley explained: "One of the issues in the courts was that patients were forced to work without compensation. They did not have to work and most of them wanted to do it to get off the wards." Joe Pearce added: "The feds got involved and said we were exploiting patient labor and that we had to pay the patient." Thus, good therapy or not, many of the patient jobs soon disappeared for lack of funds. As Don Howell explained: "We had industrial therapy and that worked very well until the federal government said we could not do this without paying patients. It gave them [the patients] a social outing as well as a sense of achievement. The Fair Labor Standards Act prevented a continuation of this."[99]

The shift in policy meant a substantial change in the daily lives of many patients, since in 1965 alone, 2,111 had held various jobs in the institution. From the hospital's perspective, the loss of patient labor added to its already serious staffing problems. Superintendent Miller's report for 1967 indicated an employee turnover rate of 37.76 percent.[100]

While the legislation effectively curtailed vocational therapy, other innovative forms of treatment continued. For example, the beauty shop served as the site for "beauty therapy," which an article in the *Austin American* described as hair styling, facials, manicures, and style shows. Paula Shea, volunteer coordinator for the hospital, believed that "When a woman starts fussing with her hair-do and her make-up, particularly when doctors or male patients are around, it can mean she's on the road to recovery."[101]

Volunteers from the community often participated in some aspect of beauty therapy, donating clothing or taking patients shopping. The Volunteer Service Councils began in the mid-1950s. Eleanor Eisenberg, executive director of the local Mental Health Association from 1956–62, organized volunteers for the former Confederate Home for Men, which served as an annex to the hospital, housing elderly male patients.[102] By 1963, a typical month saw 1,374 volunteers contributing 10,217 hours of work to assist programs at the hospital. In his master's thesis on mental health care, James Evans wrote: "The contributions of the volunteers cannot be estimated on a monetary basis. The program has been of incredible value in constantly reminding patients that people outside had not forgotten them."[103]

Volunteers might teach art classes, translate for deaf patients, trim toenails, or wrap Christmas gifts. Evans identified Mrs. De Witt Jennings as a volunteer who regularly escorted patients to shopping centers, an activity more readily identified as therapeutic by women staff members. Executive staff minutes for February 1, 1960, recorded: "Mrs. Holbert handed Dr. Hoerster a note from June ___ requesting permission to do some shopping. Dr. Hoerster asked who was going to accompany her, and then asked Mrs. Holbert to tell Mrs. ___ to make a list of the things she needed and they can be sent out here." Mrs. Holbert persisted, however, and minutes for the next staff meeting on February 5, 1960, recorded: "Mrs. Holbert talked to Dr. Hoerster about June ___ wanting to go shopping and asked him whether it would meet with his approval if Mrs. Inez Nauman accom-

*Recreational activities included outdoor bowling as well as baseball, swimming, croquet, and dancing. Courtesy ASH*

panied her to town. Permission was granted."[104]

Recreational therapy served as another form of treatment. An untitled report dated November 4, 1939, pronounced: "Recreational therapy is also used as a means of recreating interest in activities outside of themselves. Among the recreational facilities is a large park, baseball diamond, tennis court, croquet grounds, as well as an auditorium where weekly picture shows are held and dances, community singing, and church is carried on. The library has 600–700 books and subscribes to about 50 magazines."[105]

The professional staff considered baseball a highly therapeutic recreation for the patients and justified participation in the sport for medical reasons. As P. Tobin, a recreational therapist, wrote: "[T]o establish a stronger bond of unity between me and the patients, I join in the games. The better players will be granted the job of giving me practice during the day for improving my playing. This will give them a sense of responsibility and importance that will be beneficial."[106]

Baseball games occurred throughout the year. Tobin recorded: "Three nights each week men's teams play against women's teams and on Sunday games are arranged by a patient with outside teams." The asylum nine, which included not only patients and employees but also the occasional "ringer"

*Summer parties for Juneteenth and the Fourth of July were held on the southwest corner of the grounds near the baseball field. Courtesy ASH*

from the Austin community, played the nearby small towns of Elgin, Buda, Kyle, and Creedmore and enjoyed some success, winning the area title in 1933.[107]

Other popular forms of recreational therapy included movies and dances. The asylum acquired its first moving-picture projector in 1915, as Superintendent Preston's annual report attested: "A year ago a moving picture machine was installed. In summer there's a moving picture every Friday night. In winter alternate with dances."[108] The staff screened the movies to ensure their suitability before the patients saw them.

The children of hospital staff and those from the nearby Hyde Park neighborhood especially looked forward to these movies, as Charles Stanford recalled: "They had scary movies and funny ones. The patients seemed to enjoy them as much as we did."[109] In warm weather movies were shown outside with chairs set up for the adults. The children sat on the ground, turning somersaults to amuse themselves during the frequent intermissions that occurred whenever the film broke.[110]

The dances and movies were equally successful. Myrtle Seiders Cuthbertson wrote of her parents' courtship while employees of the asylum: "At that time [1890] there was a large dance hall at the Asylum. It was attended by some of the 'trustees,' as the more intelligent and trustworthy patients were called, and also by all of the hospital staff and employees. As most of the employees lived at the Hospital, this seemed to be the center of their social life—that, and visiting in the park."[111]

During the period of beautification of the grounds in the 1890s, workers had constructed a bandstand near the wards so that even those patients who were restricted to indoors could enjoy the music. The staff organized a brass band composed of both patients and employees.[112] Dances continued to be one of the most popular entertainments for decades, with dances for whites and blacks held on different nights. Otto Schultz recalled, "Employees went to the patient dances. They had little bands that would come in and play. People would talk about it for days afterwards." At such dances, patients frequently asked staff to dance, because "everyone knew everyone else."[113]

Mary Worley Hopkins recalled that as a child in the 1940s she would sneak over from her home on the asylum grounds to watch the dances, even though her parents had forbidden her to observe this sinful activity. She commented: "To this day when I hear 'San Antonio Rose' I think about those dances. My little feet would get to going and I'd go over there. I loved that music."[114]

*Ruby Knight, recreation therapist, directed music therapy. Courtesy ASH*

For many patients, religious services also provided welcome breaks—both therapeutic and spiritual—in the ward routine. While not all members of the board of managers agreed with the practice, some form of worship services had been provided for patients from the asylum's beginning. In his 1866 report Dr. Graham thanked Reverend Mr. Roud of the Iowa Volunteers "lately stationed at this point, for ministrations last winter; and also Rev. T. McRhea, for several visits of a similar nature this summer." Years later, Superintendent Wallace also thanked the clergy for volunteering their services but noted: "The experiment was tried of holding services in the corridors, but it is greatly to be regretted that the attempt was attended with so much confusion, it was given up in the belief that the good it was possible to accomplish under such untoward circumstances would be little recompense for the annoyance with which the effort was attended to these self-sacrificing pastors."[115] In spite of less than ideal circumstances for worship, clergymen continued to volunteer their services. A resolution written by the asylum's board of managers upon the occasion of the Reverend H. N. Sears's death in 1915 stated: "Every Sabbath evening at 3 o'clock with great regularity though enfeebled by age and disease, he would come to hold services and engage in singing with them. His audience was most appreciative and always enjoyed his comforting words."[116] Reverend Sears also served as chaplain for the Texas state legislature.

Since most of the patients were Protestant or Catholic, rabbis conducted Jewish services at the hospital only rarely. In the 1950s, after a young Jewish patient requested to attend Friday services, the president of her temple contacted Bert Kruger Smith, a local advocate for the mentally ill. Smith then invited the girl to her home every Friday for dinner, then escorted her to temple. The patient told the Smiths that her boyfriend, a Rhodes Scholar at Oxford, had proposed. They interpreted this story as delusional, but after successful drug therapy the patient and her Rhodes Scholar married.[117]

Laymen also led religious services. Rodney Montfort, a participant in First English Lutheran's men's brotherhood project (later combined with the Northwest Baptist Church men's group), began visiting the hospital in 1952 to deliver a short message and to lead the singing if no one else could do it. Once a patient stood up in the congregation and informed baritone Montfort, "You sang that way too low." Then the man, a University of Texas graduate in music, hit a perfect pitch and resang the whole song.[118] Another patient always volunteered to play the piano, but since she put in so many extra notes, singers found it difficult to follow her. Patients' idiosyncracies sometimes disrupted the services, as in the case of one woman who insisted on belting out "Beer Barrel Polka" instead of the hymns. If patients became too disruptive, attendants escorted them back to their wards.

Seriously disturbed patients rarely left the wards for church or anything else, and the distinction between those who could leave and those who had to remain behind clearly divided the "good" patients from the "bad." As one former back-ward patient lamented, "If we just had something to do, there is just nothing to do but wait."[119] These back wards housed the chronic patients for whom there was little hope of recovery and the maximum security units that contained the most disturbed or violent patients. Life on these purely custodial wards did not include the diversions of recreational or vocational therapy and, indeed, often resembled the hopeless "snake pit" author Mary Jane Ward had so feared.

# CHAPTER 6

# The Patient's World:
# Life on the Wards

*"Learning the Ropes"*

A new patient passed through an adjustment period to life on the wards similar to that of a newcomer in a foreign country. One day a person walked familiar streets as a free citizen; the next day he or she faced confinement in a strange new social world. Once admitted to a mental institution, persons lost their civil rights—could not vote, incur debts, or enter into contracts. In fact, legal responsibility for a patient often shifted to the superintendent of the hospital, who could assume guardianship if no relatives would. Once institutionalized, the new patient had to learn the culture of the mental hospital that he or she had entered. Belknap wrote: "[T]he new patient spends a good deal of his time in being informally instructed in ward rules by his observation, by other patients, and occasionally by attendants, in adjusting himself to these rules, in occasional diversional therapy programs conducted by the hospital, and finally in sitting or milling about with other patients on the ward as he goes through his individual process of adjustment to the hospital."[1]

Some ward rules were written and formalized; others were informal and customary. Patients soon learned that the latter included customs about who could talk to whom, and under what circumstances. For example, new patients quickly found out that they were not to initiate conversation with the doctors without intercession of the attendants. Attendants had the power to grant or refuse access to the physicians and sometimes used this power to reward or punish individuals on their wards. With caseloads of hundreds of patients, physicians rarely questioned attendants' judgments about whom they should see.

Most patients rapidly learned which rules could not be broken without

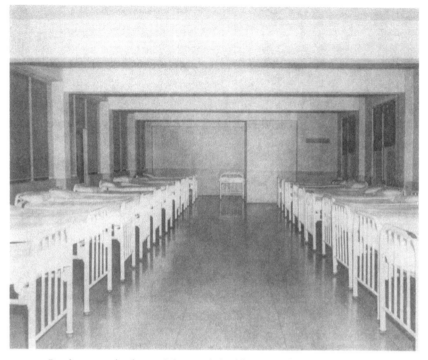

*By the 1940s the decor of the wards had become more austere. C05381.*
*Courtesy AHC*

serious consequences. According to Erving Goffman, "In Central Hospital many patients were entirely mute, were incontinent, hallucinated, and practiced other classic symptoms. However, very few patients, as far as I could see, had the temerity purposely and persistently to drop ashes on the linoleum floor, just as few declined to line up for food, take their shower, go to bed or get up on time."[2]

The process of acculturation to hospital life included adjustment to a rigid daily schedule, which in the nineteenth century began with the wake-up bell at 4:30 or 5:30 in the morning, depending on the season. The hospital later replaced the wake-up bell with a steam whistle, which also announced meal times and blew special codes for escapes, fires, or deaths. At the Austin State Hospital, the whistle system continued until the mid-1950s, at which time the wake-up whistle sounded at 7:00 A.M.[3]

For most patients, the first act of the day was to take their medications. Patients then dressed, combed their hair, washed their faces and hands. and went to breakfast. In keeping with the almost military regimentation during some periods, male patients actually marched to meals or to the grounds for exercise or other recreation. By the 1950s, a smoke break immediately followed breakfast, with cigarettes provided by the state. In all, the daily schedule contained eleven smoke breaks and two "Coke runs" for soft drinks from the canteen. Punctuated by classes for some, various forms of therapy for many, and the numerous smoke and Coke breaks, the day ended at 10:30 P.M. for the majority, although the most disturbed patients might be put to bed immediately after supper.[4]

Goffman viewed the routine of admissions as the first step in acclimatizing the patient to the culture of the hospital.

> The inmate finds certain roles are lost to him by virtue of the barrier that separates him from the outside world. The process of entrance typically brings other kinds of loss and mortification as well. We very generally find staff employing what are called admission procedures, such as taking a life history, photographing, weighing, fingerprinting, assigning numbers, searching, listing personal possessions for storage, undressing, bathing, disinfecting, haircutting, issuing institutional clothing, instructing as to rules, and assigning to quarters. Admissions procedures might better be called "trimming" or "programming" because in thus being squared away the new arrival allows himself to be shaped and coded into an object that can be fed into the administrative machinery of the establishment, to be worked on smoothly by routine.[5]

During this initial period of life on the ward, patients had to adjust to an almost total lack of privacy. Mary Jane Ward recalled moving from stall to stall in the restroom of the New York mental hospital only to discover that none of them had doors.[6] Similarly, bath time was a communal affair, often with less disturbed patients helping to bathe the more disturbed ones. While many patients objected to this loss of privacy, some took comfort in the continual presence of others, as did one woman who recalled the pleasant barnlike odors associated with nocturnal uses of the chamber vessels.

An important part of the adjustment to life in the mental hospital involved assuming the look of a mental patient in terms of dress and personal grooming. Early patients at the asylum wore similar clothing: khaki work clothes for the men, and "Mother Hubbard"-type smocks for the women. These were sewn on the premises, as Dr. Beriah Graham's 1866 report to the governor noted:

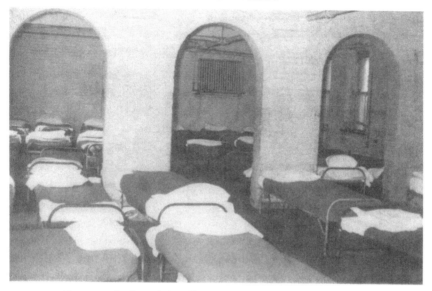

*Some wards showed the effects of overcrowding. Courtesy ASH*

There has been made into mattresses, pillows, towels, pillowslips, sheets, ladies and gentlemens' [*sic*] garments, appropriately charged, about eight hundred yards osnaburgs [a coarse heavy cloth of linen or cotton]; there had also been made into ladies' and gentlemen's garments, and appropriately charged, about two hundred yards of white woolen jeans: There has been exchanged for such goods as were needed for spring and summer use of patients, consisting of prints, denims, hickory stripe, domestic, etc., about five hundred yards of osnaburgs, and two hundred yards of jeans. The balance of cloth is still on hand.[7]

Almost a century later, executive staff minutes for November 13, 1958, recorded: "Discussed dresses and pants for next summer. Dr. Hoerster said we are short of funds and we could get some material of cheaper qualities such as seersucker or denim."[8]

The hospital purchased the most modern equipment for clothing construction. Superintendent Worsham's report for 1898 stated that the sewing room had acquired four power machines.[9] The hospital's matron, Mrs. E. L. Garrison, directed the activities of the sewing room; testifying at a legislative hearing in 1917, she stated that her duties included keeping the time of the sewing-room girls. The committee asked her about records for the amount of material that went into the seamstress shop, and Garrison admitted she did not keep any. However, she said she knew how much material it took to make a dress and how many dresses came out of the shop.[10]

A tailor shop produced clothing for men. Superintendent Hanretta's report for 1949 identified Ann Ermis as the head of this department, noting: "She has the unique assignment of teaching a corps of men patients to sew and make garments—450 pants a month, pressing 312 garments, repairing 1588 garments. She has the assistance of 8 student patients, who are quiet, orderly, industrious men."[11]

When Bess McCord started work at the hospital in 1930, the sewing room produced much of the patients' clothing. She remembered: "In the past they had a sewing room and made one style of dress and about all that we could do was tie something around the waist so it would fit. All of them were checks, red check, blue check and so on. We had everyday clothes and Sunday clothes and dance clothes. We had those in the clothing room, and they did not wear those to clean up." Even as late as the 1960s, according to Willie Crow, "all patients wore those big old thick dresses."[12]

Shoes were "just plain oxfords."[13] In the teens, the hospital employed James McConnechie, a native of Scotland, as shoemaker, but by the late 1940s, the shoe and leather shop, under the supervision of H. J. Peugh, mainly repaired shoes—two thousand pairs in one year. Superintendent Hanretta wrote of this shop, "These men are always busy, always quiet and courteous in their public service, and are ever ready to help the big 'hospital family' out in its foot troubles."[14]

In 1967, the sewing room still produced most of the clothing for the hospital. Superintendent C. R. Miller's annual report recorded that the sewing room had made 56,570 garments that year.[15] After deinstitutionalization, which greatly decreased the patient population, the only clothing still produced on the grounds was "underwear for the large ladies."[16]

As Bess McCord noted, hospital clothing tended to fit loosely and not too well.[17] Pant legs might stop well before socks began, and some male patients even held up their pants with ropes.[18] Such idiosyncracies of dress immediately marked an individual as a mental hospital resident and, prior to release into the community, necessitated trips to local stores to purchase clothing conforming more closely to current fashions.

Hospital barbers clipped the men's hair short, and by the 1920s beauticians trimmed women's hair in a uniform institutional cut. Ethel Brack remembered: "There were no mirrors. The women probably didn't want to look at themselves. They had those bobbed hairstyles." Willie Crow remarked, "You could tell a patient by their hair styles — bobbed hair."[19] As in the case of clothing, the bobbed hair marked a person as a mental patient and was a visible symbol of the conformity the institution sought from its residents. One former chaplain recalled: "Many of them didn't have their glasses, didn't have their teeth, didn't have shoes that fit them. Some of them weren't allowed to have shoelaces, because they might hurt themselves. None of them had jewelry, no rings or watches. They didn't know what time it was. It was worse than being in prison. And all the people around you [were] at least as nutty as you and maybe nuttier."[20]

Getting used to the peculiarities of other patients was a large part of patients' adjustment to life on the wards. Patients had experienced their own insanity, but few had been in the company of large numbers of other insane people. Bess McCord remembered: "You had some that was loud and some that talked all the time; some sang, some was happy in their own way. We had some that wasn't very sick, and you felt sorry for them, and they were the ones that stayed around the attendants a lot." Being around people who might begin to hallucinate and shout at any moment, even during church services, could be disconcerting. Occasionally at his services, lay preacher Rodney Montfort would encounter delusional patients who announced that they were God. Montfort never argued with them.[21]

Daily life on the "good" wards and the "bad" wards varied greatly. Assignment to particular wards held much social meaning, and patients' relatives might exert political influence to manipulate such placements, as indicated by executive staff minutes for October 19, 1959. When her husband was moved to another ward, one woman went straight to the Lieutenant Governor Woodul, who called Raymond Vowell, executive director of the board for Texas Mental Hospitals and Special Schools, who then queried Superintendent Hoerster for an explanation of the transfer. Hoerster explained that the patient had been placed on insulin treatment, which accounted for his move.[22]

The 1931 report of the Joint Legislative Committee on Organization and Economy described the general rules whereby patients were assigned to wards: "Patients are classified according to sex, color, and mental condition. The sex and color classifications are, of course, rigidly adhered to, but lack of facilities prevent the classification by mental condition beyond a broad, general one as: harmless, including seniles, imbeciles, idiots, etc.; quiescent, including those who may be expected to remain tractable; and disturbed, including those who are, or are liable to become, violent."[23]

Patients might be relegated to a back ward immediately if clearly senile or retarded, or they might "follow a fairly predictable process of transfer moving down through certain stages into what may be termed the wards of final destination, or into a position on other wards occupied by patients who are expected to live out the remainder of their lives in the hospital."[24]

In general, a patient's "goodness" equated mainly with the level of disturbance he or she manifested. According to Belknap, the patients with the highest level of functioning "regarded themselves literally as mentally sound and the patients below them as 'crazy people.'" These patients felt they had the right to socialize with the attendants and tended to monopolize their time, repulsing lower level patients who tried to engage them in conversation or to join games of dominoes or cards. Lower-level patients could even be obliged to give up their seats to higher-status patients.[25]

Not only was contact with attendants gratifying in itself as an indication of a patient's ability to function in "normal" society, but attendants also had the power to grant privileges. These included assignments to the best rooms and best jobs, ready access to the doctors, and various other rewards.[26] A fall from "good"-patient status could result in the removal of these privileges or even reassignment to one of the back wards.

Patients and staff alike understood the significance of ward assignment. Normally, a new patient went to one of the better wards where there was hope of improvement and even discharge. If after a certain period, usually a year, a patient seemed to have little chance of improving, he or she was assigned to the chronic wards, with the tacit understanding that they had little chance of improving. Assignment to a chronic ward provided Mary Jane Ward the shock needed to begin to regain her sanity. The significance of the title of her book, *The Snake Pit*, refers to the practice in some early insane asylums of subjecting mental patients to horrifying experiences, such as being placed in a pit of snakes, on the assumption that whatever would drive a normal person crazy might restore the sanity of an insane one. For Ward, the back ward functioned as her "snake pit"; the horror of her new situation and the realization that doctors no longer considered her likely to get well made Ward determined to regain her sanity.[27]

Even the back wards had a certain order to them. As Goffman noted, the "better patients'" conception of the back wards tended to be as erroneous as outsiders' general conceptions of life in a mental institution. The "better patient" believed that "Life in the locked wards is bizarre and while on a locked admissions or convalescent ward he may feel that chronic back wards are socially crazy places. But he need only move his sphere of sym-

*Patients who lived on back wards had fewer privileges than those with grounds privileges. Courtesy ASH*

pathetic participation to the 'worst' ward in the hospital and this too can come into social focus as a place with a livable and continuously meaningful social world."[28]

Attendants also categorized the different levels of patients. According to Belknap, attendants at ASH commonly believed that "There is a difference between incoming patients and those who have been in the hospital more than a year. Nearly half the incoming patients are not seriously ill, are curable, and will leave the hospital for good within the first year. These people are benefitted by the hospital and owe their cures to hospital treatment." A second, more disturbed group "have something seriously wrong with them, which is probably permanent and in all likelihood something in the family but it is something they can learn to live with eventually." The bottom group are the incurables who have "inherited weak or distorted minds or are degenerating with old age" and who will have to stay in the hospital for the rest of their lives. Most of the patients who had been institutionalized for two or more years fell into this last category and the wards on which they lived reflected this status.[29]

In addition to patients' institutional categorization into hopeful or hopeless groups, ward placement depended on their dangerousness and their tendency to escape. From its beginning, the hospital had maintained a separate ward for the criminally insane, "the Cross Place," which exercised the greatest restrictions on personal freedom. By 1870, the Cross Place housed at least twelve violent patients and by 1879 it had been enlarged to accommodate seventy-two patients.[30] Many of the violent patients were transferred to the East Texas Hospital for the Insane in Rusk when it opened in 1919. By 1955, only sixty-eight patients remained in the maximum security unit at Austin compared to 222 at Rusk.[31]

Later, placement on the violent wards depended on certain criteria, including a history of crimes of violence, the use of force or threat of the use of force, aggressive or assaultive behavior, or psychotic processes associated with dangerous behavior.[32] As might be expected, attendants maintained high security on these wards. Otto Schultz recalled: "Some of the buildings where they kept the violent patients, you couldn't get into those at all. The few times I went through those I had J. R. Sims [his supervisor] with me." Similarly, children living on the grounds rarely saw these areas. Mary Worley Hopkins never went into any of the wards except for that of attendant Johnny Mucha, which was considered one of the better ones, and her sister Margie Worley Case recalled going into a back ward only once. She reported, "I was stunned that they were locked in there and were, in fact, prisoners."[33]

Even in times of greater family tolerance for relatives' eccentric behaviors, anyone showing signs of dangerousness tended to be incarcerated—in a jail if not in a mental institution. In truth, life on these wards greatly resembled life in prison. Goffman observed that, among new patients, former prisoners adapted the quickest to life on such wards. They obtained the best jobs and the most privileges.[34]

As might be expected, violence frequently broke out on such wards, and patients assaulted each other as well as the attendants. One patient, a former doctor convicted of murder, kept a first-aid kit for treating the cuts and scrapes that resulted from the frequent fights among his fellow patients. In spite of very high levels of surveillance, these patients often found ways to obtain weapons—sharpening spoons or honing case knives to a razorlike edge against the limestone windowsills.[35]

Not surprisingly, attendants on maximum security wards mostly feared riots involving several patients. Such a riot occurred at the Rusk State Hospital on April 16, 1955, when "a gang of criminally insane Negroes, led by a 212 pound giant who calls himself the 'son of God' rioted for more than five hours in Rusk State Hospital Saturday, wounded at least nine men with icepicks and clubs and held the top officials of the hospital hostage."

The superintendent of the hospital, Dr. Charles Castner, volunteered to serve as hostage if the patients released Dr. L. D. Hancock, who had been wounded and appeared in shock. The switch of hostages occurred. The patients then tried to deliver electroshock at the maximum setting to Dr. Castner.[36] The inmates' choice of this particular mode of attack on the superintendent dramatically reversed their usual roles, giving them the power to control his brain activity. Fortunately, "They pushed the button but didn't have the spring set right—it probably would have killed him."[37]

The leader of the riot, Ben Riley, had been in a Kansas asylum and said he knew the hospital at Rusk "was not run right." He complained, "This is not any state hospital, this is a hellhole." The rioters demanded better food, better recreational facilities, and the firing of abusive attendants. Riley called off the riot after a conference with Texas Ranger Capt. Robert A. Crowder and the publication of his complaints in the local newspaper. Weapons collected from the patients following their surrender included a hammer, scissors, whips, sickles, knives, screwdrivers, tin snips, mop handles, and baseball bats.[38]

In addition to exhibiting high levels of violence, patients on maximum security wards often escaped. Attendants had to guard their keys, carrying them in their pockets at all times and never surrendering a key to any unauthorized person. Underscoring this concern, the lecture course for hospital attendants noted:

The escape of a patient may be a very serious matter. Depressed patients may attempt suicide; paranoid, that is suspicious patients feeling, as they often do, that certain individuals are responsible for their fancied wrongs, may act on these false beliefs and inflict bodily harm or property damage on the people they believe responsible for their troubles. Occasionally an escaped patient will make sexual assaults on women or children. Other patients may shamelessly expose themselves.

The lesson bluntly concluded: "Relatives blame the hospital. A high escape rate cannot be tolerated."[39]

Certainly, the hospital received the blame for one escape, which resulted in the murder of two deputy sheriffs by the escapee. Douglas MacArthur Stewart shot and killed Falls County deputies Dean Humphus and Elbert Watkins as they attempted to take him into custody. Stewart had escaped from ASH and was captured at the home of his aunt. Following the murders, Sheriff Brady Pamplin of Falls County told the press: "It's just pitiful that they [state hospital officials] don't think enough of the average citizen to protect them from those people. We've taken a dozen to the state hospital and a dozen have escaped and almost beaten us home. Many of the ones we take up there are back in 24 hours."[40] However, Superintendent Luis Laosa denied that the hospital was in any way negligent in Stewart's escape, noting, "During fiscal year 1973 seven persons were committed to the hospital from Falls County and only one walked out."[41]

When a patient with a violent record escaped, the alarm whistle blew, hospital personnel launched an intensive search, and local radio stations warned the public of the escape.[42] Residents of the adjacent neighborhood locked their doors at such times, but most believed that their homes were too close to the asylum for the inmates to stop.[43] Security might be tightened in special circumstances. Margaret Standifer Fox recalled, "Once a crazy dentist escaped and threatened to kill my father [Superintendent Standifer], and they posted a guard on our house."[44]

Margie Worley Case recalled another dangerous patient's escape.

There was a patient named Leon, and Mother would say, "Stay away from Leon, he might hurt you." But she never would tell us why. He was dangerous to little girls. Leon was nice and very attentive to us. And Leon escaped one night, and Mother and Daddy and the boys all went out looking for him, and they told us to stay inside and keep the doors locked. After they got out of sight, I told Mary, who was about four or five years old, "Come on, we're going to go find Leon and show him where the ladder is so that he can get away." So I take her by the hand and lead her out to where Mother has all these beautiful zinnia beds and called him, telling him that we want to show him how to get away. But he does not trust us and thinks they've set a trap. The next day you could see his form in that zinnia bed where he had lain there."[45]

Leon was never heard from again. Hopkins concluded that he probably joined the service, since at that time the hospital did not fingerprint the patients, and he would not have been detected.

A few years later the threat of fingerprinting triggered a successful escape by one of the hospital's most notorious patients, Howard Pierson. Pierson had been indicted for the deaths of his parents, Texas Supreme Court Justice and Mrs. William Pierson on April 24, 1935. He "lured his mother and father to the cedar-covered hills 15 miles northwest of Austin on the pretext of showing them some Indian artifacts and shot them to death." Since a jury found him insane, Pierson did not stand trial but was committed to the state hospital indefinitely.[46] For several years, Pierson seemed the model patient. Superintendent Charles Standifer explained that even though hospital staff considered Pierson an excellent patient, they always kept him under close surveillance whenever he played baseball or engaged in other outdoor recreation. Pierson maintained that he liked living at the hospital. He obeyed all the rules and gained the confidence of attendants by informing them of the escape plans of other patients.

In spite of his history of violence, Pierson's classification as a "good" patient led to his socializing with attendants and their families. His relatives had given him a movie projector and periodically presented him with recent films, which he watched in the third-floor apartment of male supervisor J. M. Huff and his family. Huff's daughter, Bonnie Gautier, recalled Pierson as a very gentle man. When asked if he were afraid of Pierson, Huff always responded, "He's done all the killing he's going to."[47]

After three years as a model patient, however, Pierson heard about plans to fingerprint all patients to facilitate tracking any who escaped. He then methodically began to plan his own leave-taking, questioning other patients about how to find a job, how to ride the rails, and other survival skills. He made a key out of a spoon and then made another one when the first proved too thin. After accumulating sixty-four dollars in cash, some by gambling, Pierson put his plan into action. He was last seen at 8:30 P.M., when he returned a magazine to an attendant, and was not missed until the next morning at the 6:30 A.M. bedcheck. He had arranged his covers to simulate a man asleep. Pierson had secured a man's suit, which he lowered to the ground outside in a pillowcase, and, after letting himself out with the key when the hall guard's back was turned, he changed clothes in the shrubbery and left town on a bus. The fugitive eventually settled in Minneapolis, where he made a living collecting for *Look* magazine. Over two years later, following the mailing of over one hundred police bulletins to every large city in the Midwest by Travis County Sheriff Jim McCoy, who had vowed to catch Pierson before he left office, police arrested Pierson.

When Supervisor Huff went to Minneapolis to return Pierson to the hospital, he was so confident of the former patient's good behavior that he did not handcuff him, bringing him back without incident. Pierson escaped again some years later and again was recaptured, but this time he was punished with eight years in Rusk's Maximum Security Unit. After treatment with Thorazine, Pierson's psychotic symptoms disappeared, and, based in part on the testimony of one of Thorazine's developers, Dr. John Kinross-Wright, a jury found him sane (but insane at the time of the crime) and released him in 1963.[48]

Discussions of the escape problem occupied much time in executive staff meetings in the 1950s and 1960s, with topics ranging from whether to shift to the use of plastic spoons (since patients continued to steal the metal ones to convert them to weapons or keys) to how best to install physical barriers at locations where escapes had previously occurred. As in the case of their suicides, patients showed great ingenuity about escaping, and staff were forever "locking the barn door" after the worst had happened. The minutes of April 11, 1960, noted: "Dr. Miller reported that Saturday afternoon one of our 80 year old patients crawled under the fence at the Rush Unit and an attendant spotted her walking toward Rush F where there is a double gate. The maintenance department drove some iron stakes in that area but a concrete slab is needed." Again, at another meeting:

> Dr. Lara discussed the matter of patients climbing the posts that hold up the roof of the patio on Receiving and Intake Unit. He commented that the best solution seems to use some sort of protective shields right under the roof to prevent patients from climbing onto the roof. Someone present suggested plow shears which could be cut in half and placed on top of the posts close to the roof to where the patients cannot hang on and try to climb onto the roof. Dr. Hoerster commented that grease paint might be another solution.[49]

The need to protect the more severely disoriented patients, even if nonviolent and disinclined to try to escape, led to high levels of surveillance for them as well. Joe Pearce recalled of one of the back wards:

> The women employees made the patients their families, their pets. . . . The men at least were given some kind of job and had ground privileges. The women were not allowed to leave the ward except in the company of attendants. I started getting the women out and giving them hospital assignments, primarily to get them off the wards, and this was met with a lot of resistance, particularly from the women employees. They did not want their women getting off the wards, no telling what those men patients might do to them. Also, they did not want to lose control of their patients.[50]

As Pearce suggested, sex joined escape attempts and violence among the most disapproved behaviors within the asylum, and one of the purposes for the high levels of surveillance and the strict gender segregation was to prevent patient sexual activity. The staff cliché about the possibility of sex among the patients was, "They're sick but they're not that sick." A nutritionist for the hospital defensively remarked: "There was too much promiscuous sex in mental institutions, and other people would think you were of low standards if you worked there. I'd tell them, 'Maybe I am of loose standards but I figure my standards are better than the people that I know.'"[51]

Willie Crow, who worked first in the big kitchen and later on one of the criminal wards, admitted that "there was always a lot of sex between the patients." Concerns about sexual relationships (and possible pregnancies) often show up in staff minutes. For example, those from a meeting on April 4, 1960, recorded:

Dr. Hoerster inquired about the incident concerning patients Charles ___ and Mary ___. Dr. Sedberry stated that the stories as related to her are somewhat confusing. Patient Mary ___ reported that when she returned to her ward, patient Annabelle ___ told Mary that a patient from Ward 2 had been coming to her home when she was on leave from the hospital, and that they have been "having affairs." Dr. Haslund has examined patient Mary ___ and a smear test was also made, but results were negative. The two patients in question have been meeting on Ward I (the old hospital building). Dr. Sedberry commented further that it has also been reported that Douglas ___ from Ward 2 has been "propositioning" many of the female patients, but he denies this. Dr. Hoerster suggested that all these patients be confined to their wards.[52]

Patients proved as ingenious about arranging trysts as about escaping the institution. Ruth Howard commented, "The lakes had been drained, and a culvert system installed by the 1950s, and that was where folks would slip on off and have intercourse." Hiding under the shrubbery was another popular alternative. One superintendent, determined to prevent this type of activity, went so far as ordering all the bushes around the buildings removed. However, it proved virtually impossible to eliminate patients' sexual activity. Writing about the Georgia State Lunatic Asylum in Milledgeville, psychologist Peter Cranford told:

In 1895 two female patients became pregnant while in seclusion. Seen only by female attendants and an elderly physician who nevertheless came under suspicion. Both patients had rooms, with one high iron barred window, on the ground floor. A day and night watch on the building finally disclosed that a patient lover on his way to the morning plowing, could by standing on his mule, greet his paramours through the cold asylum bars. The superintendent had wire mesh nailed over the windows and both female patients were discharged as improved.[53]

Several states enacted laws permitting the involuntary sterilization of both male and female patients in mental institutions, but Texas never passed such a law. However, the 1948 training outline for new employees at ASH contained a favorable quote on the matter from the September 1934 issue of *State Government:* "Modern sterilization may be said to have begun in Indiana, where in 1907, the first important sterilization law was passed. Since that time thirty-one states have enacted sterilization statutes, twenty-five of which are still effective. In *Buck v. Bell* the Supreme Court sustained the Virginia Sterilization Statute with Mr. Justice Holmes stating the majority opinion 'Three generations of imbeciles are enough.'" The training outline continued by noting that California had recorded 9,130 cases of sterilization since passing a sterilization law in 1917 and suggested that Texas would benefit from such a law.[54]

Texas officials certainly knew of the passage of such laws in other states. In fact, prior to the passage of the California law, John R. Haynes of the State of California Board of Charities and Corrections had written in 1916 to Superintendent Preston seeking his opinion on sterilization. The letter asked: "Do you believe that it would be to the best interests of society that every inmate before discharge from the institution should be sterilized? Or in view of the fact that few of the insane discharged as cured, remain permanently cured, should not the vast benefits accruing to Society in the prevention of the propagation of the unfit, outweigh an occasional injustice to an individual?"[55] Dr. Preston's reply to the leading question was not recorded.

While many Texans including Dr. Marvin Graves, superintendent of the Southwestern Insane Asylum in San Antonio, agreed with Haynes's position, and the hospital's Board of Control strongly advocated such policy, the Texas legislature refused to pass a law requiring the involuntary sterilization of mental patients. A panel of national experts who studied Texas' care of the insane in 1924 had refused to endorse sterilization noting, "There is still doubt about the constitutionally of such laws, but there is no doubt about the unenforceability of them in the very cases in which enforcement is most needed: that is, in the cases of the good-looking, attractive, and financially or socially prominent."[56] Individual instances of sterilization did occur, however, primarily of women who became pregnant repeatedly. In these cases, the informed consent of the patients had been obtained.

Sometimes other measures for birth control were initiated, as the following letter to Superintendent Springer from Chairman of the Board of Control H. H. Harrington dated February 4, 1926, indicates:

> Some ladies were in my office this morning from San Marcos on behalf of some feeble-minded children for entrance into the Austin State School, Dr. Bradfield's institution. In connection with this application, they told me that the father of these children, ___, by name, has been out on furlough two or three times, and that two children have been born to his wife as a result of this furlough permit. I am writing to ask that you do not grant ___ another furlough.[57]

A legislative committee investigating the Austin State Hospital in 1970 looked into allegations of sexual promiscuity there, but heard different accounts depending on whom it asked. Hospital unit administrators said sexual activity occurred only rarely. Security guards, on the other hand, said they commonly discovered male and female patients on the grounds in what one described as "compromising positions." A guard recalled only one incident during regular working hours but noted: "Sex is more common after supper. There are only two guards on duty then." Describing the procedure commonly followed in such incidents, he explained, "When two patients are observed actually engaging in an act of sexual intercourse, they are separated and returned to their wards, and a brief notation of the incident is made in the security log." The legislative committee noted further: "It was reported to us that the husband of a former patient had complained on about December 4, 1969, that he was being treated for gonorrhea. He assumed his wife had contracted the disease at the hospital and had passed it on to him. The wife was tested and had no venereal disease at that time. Also, her records had no evidence that she had had sex at the hospital."[58] However, the husband's suspicions concerning the possibility of extramarital sex at the hospital were not totally unjustified. Erving Goffman discussed "the marriage moratorium" in mental institutions in which staff and other patients "tolerate coupling among mental patients even though both are married and have spouses who visit regularly. The analogy is the shipboard romance." He added, "Playing around [multiple partners] is not as well tolerated." Reflecting the casual attitude of many patients toward marriage, a couple once approached lay preacher Rodney Montfort after the service and asked him to marry them. He said, "I explained I was a layman, and they consulted together and said, 'We won't tell if you won't.'"[59]

No one could prevent male patients with grounds privileges from engaging in sexual activity. Joe Pearce recalled:

We had one young man who was psychotic by the time he was thirteen. He was about nineteen years old, and his hormones were raging. He had ground privileges, and he got a twelve-hour pass and he only had two or three dollars. He took a bus out South Congress to Hattie's [a well-known house of prostitution in the 1940s–1960s located in South Austin]. He told her he was from ASH and told her he never had been with a woman before and he only had two dollars but he would really like to be with a woman. He was good-looking and engaging so she said, "okay." But then he didn't have any money left and had to walk all the way back to the hospital [approximately twelve miles], and it was way after midnight when he got back. He had already been listed as missing, so the report was on the superintendent's desk by the next morning. And the superintendent had the young man placed on the maximum security ward, which everyone thought wasn't really right.[60]

Viewed as considerably more serious were the occasional allegations of sexual activity between patients and staff. The 1970 legislative report investigated the case of a sixteen-year-old pregnant patient and recorded:

She told us she was pregnant by a former employee by the name of ___. The person was hired as a ward attendant at the Adolescent Center on February 1, 1970, is nineteen years of age and resigned his job on May 20, 1970, stating he had received an offer of another job the previous day. ___ told us she had had intercourse with Mr. ___ approximately 50 or 60 times. She said all of the incidents occurred at a motel, on picnics at the lake, at friends' houses, etc. and that none of them occurred at the hospital.[61]

Hospital rules tried to prevent this form of misconduct by employees. Howard Brack recalled: "Single men had a special route for navigating the hospital grounds. You couldn't go near the female wards. Said, 'They'll fire you for walking down there.'" Similarly, John Supak remembered being warned "not to go near the nyphomaniac ward," which no matter how hard he searched he never found. However, Otto Schultz told: "On the women's ward the attendants had to watch the women closely. They wanted to get to us. They would holler at us. They were off their rocker."[62]

Even the strictest gender segregation could not eliminate illicit sexual activity, and, as in prisons, probably actually encouraged homosexual activity. The 1970 legislative investigation took testimony from a former patient, then incarcerated in the Austin City Jail, that alleged homosexual relations between patients, between patients and attendants, and between patients and doctors. However, this patient's psychotherapist told the committee not to believe anything he said unless it was independently verified.[63] The question of the credibility of patients or former patients made such investigations difficult. A similar legislative probe of the Alabama State Hospital in 1907 caused mental patient Alexander Sheffield to write that while she was certain many abuses had in fact occurred, she was equally convinced that many of the allegations were lies.[64]

The verification of homosexual activity proved particularly difficult. Unlike the telltale pregnancies resulting from heterosexual acts, which constituted incontrovertible evidence, the proof of homosexual activity required an eyewitness. And in one instance, a superintendent reportedly resigned rather than fire a doctor whom other staff members had spotted *en flagrante* with a male patient. The superintendent's refusal to act on such a gross violation of professional ethics may have stemmed from his realization that he faced a situation that, once it became public, would undoubtedly result in his removal regardless of his actions. Explaining his resignation to the press, the superintendent noted that he left because of disagreements with the board over policy issues, not because a state legislator had requested an investigation of the hospital.[65]

Possibly even more difficult to prohibit than sex was patients' use of illegal drugs and alcohol. Alcoholics sometimes drank Vitalis hair tonic purchased at the small store located on the hospital grounds.[66] A work program that involved picking up cans had to be discontinued because the "patients would drink the last little bit of beer in the cans and get drunk." A training film from about 1960 lectured new employees about the extent to which drug addicts would go to get drugs and warned them not to give in to patients' hounding for medications. The narrator told of a patient who received narcotic-saturated letters that he either ate or soaked in water to make a narcotic "tea."[67]

Staff testified to the legislative committee investigating complaints against the hospital that they believed nonpatients sometimes brought drugs onto the grounds to sell to patients. However, the committee could find no concrete evidence of this. Staff also testified about various incidents of substance abuse, such as one occasion when three male and one female adolescents put lighter fluid on tissue paper and inhaled until they fell over and began to shake and laugh.[68]

Patients more commonly used alcohol than other forms of drugs, and one security guard reported that he frequently discovered patients and former patients drunk on the grounds. The committee found one incident of alcohol being sold to a patient by another patient but none in which alcohol was sold by an attendant. Erving Goffman's 1961 field study of a mental institution found that patients could easily purchase liquor, and Goffman even recorded one incident in which an attendant parked his car outside the canteen and drank bourbon with a patient friend while they made comments about passing females.[69]

The family of a patient at ASH sent him grapes and sugar from which he made wine, later selling the beverage to other patients.[70] One person reported that attendants at the Austin hospital sometimes gave bottles of wine to patients as a reward for helping manage other patients. Certainly, this had to be done surreptitiously, since it was grounds for immediate dismissal. Also forbidden, gambling with patients nevertheless occurred with some frequency. The 1970 investigation found that attendants often played poker with patients, a tradition that went back at least as far as 1933, when Otto Schultz and his friends played "Coon Can" on rainy days with the patient members of their concrete gang.[71]

As all this suggests, inmates at ASH were far from powerless in their dealings with the so-called "total institution." Patients learned the "underlife" of the asylum—the customary rule violations whereby the system was defied—as thoroughly as they learned the system itself. In truth, knowing both the official rules and the traditional ways in which rules could be violated was part of "learning the ropes" about life in a mental institution. In addition to acquiring the mores for ward routine and for interactions with staff and other patients, acculturation to the asylum meant that inmates learned how to obtain drugs, sex, and other prohibited goods and services. Even more basic was the knowledge of how to escape surveillance, and many residents demonstrated their specialized knowledge of the place by a daily disappearance to their hideouts, though these might be only an old chair hidden somewhere in a gully.

Whether assigned to a good ward or to one of the back wards, most patients adjusted to life in the asylum. Some quickly got better and were released. A survey conducted for 1951–54 by the Board for Texas State Hospitals and Special Schools reported "a majority of all newly admitted patients are discharged within one year. Overall, only 28.27% of males and 31.76% of females remain at the end of one year."[72] For other chronically ill patients, the sheltered environment allowed fuller participation in a community than would have been possible outside.

Deinstitutionalization produced an upheaval in the lives of such long-term residents, the so-called "institutional cures," and some used their insider's knowledge about how to "fade into the woodwork" to resist discharge during the great exodus from mental institutions of the 1970s and 1980s. Few succeeded for very long, however, as deinstitutionalization triumphed, and the focus of treatment shifted almost completely to community care. The centralized mental institution—whatever its advantages and disadvantages—became largely a thing of the past.

# CHAPTER 7

# The End of Asylum

## *"People are of Families and Communities"*

By the 1940s, few believed that living in the structured environment of an asylum, sheltered from the ordinary stresses of daily life, could cure mental illness, and some even doubted its custodial benefit. World War II created shortages of personnel so severe that in some instances patients had to take charge of wards, and mental hospitals became so crowded that patients sometimes slept on mattresses on the floor.

During the war, journalists began to write exposés of the terrible conditions in mental hospitals, such as Edith Stern's "Our Ailing Mental Hospitals," published in *Reader's Digest* in 1941. Stern called for an increase in spending for mental hospitals, noting that legislatures were often "pennywise and pound foolish" about appropriating funds for mental health unless beset with public pressure to do so. While Stern felt that the problems could be solved with sufficient funds, others began to challenge the very concept of mental hospitals. An article in the *American Journal of Psychiatry* concluded, "On the basis of this analysis we contend that the state mental hospital has developed a kind of dual cultural system which actually prevents it from achieving the expected goal of any hospital, which is therapy."[1] Public opinion of mental hospitals changed significantly during this decade, influenced by articles such as these and by best-selling novels such as Mary Jane Ward's *The Snake Pit*.

Legislators in Texas and elsewhere got on the wartime-reform bandwagon. The Texas Committee on Eleemosynary Institutions chaired by Bill Bundy began an investigation of all Texas institutions on July 27, 1941. The committee's report stated: "We made a full and complete inspection of each institution, most of them we visited two or three times. We held hearings at each institution, put all witnesses under oath and making [*sic*] a record of all testimony, which is very voluminous, and because of the volume of this testimony we are unable to include the details in this report."[2]

Conclusions were profoundly negative. The report continued: "We found shortages of food, inefficiency in management, [and that] cruelty beyond belief has been allowed and condoned by those in charge. Patients beaten, starved and even held in the most disturbed wards after being 'staffed' as being capable of living a normal life, if but given the chance." The report especially criticized superintendents, noting: "We found a number of Superintendents at the present that have the attitude that they are the 'power that be' and do not have to listen to anyone. They even resented your Committee and exerted every effort possible to stop us from making an investigation." Among other suggestions, the committee recommended that the Board of Control be given the power to fire superintendents.[3]

Regarding Austin State Hospital, the committee found that "the patients who do the manual labor did not receive any different food than the patients who stayed on the ward, while the employees received a well-balanced diet. The committee found that the per capita food cost was far below that of the employees and less than one-half of the amount for officers and doctors." The report also described the hospital's buildings as in fair condition but reported need for great improvement in sanitary conditions. It recommended abolishing the dairy, poultry, and farm operations, since these operated at a loss.[4] This committee also investigated allegations of ill treatment of patients by Austin attendants and reported: "We have made an earnest attempt to run down these complaints and have been unable to find or file any specific complaint or charge. We believe that the majority of the attendants endeavor to treat these patients in a humane way." However, the report concluded, "Your committee was reasonably convinced that there are many patients at the Austin State Hospital as well as other insane institutions that have sufficiently recovered in their mental state and are sufficiently well and could and should be released."[5] For the first time, the possibility of deinstitutionalization of large numbers of Texas patients had been raised.

A follow-up investigation by the committee reported: "The committee called at the Austin State Hospital on July 20, 1943, held a conference with the storekeeper and the dietitian; found conditions fairly good. We are glad to report that there has been a change in the superintendent at this institution. Dr. Henrietta [Hanretta] being placed in charge some months ago and it is the general opinion that he has brought about a more stable and satisfactory condition of this institution."[6]

During the late 1940s most of the critics of Texas mental institutions felt that additional expenditures for facilities and personnel could remedy conditions, and that these improvements would at long last allow the asylums to control if not cure mental illness. To this end, in 1950 the Texas legislature passed the "penny-a-pack" tax on cigarettes to create funding for these reforms. Joe Pearce explained:

When Governor [Allan] Shivers became governor in 1949 there was a great scandal—lots of newspaper articles about state hospitals and schools and the terrible conditions there. He called a special session of the legislature about this. They came out with the penny-a-pack tax on cigarettes for a building fund for the state hospitals and schools. The central office was founded to administer the funds. This did away with some of the autonomy of the superintendents since they were now accountable to the central office and a straight-line administrator. All these manuals and criteria for this and that came out of the central office.[7]

This reorganization involved the abolition of the old Board of Control and the creation of the Board for Texas State Hospitals and Special Schools in 1949. For the next sixteen years, until the legislature created the Texas Department of Mental Health and Mental Retardation in 1965, this board administered the state mental hospitals and schools for the retarded. During this time, they attempted to improve the care of the mentally ill within the confines of the asylum model. Ironically, the seeds for its dismantling had already been sown with the passage in 1946 of the National Mental Health Act, which for the first time made the federal government a major participant in mental health care.

Those committed to reform often focused their efforts on food—an old emphasis of reformers. Decades before, the legislative report for the Committee to Investigate State Departments and Institutions recorded that one committee member had strongly questioned Superintendent Preston about the institution's use of "deodorized" meat, spoiled meat treated with chemicals to improve its smell, but Dr. Preston denied any knowledge of this practice.[8] The concern with food resurfaced during the 1950s. A survey of Texas mental institutions by National Institute of Mental Health, done at the request of Governor Allan Shivers, described food service at ASH in unflattering terms:

There are two trained nutritionists, neither of which are graduate dieticians, who are responsible for the preparation and service of food. There are fifteen dining rooms, eight of which are improvised cafeterias. Most of the dining tables are made of wood, have no table covers and many benches are used, while a few have chairs. Metal trays and cups are used throughout the hospital, most patients are allowed only spoons, but a few patients are permitted to have knives and forks. Meals are usually plain, but appear to be adequate. The largest meal is at noontime, while suppers are relatively light. The patients are weighed monthly. Garbage is given to the State dairy and hog farms, including raw garbage from the tuberculosis units.[9]

Early mental institutions, including ASH, had tried to provide well-balanced and nutritious meals as part of their emphasis on moral treatment. To this end, many of them operated vegetable gardens and fruit orchards, and raised chickens, hogs, and cows so that patients benefited from the availability of fresh foods. However, as institutions lost their self sufficiency, the quality of their food suffered. Howard Brack remembered that the canned vegetables came from the prison system. And Joe Pearce added: "You never knew what would come out of those cans. Once, a pair of socks was in a can."[10]

As some professionals well recognized, the importance of food therapy went beyond moral treatment. Disorders such as pellagra produced mental symptoms as a direct result of vitamin deficiencies, and Dr. Harvey Watkins treated one such patient. He recalled, "This old lady was one of the top social lights in Austin and she had gotten so bad mentally that the family had decided that they were going to have to commit her. I took one look at her and recognized an advanced case of pellagra and put her on a high concentration of niacin, and in a month's time she was back as a leader of society."[11]

Certainly, the psychological effect of good food could not be underestimated. As the Texas Research League reported, "Food can be one of the most effective therapies when it is well prepared, well balanced and attractively served." The report continued: "Food service [at ASH] has improved in the last few years. Reports of former conditions indicated that the amount and quality of food served was inadequate, especially in the last quarter of the fiscal year when budgetary allocations began running out." Joe Pearce agreed: "The last three months [of the fiscal year] we would have goat meat three times a day." Another former employee noted, "we had lots of mutton during the war." Similarly, Jo Jureka, who worked in Food Service in the mid-1950s, confirmed: "I used to fix lamb or mutton once a week, but the patients didn't eat it well. We served beans and rice and they ate that fairly well." Jureka identified the patients' favorite foods as fried chicken, roast beef, and hamburgers.[12]

Breakfast for the patients consisted of oatmeal, eggs, toast, and biscuits, and some resisted any deviation from this traditional menu. Executive staff minutes for March 21, 1960, record that Dr. Miller "commented on the insufficiency of biscuits this morning at breakfast and stated that it would not have been so bad if there had been some light bread. He referred to this elderly patient who was just waiting for his biscuits and, finally, someone found a couple of them in the other dining room and let him have them."[13]

Food cost more than any other part of patient care at the state hospitals, and the Texas legislature pinched pennies in appropriating money for it. A monthly report for expenditures of eleemosynary institutions in Texas for September 1926 listed the per capita cost for ASH at $22.33, which included staff salaries and construction costs as well as food. Zilphia Davis, who directed Food Service in the 1940s and 1950s, recalled that her budget per patient was well under fifty cents per day, and Bob Lefteau, who started work in 1964 as assistant Food Service manager, recalled a food allotment per patient per day of only fifty-two cents. On this amount of money, he and his staff prepared meals for thirty-five hundred patients following ten different diets, among them diabetic, low salt, and ground (for the elderly). They served hot breads four times a week. A few times he and the workers spent the night in the kitchens when it was snowing or sleeting. As he recalled, they would "just pull out mattresses and bedding and sleep on the floor. We never missed [preparing] a meal."[14]

Just as the caste system pervaded other aspects of life at the institution, so did it influence the allocation of foodstuffs. The doctors' dining hall had the best of everything, but the rest of the staff also ate well. Ethel Brack recalled: "Bertha Sides was the head dining room lady. She'd make toast. She'd send up platters of at least a dozen eggs. I sent up a plate of eighteen eggs. Sent it up in the dumbwaiter. Five minutes later it came down again. Chief Griffin ate twelve eggs each morning."[15]

World War II brought shortages of certain foods. Bess Greene recorded her memories of cooking at the hospital during the war. She wrote: "My work with Austin State Hospital began in 1941 as a cook. I well remember during the war. No sugar or shortening. During that year I canned 100 gallons of apples." Ethel Brack, a war bride from Great Britain when she started working in Food Service, recalled: "I had to be in the kitchen at

*Segregation meant that a separate kitchen prepared meals for African-American patients in the 1950s. Courtesy ASH*

5:30 in the morning. We went to the female colored ward and then the male colored ward where they let out the kitchen help. That was traumatic for me. I had never been around blacks, much less psychotics. It was dark when we walked them over to the kitchen. I also had to get used to the food—cornbread, okra, sweet potatoes, corn. In Britain, corn was fed only to animals." She also had to adjust to wasted food. "More stuff went in the garbage than people had to eat in England during the war," she claimed.[16]

Later, during the early 1950s, the Board for Mental Hospitals and Special Schools tried to regularize food service. Ruth Howard recalled: "At that time the operation of the hospitals was made as uniform as possible. For example, if we were having blackeyed peas and cornbread at Wichita Falls, they were having blackeyed peas and cornbread at the Austin State Hospital and the San Antonio State Hospital and all the hospitals." She continued: "I never did eat there, but the coffee was terrible. I took my own coffee to work."[17] The patient helpers who roasted the coffee sometimes let it burn and sometimes ground partially green coffee beans.[18] During the 1950s the hospital continued to serve surplus coffee from World War II, diluted with war-surplus powdered milk in place of cream.

Central Office dietician Cynthia Bishop tackled the issue of wasted food during the late 1950s and took on the Austin superintendent on the issue of stale powdered milk. She weighed the plate waste to determine what the patients ate and what they did not eat, showed up to inspect institutional kitchens before daylight, and even rode the garbage trucks in the early mornings to see exactly what was being thrown out. If Bishop discovered that a particular ward did not eat a certain food, she ordered that it stop being served there. For example, beans were not popular on the geriatric wards, black patients preferred fried eggs to scrambled, and Hispanics preferred beef to pork. Nobody liked mutton.

Bishop also specialized in unannounced inspection visits to kitchens and dining halls. Executive staff minutes for October 12, 1959, recorded: "Mrs. Holbert reported that we had a couple of visitors last Saturday, and stated that Miss Bishop was here with a Board member. They were in the Rush kitchen when she was notified by a food service worker. Mrs. Holbert then reported further that from the Rush kitchen they went over to the New Building kitchen, then from there to the Doctors' Dining Room. All she had time to do was to phone the kitchens in question to notify them of the visitors."[19]

Bishop also quizzed the dietician about her unauthorized changing of certain items of the menu contrary to the menu submitted by Central Office, and she criticized the kitchen in the Doctors' Building, stating that it was dirty. Bishop and the board member were on the dark grounds before 7:00 A.M. and left approximately forty-five minutes later, but the food staff knew they would return.

These unannounced visits did not endear Bishop to the staff of any of the state's mental hospitals, and the proximity of Central Office to Austin State Hospital meant that her relations with that institution became particularly strained. The matter of the war-surplus dry milk soon came to the fore. Bishop recalled: "He [Superintendent Hoerster] ordered all of that nonfat dry milk and then cancelled his order of fresh milk. He ordered the security men never to let me on the grounds. One man told me about this order, and I just laughed. And he said, 'Aren't you afraid of him?' I said, 'My dear man, I go where angels fear to tread.'"[20]

During an inspection of the hospital's storeroom, Bishop had discovered a twenty-seven-year supply of war-surplus dry milk. Federal guidelines prohibited serving patients powdered milk instead of fresh milk for drinking, but the vast stores indicated that management intended to do this. Bishop told: "So I said, 'This stops right now. From here on in, every order going to Food Service will come over my desk and have a red CB in the corner and a date.' And it becomes my responsibility then. So, I called [Texas governor] Price Daniel and I said, 'Mr. Daniel, I need you and the attorney general to pay me a visit today.' And he said, 'We'll be there.'"[21]

With help from friends in high places, Bishop managed to get food service operating in a manner that she thought appropriate. Her former boss at Central Office commented:

> Cynthia Bishop was the greatest thing that ever happened to that program there. She was a sergeant. When she issued an order she expected it to be carried out. I had a supply officer who handled all the purchasing of food for the entire institution. Cynthia was just all over him all the time, and she would come to me to get things resolved. I got tired of fooling with them and I told the purchasing officer, I said, "Now Ted, if Cynthia orders cow chips, all I want you to do is ask her how many, how fresh, and how big around!" It kind of settled things down.[22]

Cynthia Bishop worked closely with board member Mary Holdsworth Butt, wife of grocery-chain owner Howard E. Butt. After Mrs. Butt became a member of the Board for Mental Hospitals and Special Schools in 1955, she immediately began a personal investigation of institutional food quality and dining conditions and became appalled at some of what she found. Butt particularly objected to meals being served on metal trays with metal cups and only a spoon as a utensil. After the board ignored her pleas to improve dining conditions, she sent each board member a patient's metal tray and cup as a Christmas present. The board approved the changes she wanted shortly thereafter.

Besides the reforms in Food Service, the 1950s also saw dramatic improvement in facilities at ASH, with the addition of 1,012 beds at a cost of over five million dollars.[23] The increase in beds resulted from a recommendation by the National Institute of Mental Health following a study that had been commissioned by Governor Shivers. The investigation examined all of Texas' mental hospitals and special schools and found the Austin facility to be in reasonably good repair, although seriously overcrowded, with 3,198 patients in residence despite the calculated capacity of 2,810.[24]

The new hospital, the first building constructed with penny-a-pack funds, contained state-of-the-art surgical facilities. The medical staff "did all kinds of surgery, including brain surgery, hysterectomies, gall bladder, etc."[25] The new hospital had four operating rooms and an emergency room.[26] In spite of such improvements, critics continued to lament conditions in the state's mental hospitals in voices that grew ever more strident with the passing of time. Nationally, agitation for reform of what many now viewed as "warehouses" for the insane increased, and some began to call for the closing of state hospitals.

A series of critical articles by Bert Kruger Smith of the University of Texas' Hogg Foundation for Mental Health ran in the *Austin Statesman* and sixty other Texas newspapers in 1952. While noting that much had been done, Smith drew attention to areas still needing improvement, such as record-keeping and staff training. These articles "humanized" the fourteen-point plan for improvement established by the Board of State Hospitals and Special Schools under the leadership of Dr. George W. Jackson and were consolidated into a pamphlet, *My Brother's Keeper,* published in 1953 by the Hogg Foundation.[27] This pamphlet helped draw public attention to the problems of mental health care in Texas, and Smith and Dr. Robert L. Sutherland, director of the Hogg Foundation, further increased public awareness by traveling through the state lecturing about mental hygiene and calling for reform. Writing in the *Austin American,* Bill Brammer voiced harsher criticisms of Austin State Hospital. He wrote: "There were 3,000 patients mentally ill, mentally retarded, psychopathic personalities, alcoholic and the aged crowded into the hospital in 1949 when a series of newspaper articles revealed the plight of the inmates, the overcrowded facilities, inadequate staffs, and filthy, unthinkable, sickening conditions. Nothing has changed." He quoted Superintendent Ristine's comment, "It hasn't changed one iota since that time." A later article again quoted Dr. Ristine: "I have heard state officials brag that Texas now has one of the best mental hospital systems in the nation. They are either badly misinformed or just spouting political claptrap."[28] Dr. Sam Hoerster replaced the outspoken Dr. Ristine as superintendent shortly thereafter, as Joe Pearce recalled.

Hoerster came in 1955 and lifted that place up by the boot straps. He was a taskmaster and also a bully in every sense of that word, but he brought in some qualified staff. He got ASH accredited by the Joint Commission of Hospitals, and it took a number of years since so many things had to meet their standards—numbers of staff and physical conditions, etc. ASH gained a reputation of being one of the best mental hospitals in the U.S. We had a three-year residency psychiatry program and a vocational nursing program. We had graduate social workers. Our chaplain trainee program had national accreditation. We had occupational therapy. All areas had some sort of academic affiliation. We saw ourselves as not only a treatment facility but also a training facility and, thirdly, research, particularly in neurology and pharmacology.[29]

Executive staff minutes revealed incredibly detailed preparations for the visit of the accrediting team from the Joint Commission of Hospitals. Minutes for May 16, 1958, noted:

The Survey Inspection Team will be here May 20th for inspection of the grounds. Dr. Hoerster suggested to put the trash cans in the gutters around the Administration Building and on fire escapes around other buildings. Dr. Miller suggested keeping the grass cut, especially in areas that will be seen by the committee and also road repair in front of Dr. Hoerster's house. Dr. Hoerster recommends showing of posters on the wards. Dr. Hoerster also mentioned showing of books at the Library at the New Building. Dr. Hoerster recommended Mr. Williams and Mr. Pennell take care of Mr. Heath while the others are on tour. Dr. Hoerster stated he would do the selling end.[30]

On May 19, 1958, the day before the inspection, the minutes recorded last-minute preparations: "Dr. Hoerster asked if everything was set for the visit. Garbage cans to be picked up, tour route to be policed (Mr. Sloan to head detail). Grass in and around New Unit to be mowed. Ward D will be first place of assembly. Mrs. Eidelbach to see that wards are cleaned up. Team to enter through visiting room in Lot I Unit and all doors to be open."[31]

A letter read by Dr. Hoerster at the May 21, 1958, staff meeting proved that the inspection went well. The Joint Commission informed ASH that it had been approved for one year, becoming only the second mental hospital not affiliated with a university to receive this accolade.[32] By the late 1960s, the hospital had become fully accredited by the Joint Commission

*Superintendent Sam Hoerster awards a certificate to an unidentified patient.*
*Courtesy ASH*

of Accreditation of Hospitals, which indicated that the prescribed standards of the American Medical Association, American Hospital Association, American College of Physicians, American College of Surgeons, and Canadian Medical Association had all been met or surpassed.[33]

Despite this hard-won recognition for excellence achieved by the hospital, and despite the attempts to reduce crowding by increased spending for buildings, by the late 1950s some authorities had begun to call for the massive deinstitutionalization of patients. Such critics believed that the asylum concept for the treatment of mental illness not only had not worked but also could not be made to work. A former chair of the Board for Texas Mental Hospitals and Special Schools asserted: "There was just no humane way to take care of people in an institution. You don't need to lock people up. The institutions were worse than being in prison. And people were put there completely illegally in those days. Your family could get a doctor to sign a certificate and you'd go before the county judge—no lawyer, no one to defend your rights—and the judge signs an order, and you're off to Rusk for the rest of your life."[34]

Such opinions were part of a national groundswell against traditional asylums. Describing the forces behind deinstitutionalization, Dr. Gary Miller, former deputy commissioner of the Texas Department of Mental

Health and Mental Retardation, and Dr. Ira Iscoe, a professor of psychology at the University of Texas, wrote: "It was a combination of the newly emerging community care movement and the recognition of the inadequacies of many state mental hospitals described in the *Shame of the States* [by Albert Deutsch] that led Congress to appoint a Joint Commission on Mental Illness and Health in 1955. The 1961 report of this commission, *Action for Mental Health,* recommended smaller, more specialized state psychiatric hospitals and a network of community treatment centers."[35]

While some members of the Board for Texas State Hospitals and Special Schools, such as Mary Holdsworth Butt and Methodist minister Robert S. Tate, Jr., embraced the concept of community mental health centers very early, others continued to prefer modification of the existing centralized system. However, after 1963, when President John F. Kennedy signed the bill providing matched federal funding for community mental health clinics, deinstitutionalization proved irresistible. Describing the changes in Texas mental health policy, researcher Jean Brightman wrote in 1971:

> The Texas Plan for Mental Health Services began officially in August, 1962 when Congress appropriated $4,200,000 as additional grants-in-aid for support of the development of comprehensive mental health in each state. The first Texas allotment of $182,800 came in July, 1963 with the remaining $185,000 in June, 1965. Nationally, the origins of this plan date back to the 1946 National Mental Health Act which established the National Institute of Mental Health which authorized grants-in-aid to states to help in the development of community programs.[36]

A statewide citizens' committee for mental-health planning headed first by Dr. Spencer Bayles and later by Dr. Moody C. Bettis recognized "that people are of families and communities" and stressed the "need for joint action, for a community climate for improvement of mental health of all citizens; that one single mental health authority be established; and that comprehensive mental health centers be established in at least 21 metropolitan areas."[37]

In Texas, legislation providing for these community mental health centers, the Mental Health and Mental Retardation Act (House Bill 3), "as enacted by the 59th Legislature and amended by Senate Bill 465 of the 61st Legislature effective September 1, 1969 was to provide for the effective administration and coordination of mental health services at the State and local levels."[38] This bill also replaced the governing board for State Hospitals and Special Schools with the Texas Department of Mental Health and Mental Retardation, providing a mechanism for the funding of the local centers that virtually eliminated centralized state control. One former commissioner of the Texas Department of Mental Health and Mental Retardation recalled: "The community centers had their own appropriation, but it was a pass-through type thing. Their appropriation was tacked on to our appropriation bill, and we were technically the custodians of their funds. But we just passed those funds out to them according to a formula that had been worked out."[39]

This new arrangement diverted power from the central office to the local communities. Not surprisingly, the commissioner of Mental Health and Mental Retardation at the time, Dr. John Kinross-Wright, strongly resisted it. According to another former commissioner, Kinross-Wright "did everything in his power to keep it from happening, including creating small institutions under the board, called State Centers for Human Development. You see, Kinross-Wright's strategy was to prove that we could have community treatment under the board, rather than under a separate board."[40]

However, the board supported the strongest version of the community mental health care system, effectively shifting control and responsibility for the care of the mentally ill and the mentally retarded back to the communities and vastly curtailing centralized mental health. Upper-level staff at Central Office also disagreed about this issue, and conditions there became very acrimonious, with debates descending to the level of personal attack. A letter dated July 1, 1969, from one of the deputy commissioners to Dr. Kinross-Wright stated:

I would like to comment on your talk at last Monday afternoon's staff meeting. You seemed to assume that the factionalism and failure of Central Office staff to work together are things which sprang up de novo because Central Office people just don't like to work together, or because some of them are not "loyal" to you as Commissioner. I contend, however, that at least 90 percent of the problem stems from your consistent failure to clearly define roles of Central Office personnel, your insistence on unworkable administrative and organizational methods, your uncritical support and defense of three favored Central Office staff members, and your failure to respect your own organization, by which I mean your promoting direct personal reporting to you of people at all levels of the organization.[41]

Although Kinross-Wright fired his deputy commissioner shortly after this insubordination, the deputy refused to leave, maintaining that only the board had the right to fire him. A former staff member recalled the conflict: "Dr. ___ had got crossways with Dr. Wright. And he had this huge, horrendous dog. I don't know what breed he was, but a big dog. And the story goes, Dr. K-W was gone for several days, and on Friday afternoon, ___ brought the dog up to Central Office after having given him a dose of purgative. And he left the dog in Dr. K-W's office suite over the weekend. And that was the talk of the department for quite some time."[42]

Shortly after the "big dog" incident, an anonymous letter to the board advised that Kinross-Wright should be fired immediately, since he was trying "to hang on through bad publicity for the board especially in Houston." Kinross-Wright had lost the battle. Six members of the board—Barnie E. Rushing, Dr. Charles H. Brown, Mary Holdsworth Butt, Robert S. Tate, Jr., Ward Burke, and Jess Osborn—signed a request for his resignation.[43] The Houston press did indeed support Kinross-Wright; the headline announcing his resignation read, "Petty politics did Kinross-Wright in." An article by Norman Baxter of the *Houston Chronicle* concluded that a "rule or ruin" faction of the board had succeeded in ousting Kinross-Wright to the detriment of the "most defenseless people of all—the mentally ill and the retarded."[44]

Besides the federal policy changes and rising public concern regarding conditions in large state-run mental institutions, other factors influenced the decision in favor of community mental health care. Outpatient clinics authorized by the Fifty-fifth Legislature had already resulted in the treatment of four thousand outpatients at ASH in 1964–65—persons who otherwise might have been committed to the hospital.[45] The success of psychotropic drugs in alleviating the worst symptoms of schizophrenia created the possibility for many schizophrenics' successful functioning in the community, and lithium did the same for persons suffering from mania. Similarly, following the development of antibiotics, communicable diseases with disabling mental symptoms, such as tuberculosis or syphilis, decreased dramatically, lessening the need to isolate these patients from the public.

In 1957, the legislature passed the Texas Mental Health Code (H.B.6), excluding epilepsy, senility, alcoholism, and mental deficiency from the definition of mental illness. These conditions per se no longer constituted mental illness; however, a person diagnosed with one of these conditions might also be mentally ill.[46]

Previously, one of the largest populations of mental patients, the senile, had been housed at ASH. Now, nursing homes began to care for them. The concept of "furloughing" elderly mental patients to nursing homes was novel enough in 1959 for a report of the success of this type of program to be published by *Mental Hospitals,* a professional journal. In a revised version giving more recent statistics, John Middleton, the director of Psychiatric Social Services at ASH, wrote: "On June 30, 1964 the Austin State Hospital furloughed its 2542nd patient to a private nursing home. This represented an increase of over 1736 since the last report in *Mental Hospitals* in January, 1959. The program started as a small-scale attempt to reduce over-crowding of chronically ill seniles but progressed to a very practical full-scale operation with placements now being made from admission wards and the outpatient clinic."[47]

Changes in insurance coverage also encouraged the community-care movement. In his master's thesis, James Evans noted that "Many health insurance plans, especially group plans, have recently extended their coverage to include mental illness and thus have enabled many more persons to obtain treatment in the psychiatric units of the local hospitals." At the time, new federal programs such as Medicare meant that the elderly could receive care in nursing homes with federal rather than state support. Gerald Grob wrote of the shift in location of the senile population: "From 1963–1969 the number of people in nursing homes with mental disorders rose from 221,721 to 426,712. . . . The change in the source of funding . . . was the occasion once again for redefining aging and senility but in nonpsychiatric terms."[48] Other populations previously routinely placed in state mental hospitals, such as alcoholics and substance abusers, now could be treated in outpatient settings or in other facilities, with medical insurance often footing the bill.

The civil rights movement of the 1960s, which heightened public awareness concerning the value of personal freedom, gave additional impetus to deinstitutionalization. Civil rights advocates, such as the National Alliance for the Mentally Ill founded by relatives of mental patients, favored the least intrusive means as the most desirable forms of treatment for mental illness. Several advocacy groups for the mentally ill organized in Texas during this time, including Advocacy Inc., The Texas Alliance for the Mentally Ill, and Texas Mental Health Consumers.

Passage of Texas House Bill 3 in 1965 meant that community care in Texas would become a reality. To facilitate the anticipated transition from centralized care in large "total institutions" to community-based care, Austin State Hospital shifted to a geographical unit system in 1968, whereby patients' assignment to wards depended on their area of origin rather than their diagnoses.[49]

Lolita Roberson, who worked on the Harris County Unit, recalled, "They did keep the geriatrics together; [but] had MRs, depressed house-wives, people with problems with sexual identity all together." The *Austin Daily American* reported that the change would allow "better treatment through more personal interaction between patients and staff."[50]

Unit administrators had complete authority over their units and tended to relish the new autonomy. Dr. Margaret Sedberry, administrator for the Travis County Unit, stated: "The geographical unit system was a big improvement. Each unit was autonomous, and you could avoid a lot of the bureaucracy."[51]

People who lost authority under the reorganization, however, held different views. Lillian Eidelbach complained: "When they went to the geographic system my role [as chief of Nursing Services] completely changed, and I never really found my role after that. I didn't have any authority. The nurse administrator of each unit was the head of each unit and took orders directly from the doctor." Similarly, Joe Pearce, who lost some of his authority to manage the rehabilitation program, recalled:

In 1968, this was a fad all over the U.S. It got away from central authority and divided the hospital into geographic units, and each unit became very autonomous and established their own treatment programs. I was particularly resentful because I had responsibilities for rehabilitation but the unit administrator had complete say-so. Some of the units had good programs and some of the others I was ashamed of. You could see good care in some units. Travis Unit was excellent under Dr. Sedberry. Other units I would not recommend a patient be admitted to. It was very inequitable.[52]

University of Texas law student Hugh Lowe observed conditions at the hospital for a criminal justice seminar project in 1970 and concluded: "The single most important stimulus [for change] was that the shift to the new system effected a decentralization of authority; each of the units is now a largely autonomous hospital. The director and staff of each are free to experiment with new treatment programs, to take chances on early release and to allow maximum freedom in the wards." He observed three of the units and concluded that the Central Brazos Unit worked very well but the others were less effective.[53]

*Dr. Margaret Sedberry converses with Texas governor Preston Smith on the grounds of the state hospital in 1959. Courtesy ASH*

Phillip Otting commented on the changes: "Stable, trustworthy patients were given keys to go in and out as they pleased. This would have been unthinkable before. Personnel were no longer required to wear white uniforms. I transferred to a back ward and got into trouble there trying to implement the changes. Had ward government to give patients more responsibility. I opened up a little coffee shop on the ward that the patients ran, sold cigarettes etc. From the profits they bought a TV for the ward."[54]

Such internal restructurings were only a prelude to major changes that ended the mental hospital as it had existed for over a century. Deinstitutionalization soon drastically affected conditions at ASH and other institutions, with Texas mental-patient populations reduced by more than half in the period from 1966 to 1975.[55] The big change sometimes caused problems for patients. Sue Pearce described: "At first you could not release the patients unless they went back to their families, and so many of the families had already told everybody that the patient was dead, and they weren't just fixing to take them back." Joe Pearce added: "Finally, the laws changed and you could release them on their own. We'd give them a two-month supply of meds, but they wouldn't get the prescription refilled and the symptoms would come back."[56]

Some patients resisted deinstitutionalization. Once they had adjusted to the hospital routine and had established a comfortable niche for themselves, some felt reluctant to leave. Having learned the ropes of the hospital, they knew how to disappear, and often made a point of being off the ward when a doctor or anyone in authority came around. Joe Pearce observed:

We had some patients who didn't want to leave. They didn't have to pay taxes, worry about a nagging wife or a boss. These patients didn't want to draw attention to themselves because they wanted to stay there. They would leave the wards in the morning and go to their jobs in the canteen or wherever. Part of our job was to search out these patients and to give them some skills and to get them out, and they resisted to the utmost, particularly the old alcoholics. We'd release them and give them a ticket and some of them would sit out in front of the hospital for days waiting to get back in.[57]

None of this was unique to Austin State Hospital. Erving Goffman wrote of the advantages of life in the mental hospital, where loss of freedom also meant freedom from burdensome responsibilities: "Of course, the rights

*A simulated grocery store taught patients skills they needed following discharge from the hospital. Courtesy ASH*

that are denied a mental patient are usually transferred to a relation, a committee, or the superintendent of the hospital itself, who then becomes the legal person whose authorization must be obtained for the many matters originating outside the institution; social security benefits, income taxes, upkeep of properties, insurance payments. One of the benefits of being mentally ill is you don't have to cope with these."[58]

Not surprisingly, many patients did not want to reassume these responsibilities or resisted release for other reasons. Goffman attributed release anxiety to several causes, including disculturation, in which certain cultural knowledge of the wider world has been lost and the person fears stigmatization if he or she fails to "pass" as a member of that culture. Adjusted to a high level of dependency fostered by the hospital's paternalistic structure, some patients were reluctant to leave the safety of the mental institution. Some even returned surreptitiously, as did one former ASH patient whom maintenance workers found dead of a heart attack in his makeshift bed under one of the asylum buildings.[59]

Returning to life on the outside often required courage. Mary Jane Ward wrote of her discharge from the New York Mental Hospital: "Terror of a world no longer familiar shook [me] and [I] had to clutch [my] hands together to keep from snatching the paper from Robert. I've forgotten the simplest of the social amenities and it's been so long since I've had to use my own judgment that I've lost the capacity."[60]

Employees at Austin State Hospital did what they could to ease patients' transition back to the outside world. One attendant escorted a soon-to-be-released patient to Sunday services at a local Baptist church so that the young woman could see how the worshipers dressed and behaved during the services. Fear of stigmatization as a former mental patient haunted many persons about to be released. A former patient recalled: "There was a local newspaper reporter who had been at ASH for about twenty years, and I saw her at the mall after she was dismissed and she was so upset. 'Don't you tell anybody that I've ever been out there.'"[61]

Patients about to be released from the hospital lived in special units and enjoyed more privileges than others. As one explained: "I was on the Dorothy [*sic*] Dix Unit, which was for people who worked, some of them off the grounds. The doors were unlocked until about seven or eight at night. But they did have rules. You had to be there on time."[62]

Living in these units provided the first step to independent living. Lois Gainer described another patient who enjoyed semi-independent living conditions: "This woman would sew for people and make a little money. She'd buy her groceries from Foodland and they would deliver them for her. This was on an open ward. All patients carried a key and took their own medications. This patient would also house-sit for one of the social workers for three weeks at a time."[63]

Later, halfway houses allowed patients to adjust to outside living while maintaining contact with the hospital support system. One resident recalled: "There was a halfway house on Rio Grande, and I stayed there before I could get an apartment. I had to get up and ride the bus and be there [at work] by seven. I stayed there three months. Some of the people there made so little money they couldn't help with buying the food. So their contribution would be cleaning the kitchen or helping with the preparation."[64]

Deinstitutionalization progressed rapidly in the 1970s. In that decade a series of lawsuits officially delineated the rights of mental patients, beginning with an Alabama suit in 1972, *Wyatt* v. *Stickney,* which ruled that patients had the right to treatment; that is, custodial care alone did not justify commitment to a mental institution. Subsequently, a suit brought by a Florida patient, *Donaldson* v. *O'Connor,* found that the state could not confine persons in a mental hospital if they did not pose a danger to themselves or others and if they could safely survive outside the institution. A 1979 Texas case, *Addington* v. *Texas,* further established that the need for confinement had to be clear and convincing and not just "an improvement of the quality of life."[65] During this time, several class-action lawsuits were filed by Dallas Legal Services on behalf of patients and residents of Texas mental health and mental retardation facilities to establish parameters for conditions in those institutions. The suits, *Jenkins (RAJ)* v. *Cowley* and *Lelsz* v. *Killian,* filed in 1974, asserted that "hospitals are understaffed, patients are overmedicated and living conditions are oppressive and unhealthy."[66] The suits dragged on for years under U.S. District Judge Barefoot Sanders. A settlement reached in 1981 "called on MHMR [Mental Health and Mental Retardation] to make widespread improvements. But compliance problems quickly arose. Sanders who toured Austin State Hospital at that time appointed a three-member panel to periodically review conditions in state hospitals and report its findings to the court."[67] Later the court and the Texas Department of Mental Health and Mental Retardation agreed to staff-patient ratios of one to five during the day and one to ten at night. To meet these ratios and avoid penalties, desperate superintendents sometimes had to use members of the yard crew as attendants. Finally, in 1996, after twenty-two years of court supervision, during which time patient numbers dropped from 834 to 330 and staff numbers from 1,345 to 1,316, Sanders's court released Austin State Hospital from court supervision.[68]

Authority for treatment of mentally ill Texans shifted still further away from mental health professionals with a state law that became effective September 1, 1993. Now, patients could request a court hearing to determine if they could be forced to take psychoactive drugs against their will.[69]

The threat of lawsuits extended to surgical as well as psychological services at the state hospitals. Dr. Leggett recalled: "About 1980 they got concerned about lawsuits and closed the hospital precipitously. They stopped all surgery and sent the patients to the regular hospitals. I had to make the announcement to the doctors, and they were stunned. Literally all surgery that was not then in progress was cancelled."[70]

Gary Miller, former deputy commissioner of the Department of Mental Health and Mental Retardation, and psychologist Ira Iscoe wrote of the impact of the lawsuits on staff morale: "Lawsuits are a fact of life for a state mental health commissioner. For example, there are about fifty to sixty lawsuits pending at all times against the Texas Department of Mental Health and Mental Retardation, many naming its commissioner as the lead defendant." Describing the ultimate outcome of the landmark Texas lawsuits for mental health professionals, Miller and Iscoe believed that:

The fate of the patients in their care will depend less on their view of proper treatment than on the opinion of outside monitors and consultants who are free to test their ideas on a captive state mental health system and yet bear no responsibility for the consequences. This has been the experience of the Texas Department of MHMR in contending with two class-action lawsuits, *RAJ* v. *Miller,* dealing with mental health services, and *Lelsz* v. *Kavanaugh,* dealing with mental retardation services. In RAJ a three-person panel of monitors reported to the judge that there was too much violence in the Texas state hospitals, that aggressive acts by severely mentally ill patients could be predicted and prevented by behavior management, and there were too few aides on the hospital wards, and that the hospitals were relying too much on medication and too little on social therapies. . . . [In conclusion,] The state mental health agency lost on every count. The agency was found "guilty" of excessive violence, inadequate treatment programs, and an insufficient number of aides working on the hospital wards. Among the several remedies ordered by the court was imposition of a rigid staffing formula (psychiatric aides to patient ratios of 1:5, 1:5 and 1:10 for the three shifts), although no evidence has been presented at the court hearing to support this or any other ratio.[71]

Miller and Iscoe believed that the hearings had had tremendous ill effect on the morale of mental health care workers, noting, "The employees of the mental health agency are depicted in the legal pleadings of their opponents as the 'bad guys' intent on providing poor care and depriving defenseless mental patients of their rights."[72]

In spite of harsh criticisms during the last decades of the asylum movement, many former staff of the Austin State Hospital evaluated their careers positively. Nurse Tisha Kinnard, who likened work at the hospital to being a missionary with Albert Sweitzer, asserted: "I think the staff has a right to feel proud. They made life easier for the mentally ill." Echoing Miller and Iscoe's opinion that mental health care workers were really "unsung heroes" who worked for little pay under adverse conditions, Dr. Elbert Leggett concluded simply, "We did the best we could for as long as we could."[73]

Due to the combined effects of the community mental health care movement, new federal laws, the increased involvement of the legal system in mental health care, patients' rights activists, and changed public opinion concerning treatment of mental patients, responsibility for the care of the mentally ill has shifted from centralized, state-run institutions, such as Austin State Hospital, back to communities, families, and to some degree the mentally ill themselves. The asylum movement in Texas, begun with such high aspirations in the mid–nineteenth century with the establishment of the State Lunatic Asylum in Austin, ended.

However, just as "asylum" grew to have very negative connotations in the field of mental health care, so too has "deinstitutionalization" acquired a more negative sound than it had in the 1970s. As Gerald Grob wrote, "It suggests an image of homeless former mental patients who inhabit the streets of virtually every major urban area and seem to threaten the community as well as themselves." In fact, although deinstitutionalization has benefited some categories of mentally ill persons, it has failed to benefit others. Critically assessing the state of national mental health care twenty years after deinstitutionalization, Harold Visotsky observed that economics "will always drive mental health" and deplored a "void in coverage for the severely mentally ill." Similarly, public policy analyst Charles A. Kiesler concluded that changes in Medicare's payment policies for mental health care adversely affected the treatment of affective disorders and schizophrenia while benefiting care of alcohol and drug disorders. He wrote, "My opinion regarding these changes in general hospital care is that they are an example of the unintentional effects on a total system when public policy changes are directed toward part of the system."[74]

Some of those who participated in deinstitutionalization in Texas also had mixed opinions about its success. Lolita Roberson, who later served on the board of a community mental health care center in Lockhart, Texas, commented: "Deinstitutionalization is good up to a point. Some patients cannot function in the community and are a danger to themselves and others. Now, we do not allow people to be locked up for thirty years if they can function in the community." A former commissioner of the Texas Department of Mental Health and Mental Retardation agreed: "It finally worked itself out, but for a long time we put big, big, big money into these communities that did not have the foggiest notion of what they were doing, or even trying to do. These people have now come in line, and the community centers are very, very forward thinking."[75]

Some of these observers have raised deeper concerns about the long-term effects of deinstitutionalization, however—a chorus of voices that has grown over time. For example, Roberson expressed the fear that inadequate supervision in Texas could result in exploitation of the mentally ill, noting, "Some states will put their mentally ill on a bus to another state and dump them there. I live in fear of that, of putting them out on the streets without a support system, fending for themselves and being exploited."[76]

In the end, professional judgments remained mixed about the problem of providing effective mental health care. The uneven success of community mental health care highlighted the existence of the many different disorders with quite varied etiologies and prognoses that comprise mental illness. Very possibly, no one system of mental health care could adequately serve all kinds of mentally ill people. For many, the most humane method of treatment doubtless lay in community care, but for others the refuge offered by asylum still might offer the best hope of effectively managing their condition.

# ⌁ NOTES ⌁

## Chapter 1. Introduction

1. David J. Rothman, *The Discovery of the Asylum*, p. 129.
2. Michel Foucault, *Madness and Civilization;* Andrew Scull, "Psychiatry and Social Control in the Nineteenth and Twentieth Centuries," *History of Psychiatry* 2 (1991): 149–50; Abraham S. Luchins, "Social Control Doctrines of Mental Illness and the Medical Profession in Nineteenth-century America," *Journal of the History of the Behavioral Sciences* 29 (1993): 29.
3. John S. Hughes, *The Letters of a Victorian Madwoman*, pp. 5, 7–8.
4. Peter McCandless, *Moonlight, Magnolias and Madness: Insanity in South Carolina from the Colonial Period to the Progressive Era*, p. 5.
5. John C. Perry, *Superintendent's Report for the State Lunatic Asylum*, 1857, p. 4 (hereafter cited as author, *Superintendent's Report* [year], pages); Thomas S. Kirkbride, *On the Construction, Organization, and General Arrangements of Hospitals for the Insane.*
6. *A History of the Historic Administration Building of 1857, Austin State Hospital*, p. 4.
7. Mary Ann Jimenez, *Changing Faces of Madness: Early American Attitudes and Treatment of the Insane*, p. 124.
8. John Sutton, "The Political Economy of Madness: The Expansion of the Asylum in Progressive America," *American Sociological Review* 56 (1991): 677–78.
9. Edith Stern, "Our Ailing Mental Hospitals," *Reader's Digest*, Aug. 1941, 66.
10. Ivan Belknap, *Human Problems of a State Mental Hospital*, p. xii.
11. Jimenez, *Changing Faces of Madness*, p. 48.
12. Leona Bachrach, "Deinstitutionalization: A Semantic Analysis," *Journal of Social Issues* 45 (1989): 161.
13. Rael J. Isaac and Virginia C. Armat, *Madness in the Streets: How Psychiatry and the Law Abandoned the Mentally Ill.*, p. 348.
14. Pamela J. Fischer and William R. Breakey, "The Epidemiology of Alcohol, Drugs and Mental Disorders among Homeless Persons," *American Psychologist* 46 (1991): 1115; Gerald Grob, "The Paradox of Deinstitutionalization," *Society* 32 (1995): 60; E. Fuller Torrey, "Jails and Prisons—America's New Mental Hospitals," *American Journal of Public Health* 85 (1995): 1611; H. Richard Lamb and Roderick Shaner, "When There are Almost No State Hospital Beds Left," *Hospital and Community Psychiatry* 44 (1993): 974.

15. See Leona Bachrach, "The State of the State Mental Hospital in 1996," *Psychiatric Services* 47 (1996): 1075.

16. Gerald Grob, review of "The Most Solitary of Afflictions: Madness and Society in Britain, 1700–1900," by Andrew Scull, *Journal of Social History* (Summer, 1994): 883–85.

17. Erving Goffman, *Asylums*, p. 69; Belknap, *Human Problems*, p. 75.

18. Gerald Grob, *Mental Illness and American Society 1875–1940*, p. 320.

## Chapter 2. Origins

1. *Constitution of the State of Texas*, 1845, art. 16, sec. 54; *Handbook of Texas*, p. 88.

2. James Rotton and I. W. Kelly, "Much Ado About the Full Moon: A Meta-analysis of Lunar-lunacy Research," *Psychological Bulletin* 97 (1985): 286.

3. Rothman, *Discovery of the Asylum*, p. 4; Jimenez, *Changing Faces of Madness*, p. 8.

4. George Shelley, "Some Aspects of the Founding Early Government and Incidents of Life in the Old Home Town," unpublished manuscript, p. 1.

5. Riley Guthrie, *Survey of the Mental Institutions in the State of Texas*, p. 30.

6. Texas Department of Mental Health and Mental Retardation (hereafter Texas Dept. MHMR), *Mental Illness and Mental Retardation*, p. 5. Committee of the Houston Rotary Club on the study of the care of insane. *Proposed Plan of Caring for the Insane*, p. 10.

7. Perry, *Superintendent's Report* (1857), p. 14.

8. Ibid., p. 14.

9. Henry M. Hurd, *The Institutional Care of the Insane in the United States and Canada*, p. 650; "Three Commissioners to Meet March 20 to Select Site of Asylum," *State Gazette*, Feb. 28, 1857.

10. John Supak, interview by author, Oct. 18, 1995.

11. Perry, *Superintendent's Report* (1857), p. 1.

12. Beriah Graham, *Superintendent's Report* (1869), p. 8.

13. John Preston, "Insane Asylum's Growth from Civil War Period Told by Superintendent," *Austin Statesman*, 1914.

14. S. S. Zwelling, *Quest for a Cure*, p. 30; Samuel Thielman, "Southern Madness: The Shape of Mental Health Care in the Old South," in *Science and Medicine in the Old South*, ed. R. L. Numbers and T. L. Lavitt, p. 260.

15. Nancy Tomes, "The Great Restraint Controversy" p. 190; Isaac Ray, "Observations on the Principal Hospitals for the Insane in Great Britain, France and Germany," *American Journal of Insanity* 2 (1846): 346.

16. Hurd, *Institutional Care of the Insane*, p. 652; Preston, "Insane Asylum's Growth from Civil War Period," n.p.

17. J. Sanbourne Bockhoven, *Moral Treatment in Community Mental Health*, p. 47.

18. Pliny Earle, "The Curability of Insanity" (paper presented at the New England Psychological Society, Worcester, Mass., December 14, 1876), 490; reprinted in *American Journal of Insanity* 33 (1877): 483–533.

19. Perry, *Superintendent's Report* (1857), p. 13.

20. Ray, "Observations on the Principal Hospitals," p. 318.

21. Perry, *Superintendent's Report* (1857), p. 5.

22. Ibid., p. 4.

23. B. M. Worsham, *Superintendent's Report* (1896), p. 1; David C. Humphrey, *Austin, an Illustrated History,* p. 14.

24. Beriah Graham, *Superintendent's Report* (1866), p. 3.

25. David R. Wallace, *Superintendent's Report* (1878), p. 13; L. J. Graham, *Superintendent's Report* (1882), p. 6; Kirkbride, *Construction, Organization, and General Arrangements,* p. 59.

26. Kirkbride, *Construction, Organization, and General Arrangements,* p. 59; Perry, *Superintendent's Report* (1857), p. 5.

27. Perry, *Superintendent's Report* (1857), p. 5.

28. Ibid.

29. Kirkbride, *Construction, Organization, and General Arrangements,* p. 62; Perry, *Superintendent's Report* (1857), p. 6.

30. Hurd, *Institutional Care of the Insane,* p. 653.

31. Ibid., p. 654.

32. Myrtle S. Cuthbertson, *Seiders Family History 1739–Early 1900s,* n.p.

33. Preston, "Insane Asylum's Growth from Civil War Period," n.p.

34. Cuthbertson, *Seiders Family History,* n.p.

35. Kirkbride, *Construction, Organization, and General Arrangements,* p. 42.

36. Ibid., 66.

37. B. Graham, *Superintendent's Report* (1869), p. 8.

38. Kirkbride, *Construction, Organization, and General Arrangements,* p. 58.

39. Ellen Dwyer, *Homes for the Mad: Life Inside Two Nineteenth-century Asylums,* pp. 17, 25.

40. Perry, *Superintendent's Report* (1857), p. 6.

41. Hurd, *Institutional Care of the Insane,* p. 653.

42. Perry, *Superintendent's Report* (1857), p. 7.

43. Ibid., pp. 10–11.

44. "The State Lunatic Asylum Completed," *State Gazette,* Mar. 30, 1861.

45. "The Lunatic Asylum," *State Gazette,* Feb. 15, 1859.

46. Ibid., Mar. 30, 1861; Hurd, *Institutional Care of The Insane,* p. 650; F. S. White, *Superintendent's Report* (1894), p. 3.

47. B. Graham, *Superintendent's Report* (1869), p. 6.

48. J. A. Corley, *Superintendent's Report* (1870), p. 10; Wallace, *Superintendent's Report* (1878), p. 4; Grob, *Mental Illness and American Society,* p. 10.

49. Rothman, *Discovery of the Asylum*, p. 145.

50. *By-laws, Rules and Regulations for the Government of the Texas State Lunatic Asylum* (1861), pp. 6, 7.

51. B. Graham, *Superintendent's Report* (1866), p. 6.

52. Constance M. McGovern, *Masters of Madness: Social Origins of the American Psychiatric Profession*, p. 10; quoted in Rothman, *Discovery of the Asylum*, p. 146; Kirkbride, *Construction, Organization, and General Arrangements*, p. 62.

53. Ray, "Observations on the Principal Hospitals," p. 361.

54. B. Graham, *Superintendent's Report* (1866), p. 7.

55. Ibid., p. 2.

56. *By-laws, Rules and Regulations* (1861), p. 5.

57. Joe Pearce, interview, Nov. 13, 1980.

58. *By-laws, Rules and Regulations* (1861), p. 14.

59. Mary Pinckney, telephone interview by author, Aug. 26, 1995.

60. *By-laws, Rules and Regulations* (1861), p. 4.

61. Wallace, *Superintendent's Report* (1878), p. 5.

62. Chris Brownson, "From Curer to Custodian: A History of the Texas State Lunatic Asylum, 1857–1880," p. 33.

63. "Horrible and Unprovoked Murder at the Lunatic Asylum This Morning," *Austin Evening News*, Dec. 29, 1891.

64. James Coleman, *Aesculapius on the Colorado*, p. 79.

65. *Handbook of Texas*, pp. 470–71.

66. Coleman, *Aesculapius*, p. 47.

67. Ibid., pp. 58, 79.

68. *By-laws, Rules and Regulations* (1861), p. 1.

69. "Rev. Dr. R.K. Smoot Resigns from Asylum Board," *Austin Daily Statesman*, n.d.

70. "Proceedings of the Association for Medical Superintendents of Institutions for the Insane" (hereafter cited as "Proceedings"), *American Journal of Insanity* 26 (1869): 150.

71. Coleman, *Aesculapius*, pp. 78–79.

72. B. Graham, *Superintendent's Report* (1869), pp. 6, 5.

73. Ibid. (1866), p. 11.

74. "Fourth of July By the Insane," *Daily Journal*, July 8, 1871.

75. B. Graham, *Superintendent's Report* (1866), p. 9; Committee to Investigate State Departments and Institutions, *Report to the 25th Texas State Legislature*, 1917, p. 124.

76. Wallace, *Superintendent's Report* (1875), p. 26.

77. Edith Mapes, "A Limited History of the Austin State Hospital 1857–1965," unpublished manuscript, Austin State Hospital (hereafter ASH), ca. 1965.

78. Dwyer, *Homes for the Mad*, p. 9.

79. B. Graham, *Superintendent's Report* (1869), p. 7.

80. Corley, *Superintendent's Report* (1870), pp. 13, 14.

81. The Williams Company, *A History of the Historic Administration Building of 1857, Austin State Hospital*, p. 11.

82. Wallace, *Superintendent's Report* (1875), p. 5.

83. L. J. Graham, *Superintendent's Report* (1882), p. 6; Worsham, *Superintendent's Report* (1897), p. 2.

84. Wallace, *Superintendent's Report* (1878), p. 9.

85. White, *Superintendent's Report* (1893), p. 6.

86. Ibid. (1894), pp. 4, 5.

87. Worsham, *Superintendent's Report* (1897), p. 3.

## Chapter 3. Superintendents and Professional Staff

1. *Handbook of Texas*, p. 887.

2. Preston, "Insane Asylum's Growth from Civil War Period," n.p.

3. *Handbook of Texas*, p. 886.

4. Coleman, *Aesculapius*, p. 57.

5. *By-laws, Rules and Regulations* (1861), p. 3.

6. Corley, *Superintendent's Report* (1870), p. 16.

7. "Proceedings," *American Journal of Insanity* 33 (1876): 299–300.

8. Ibid., p. 220; ibid. 42 (1885): 978.

9. *By-laws, Rules and Regulations* (1861), p. 3.

10. Kay Fleet, interview by author, tape recording, July 19, 1994, ATC.

11. Joe Pearce, interview by author, tape recording, Aug. 2, 1994, ATC.

12. Joe Pearce, "Past and Present," *The Envoy* 1 (1975): 1; "Austin State Hospital as I Remember in 1912–1913," unpublished manuscript, ASH archive, ca. 1950.

13. B. B. Perkins to R. B. Walthall, Aug. 5, 1927, ASH Archive.

14. Charles Standifer, Jr., interview by author, tape recording, Aug. 8, 1994, ATC.

15. Margaret Standifer Fox, telephone interview by author, Aug. 10. 1994; John Grimes, *When Minds Go Wrong*, p. 147.

16. "Preston Rites Are Set for Wednesday," undated newspaper clipping; *Pythian Banner-Knight*, Apr. 15, 1915, ASH Archive.

17. Belknap, *Human Problems*, p. 44.

18. J. Pearce, interview, Aug. 2, 1994.

19. Pearce, "Past and Present," p. 2; Anonymous, interview by author, tape recording, Oct. 13, 1995, Sarah Sitton Collection.

20. J. Pearce, interview, Aug. 2, 1994.

21. Jean Brightman, "An Historical Survey of the State Of Texas' Efforts to Aid the Mentally Ill and the Mentally Retarded," (master's thesis, University of Texas, 1971), p. 12.

22. John Hayes to John Preston, Feb. 10, 1916; John I. Bernstein to Preston, Jan. 19, 1919; National Committee for Mental Hygiene to Preston, May 20, 1922; A. P. Herring to Preston, Feb. 7, 1916, ASH Archive.

23. H. W. Davis to Preston, Mar. 31, 1919, ASH Archive.

24. Ernest Winkler to Preston, Oct. 27, 1913, ASH Archive.

25. R. V. Nichols to Preston, Jan. 16, 1917; L. W. Saterwhite to Preston, Jan. 24, 1921, ASH Archive.

26. George Leavy to Preston, Mar. 30, 1916, ASH Archive.

27. A. T. Hanretta to Darden, June 9, 1950, ASH Archive.

28. Ibid.

29. Raymond Habbit, interview by author, tape recording, Oct. 18, 1995; Committee on Eleemosynary Institutions, "Report to the 48th Texas State Legislature," p. 5; Bess Greene, "Memoir," ASH, ca. 1950; Joe Pearce, interview by author, tape recording, Jan. 4, 1995, ATC.

30. Fox, interview.

31. Wendell Worley, interview by author, tape recording, Oct. 6, 1995, ATC.

32. "State Eleemosynary Institutions Care for Thousands of Unfortunates," *Austin Statesman*, Mar. 4, 1923; Floyd Huff, telephone interview by author, Dec. 23, 1995.

33. J. O. Buchanon to Preston, Oct. 6, 1914; H. H. Smith to Preston, Oct. 15, 1914; Smith to Buchanon, Apr. 23, 1915, ASH Archive.

34. ASH, minutes of staff meeting, Nov. 28, 1958, ASH Archive.

35. ASH, minutes of staff meeting, June 2, 1961, ASH Archive.

36. Belknap, *Human Problems,* p. 239.

37. Worsham, *Superintendent's Report* (1898), pp. 4, 6; ibid. (1901), p. 3; Texas Dept. MHMR, *Mental Illness and Mental Retardation,* p. 9.

38. Committee to Investigate State Departments and Institutions, *Report to the 25th Texas State Legislature,* p. 7.

39. Ibid.; Texas Research League (hereafter TRL), *Fiscal Administration in the Texas Hospital System,* report no. 12, pp. 33, 9.

40. Committee on Organization and Economy, *Report to the 42nd Texas State Legislature,* 1931, p. 65.

41. TRL, *Organizational Structure and Personnel Administration,* report no. 2, p. 40.

42. Standifer, interview; Ethel Brack, video interview by Joe Pearce, Nov. 13, 1980, ASH.

43. C. H. Cavness, *Audit of Austin State Hospital,* p. 12, ASH Archive.

44. Lolita Roberson, interview by author, tape recording, Sept. 29, 1994, ATC; Dr. Sam Hoerster, memorandum, Aug. 8, 1955, ASH Archive.

45. ASH, minutes of staff meeting, Aug. 11, 1958, ASH Archive.

46. "Danger of Fire," *Austin Daily Democratic Statesman,* Jan. 24, 1875.

47. "Fire. Building Destroyed," *Austin Statesman,* Apr. 18, 1882, "Lunatic Asylum

Set on Fire by Lightning," Ibid., Aug. 1, 1892, "$33,000 Fire at SLA," Ibid., Dec. 15, 1916.

48. "'Hardhead' Wins Praise," *Austin American,* Dec. 21, 1958.

49. Tisha Kinnard, telephone interview by author, July 26, 1995.

50. ASH, minutes of staff meeting, Sept. 19, Mar. 16, both 1958, ASH Archive.

51. Otto Schultz, interview by author, tape recording, July 11, 1995, ATC.

52. ASH, minutes of staff meeting, Jan. 13, 1959, ASH Archive.

53. Worsham, *Superintendent's Report* (1897), p. 4; ibid. (1902), p. 3.

54. J. Pearce, interview, Aug. 2, 1994.

55. Worsham, *Superintendent's Report* (1904), p. 3.

56. Hoerster, memorandum, Dec. 1, 1957; ASH, minutes of staff meeting, Nov. 5, 1958, ASH Archive.

57. Howard Brack, video interview by Joe Pearce, Nov. 13, 1980, ASH.

58. Jim Cooper, telephone interview by author, June 5, 1994.

59. W. A. Davis to Preston, Aug. 15, Oct. 26, 1917, ASH Archive.

60. ASH, minutes of staff meeting, Aug. 4, 1958, ASH Archive.

61. Luke Word to Preston, Feb. 28, 1914; *By-laws, Rules and Regulations* (1911), p. 7; TRL, *Institutional Services in the Texas State Hospital System,* report no. 9, p. 58.

62. Erna Wisian Leigh, interview by author, tape recording, June 29, 1990, ATC.

63. F. M. Fairchild to J. G. Springer, Jan. 8, 1926, ASH Archive.

64. Springer to Fairchild, Jan. 12, 1926, ASH Archive.

65. Don Howell, interview by author, tape recording, Sept. 29, 1994, ATC.

66. Committee on Organization and Economy, *Report to the 42nd Texas State Legislature,* p. 66.

67. Ruth Howard, interview by author, tape recording, Sept. 16, 1994, ATC.

68. James Evans, "The Care of the Mentally Ill in Texas" (master's thesis, University of Texas at Austin, 1964), p. 94.

69. J. Pearce, interview, Jan. 4, 1995.

70. Howard, interview; Coleman, *Aesculapius,* p. 47.

71. H. Brack, interview.

72. J. Pearce, interview, Aug. 2, 1994.

73. ASH, minutes of staff meeting, Mar. 16, 1959, ASH Archive.

74. Hurd, *Institutional Care of the Insane,* p. 657; Mapes, "A Limited History of the Austin State Hospital," n.p.

75. Sam Hamilton, *A Survey of the State Mental Institutions of Texas,* p. 2.

76. J. Pearce, interview, Jan. 4, 1995.

77. Elbert Leggett, telephone interview by author, Oct. 11, 1995.

78. Margaret Sedberry, telephone interview by author, July 12, 1995.

79. Guthrie, *Survey of the Mental Institutions in the State of Texas,* p. 20; Belknap, *Human Problems,* p. 37.

80. James Lassiter, interview by author, tape recording, Aug. 5, 1994, ATC.

81. Will Van Wisse, personal communication, July 18, 1995; Leggett, interview; Wilmer Allison, "What Texas Has Not Done for Her Insane," *Texas State Journal of Medicine* 20 (1925): 483.

82. Sedberry, interview; Belknap, *Human Problems,* p. 109.

83. Belknap, *Human Problems,* p. 106.

84. Lassiter, interview; Sedberry, interview; Leggett, interview.

85. Ida Lou Bruce, video interview by Joe Pearce, Nov. 13, 1980, ASH.

86. Lillian Eidelbach, interview by author, tape recording, Oct. 26, 1994, ATC; Penny Marks, telephone interview by author, Dec. 5, 1994.

87. Belknap, *Human Problems,* p. 118.

88. Hanretta to Darden, June 9, 1950, ASH Archive.

89. Howard, interview.

90. Belknap, *Human Problems,* p. 78.

91. Ibid., pp. 69, 101.

92. Ibid., pp. 43, 75, 78.

93. Ibid., pp. 79, 151.

94. Ibid., p. 153.

## *Chapter 4. Attendants*

1. "Austin State Hospital as I Remember."

2. Ibid.

3. Bess McCord, interview by author, tape recording, Aug. 1, 1994, ATC.

4. Texas State Lunatic Asylum, application form, June 8, 1915; "Austin State Hospital as I Remember."

5. McCord, interview.

6. Otto Schultz, *Genesis of a Printer,* p. 27; J. Pearce, interview, Jan. 4, 1995.

7. TRL, *Organizational Structure,* p. 74; ASH, *Training Outline for New Employees,* p. 14; ASH, *Rules and Regulations,* n.p., ASH Archive.

8. ASH, minutes of staff meeting, Oct. 5, 1959, ASH Archive.

9. Schultz, interview; Worley, interview.

10. Leggett, interview; Mary Worley Hopkins, interview by author, tape recording, July 19, 1995, ATC.

11. Hopkins, interview. Robert Worley, interview by author, tape recording, Aug. 2, 1994, ATC.

12. Ethel Brack, telephone interview by the author, Aug. 7, 1995.

13. Standifer, interview.

14. Ibid.

15. Hopkins, interview; Margie Worley Case, interview by author, tape recording, July 19, 1995, ATC; V. D. Basey, interview by author, tape recording, Aug. 6, 1994, ATC.

16. Hopkins, interview.

17. Mary Jimperieff, "How the State Cares for its Insane," *Austin Statesman,* Nov. 23, 1921; Charles Stanford, interview by author, tape recording, Sept. 3, 1994, ATC.

18. Belknap, *Human Problems,* p. 238; Roberson, interview.

19. Sue Pearce, interview by author, tape recording, Jan. 4, 1995, ATC.

20. Roberson, interview; Eidelbach, interview.

21. Schultz, *Genesis of a Printer,* p. 25.

22. Texas State Lunatic Asylum, application form, June 8, 1915, ASH Archive.

23. TRL, *Organizational Structure,* p. 95.

24. Anne Anastasi, *Psychological Testing,* p. 508.

25. Roberson, interview.

26. S. Pearce, interview.

27. Willie Crow, telephone interview by author, July 31, 1994.

28. Committee on Organization and Economy, *Report to the 42nd Texas State Legislature,* p. 63; Belknap, *Human Problems,* p. 150; Verna Lee Ferguson Tedford, telephone interview by author, June 17, 1994.

29. Eidelbach, interview.

30. Sedberry, interview.

31. Fleet, interview; Eidelbach, interview.

32. Belknap, *Human Problems,* p. 151; Cuthbertson, *Seiders Family History,* n.p.; Lewis Brownlow, interview by author, tape recording, July 10, 1995, ATC.

33. Belknap, *Human Problems,* p. 151.

34. Ibid., p. 48.

35. TRL, *Organizational Structure,* p. 61.

36. Schultz, interview; J. Pearce, interview, Jan. 4, 1995.

37. Peter Cranford, *But for the Grace of God,* p. 131.

38. Texas State Lunatic Asylum, list of duties of employees, n.p., ASH Archive.

39. *By-laws, Rules and Regulations* (1911), p. 10, ASH Archive.

40. Committee to Investigate State Departments and Institutions, *Report to the 25th Texas State Legislature,* p. 182; Clifford Beers, *A Mind That Found Itself,* p. 165.

41. Phillip Otting, interview by Thad Sitton, tape recording, Aug. 18, 1994, ATC.

42. ASH, *Conduct Subject to Dismissal,* n.p., ASH Archive; Worley, interview.

43. ASH, *Conduct Subject to Dismissal,* n.p.

44. Committee to Investigate State Departments and Institutions, *Report to the 25th Texas State Legislature,* p. 199.

45. Rae Nadler, personal communication, 1994.

46. Dee Turner, telephone interview by author, June 15, 1994.

47. Bruce, interview; H. Brack, interview.

48. H. Brack, interview; Supak, interview.

49. H. Brack, interview.

50. Ibid.

51. ASH, *Lecture Course for Hospital Attendants, Psychiatric Nursing,* n.p.
52. ASH, *Training Outline for New Employees,* p. 18.
53. TRL, *Organizational Structure,* p. 60.
54. ASH, *Training Outline,* p. 11.
55. Lolita Roberson, interview, Sept. 29, 1994.
56. E. Brack, interview, Nov. 13, 1980.
57. Committee on Organization and Economy, *Report to the 42nd Texas State Legislature,* p. 68; untitled memoir, San Antonio State Hospital, ASH Archive.
58. Habbit, interview.
59. Otting, interview.
60. Worley, interview.
61. S. Pearce, interview.
62. J. Pearce, interview, Jan. 4, 1995.
63. Lois Gainer, telephone interview by author, July 30, 1994.
64. J. Pearce, interview, Aug. 2, 1994.
65. Roberson, interview; Gainer, interview.
66. Roberson, interview.
67. Worley, interview.
68. Roberson, interview.
69. Schultz, interview; ASH, *Lecture Course,* no. 4, n.p.
70. ASH, *Lecture Course,* no. 4, n.p.
71. Leggett, interview.
72. H. Brack, interview; Lolita Roberson, interview.
73. Gainer, interview; H. Brack, interview.
74. Howard, interview.
75. *By-laws, Rules and Regulations* (1861), p. 6.
76. Ibid.
77. ASH, *Lecture Course,* no. 3, n.p.
78. McCord, interview; Habbit, interview; H. Brack, interview.
79. Eidelbach, interview; Jo Jureka, telephone interview by author, Oct. 21, 1994.
80. Schultz, interview.
81. Howard, interview.
82. ASH, *Lecture Course,* no. 3, n.p.; H. Brack, interview.
83. TRL, *Organizational Structure,* p. 113.
84. ASH, *Training Outline,* p. 28; S. Pearce, interview.
85. TRL, *Institutional Services in the Texas State Hospital System,* report no. 9, p. 48.
86. Texas State Lunatic Asylum, list of duties of employees, n.p.; ASH, minutes of staff meeting, Oct. 5, 1959, ASH Archive.
87. "Austin State Hospital as I Remember," n.p.; ASH, *Training Outline,* p. 28; TRL, *Building Engineering and Management,* report no. 11, p. 20.

88. Belknap, *Human Problems,* p. 137.

89. Gainer, interview; Evans, "Care of the Mentally Ill," p. 131; C. R. Miller, *Superintendent's Report* (1966), p. 5.

90. Belknap, *Human Problems,* p. 44; Goffman, *Asylums,* p. 292.

## Chapter 5. The Patient's World: Admission and Treatment

1. TRL, *The Program for the Mentally Ill,* p. 16; Jaco, *Social Epidemiology of Mental Disorders,* p. 177.

2. Goffman, *Asylums,* p. 134.

3. Jaco, *Social Epidemiology of Mental Disorders,* p. 177.

4. Wallace, *Superintendent's Report* (1878), p. 24; ASH, general information, Mar. 2, 1953; C. R. Miller, *Superintendent's Report* (1965), p. 20.

5. TRL, *The Program for the Mentally Ill,* report no. 3, p. 26; Belknap, *Human Problems,* p. 55; J. A. McIntosh, "The Proper Care and Treatment of the Insane," *Texas State Journal of Medicine* 20 (1925): 483.

6. Allison, "What Texas Has Not Done," 480; C. W. Bonner to Preston, April 8, 1915; Graves, *The Care of the Insane,* p. 7.

7. TRL, *Fiscal Administration,* p. 53.

8. J. Pearce, interview, Jan. 4, 1995.

9. Shelley, "Some Aspects of the Founding Early Government," p. 8.

10. Ibid.

11. Lewis Brownlow, interview, July 10, 1995.

12. Allison, "What Texas Has Not Done," p. 482; TRL, *Program for the Mentally Ill,* p. 25; idem, *For Those Committed to Our Care,* report no. 1, p. 36.

13. "Thrower Hearing Enters Second Week," *Austin American-Statesman,* May 1, 1963, "Medic's Behavior Related in Court," Ibid., May 3, 1963.

14. "Dr. Thrower Leaves Free," Ibid., May 10, 1963.

15. Turner, interview; Worley, interview; *Austin American,* Jan. 27, 1963.

16. J. Pearce, interview, Jan. 4, 1995.

17. Goffman, *Asylums,* p. 138; J. Pearce, interview, Aug. 2, 1994.

18. Evans, "Care of the Mentally Ill," p. 12.

19. Barbara Sapinsky, *The Private War of Mrs. Packard,* p. 63.

20. Marian King, *The Recovery of Myself,* p. 8.

21. Guthrie, *Survey of the Mental Institutions,* p. 20; Anonymous, interview by author, tape recording, Aug. 16, 1994, Sarah Sitton Collection.

22. Betty McNabb, "State Hospital: A Point of No Return," *Austin American,* Jan. 27, 1963; Goffman, *Asylums,* p. 215; Cranford, *But for the Grace of God,* p. 134.

23. Belknap, *Human Problems,* p. 56; Howard, interview.

24. B. Graham, *Superintendent's Report* (1867), p. 2; White, *Superintendent's Report* (1894), p. 2.

25. Hurd, *Institutional Care of the Insane*, p. 654; ASH, general information, Mar. 2, 1953, n.p.; Hugh Lowe, "Austin State Hospital the Winds of Change," unpublished manuscript, p. 5.

26. Miller, *Superintendent's Report* (1965), p. 4.

27. Belknap, *Human Problems*, p. 56.

28. Texas State Lunatic Asylum, *An Outline for the Mental and Physical Examination of Patients*, 1919, n.p.

29. ASH, *Lecture Course*, no. 3, n.p.

30. ASH, memorandum, ca. 1950; Hoerster, *Report on Admissions*, ASH Archive.

31. Howard, interview.

32. Anonymous, interview, Aug. 16, 1994.

33. Betty McNabb, "State Hospital: A Point of Return," *Austin American*, Jan. 27, 1963.

34. Howard, interview.

35. Belknap, *Human Problems*, p. 123; Hugh Williamson, "Cure of Insane Not Confinement is Goal of Austin State Hospital," *Austin Statesman*, Dec. 5, 1937.

36. Clarence S. Yoakum, *Care of the Feeble-minded and Insane in Texas*, p. 87.

37. Horatio Pollock and Edith Furbush, *Comparative Statistics for State Hospitals for Mental Diseases*, p. 8.

38. Sedberry, interview; Gerald Grob, *From Asylum to Community*, pp. 136, 139.

39. Belknap, *Human Problems*, p. 249.

40. Sedberry, interview.

41. J. Pearce, interview, Aug. 2, 1994; H. Brack, interview; Mary Jane Ward, *The Snake Pit*, p. 17.

42. J. Pearce, interview, Aug. 2, 1994.

43. "Proceedings of the Association of Medical of American Superintendents of American Institutions for the Insane," *American Journal of Insanity*, (July, 1874),p. 228.

44. Rebekah B. Wright to Preston, Nov. 24, 1915.

45. Eidelbach, interview.

46. King, *Recovery of Myself*, p. 13.

47. Hanretta to Darden, June 9, 1950; ASH, *Training Outline*, p. 28.

48. Texas State Lunatic Asylum, patient records, ASH Archive.

49. Williamson, "Cure of Insane"; Eidelbach, interview.

50. A. W. Beveridge and E. B. Renvoize, as cited in *Abnormal Psychology and Modern Life*, ed. Robert C. Carson, James N. Butcher, and Susan Mineka, 10th ed., p. 603; Morris Benedickt, quoted in *American Journal of Insanity* (1873): 505; Lynn Gamwell and Nancy Tomes, *Madness in America: Cultural and Medical Perceptions of Mental Illness Before 1914*, p. 139.

51. Carson, Butcher, and Mineka, *Abnormal Psychology and Modern Life*, p. 603; Worsham, *Superintendent's Report* (1902), p. 5.

52. Ugo Cerletti and Lucio Bini, quoted in E. S. Valenstein, *Great and Desperate Cures,* p. 51.

53. ASH, Protocol for insulin shock, Nov. 14, 1957, ASH Archive; Eidelbach, interview.

54. David Wade, telephone interview by author, Aug. 15, 1995.

55. Worley, interview.

56. J. Pearce, interview, Jan. 4, 1995; Belknap, *Human Problems,* p. 194.

57. Howell, interview.

58. Belknap, *Human Problems,* p. 194.

59. ASH, minutes of staff meeting, April 4, 1960, ASH Archive.

60. H. Brack, interview.

61. Gainer, interview; Valenstein, *Great and Desperate Cures,* p. 225; ASH, minutes of staff meeting, Oct. 30, 1959, ASH Archive.

62. "Amazing Results Claimed in Use of Two New Drugs," *Austin Statesman,* Aug. 19, 1955; J. Pearce, interview, Aug. 2, 1994; E. Brack, interview, Aug. 7, 1995.

63. Leggett, interview.

64. Gerald Grob, *The Mad Among Us,* p. 125; Williamson, "Cure of Insane"; Allan Brandt, *No Magic Bullet: A Social History of Venereal Disease in the United States Since 1880,* p. 12.

65. Grob, *Mental Illness and American Society,* p. 293.

66. J. Pearce, interview, Aug. 2, 1994.

67. Harvey Watkins, interview by author, tape recording, Aug. 15, 1995, ATC.

68. H. Brack, interview; Lillian Eidelbach, interview.

69. Belknap, *Human Problems,* p. 56; Otting, interview.

70. Belknap, *Human Problems,* p. 129.

71. S. Pearce, interview.

72. Ibid.

73. Cavness, *Audit of Austin State Hospital,* p. 21.

74. J. Pearce, interview, Jan. 4, 1995.

75. B. Graham, *Superintendent's Report* (1869), p. 7; Worsham, *Superintendent's Report* (1900), p. 6.

76. Louis DeMoll, interview by author, tape recording, Aug. 23, 1996, ATC.

77. E. Brack, interview, Nov. 13, 1980.

78. J. Pearce, interview, Aug. 2. 1994; E. Brack, interview, Aug. 7, 1995.

79. Schultz, interview.

80. Habbit, interview; Supak, interview; Tony Garcia, interview by author, Oct. 18, 1995.

81. Ward, *Snake Pit,* p. 155.

82. Anonymous, interview, Aug. 16, 1994.

83. E. Herber, "Thoughts on the Austin State Hospital," unpublished manuscript, n.p.

84. Schultz, interview.

85. Fleet, interview; McCord, interview.

86. Doug Lawson, telephone interview by author, June 6, 1994; Lewis Brownlow, interview, July 10, 1995.

87. ASH, minutes of staff meeting, Sept. 21, 1959.

88. Goffman, *Asylums,* p. 267.

89. J. Pearce, interview, Jan. 4, 1995.

90. W. Worley, interview; Joe Pearce, telephone interview by author, July 6, 1996.

91. Beth Covey, telephone interview by the author, July 21, 1995.

92. J. Pearce, interview, Jan. 4, 1995.

93. TRL, *Program for the Mentally Ill,* p. 38.

94. J. Pearce, interview, Jan. 4, 1995; Miller, *Superintendent's Report* (1966), p. 4.

95. Covey, interview.

96. McCord, interview, Sept. 16, 1994.

97. Anonymous, interview, Aug. 16, 1994.

98. Miller, *Superintendent's Report* (1967), p. 37.

99. W. Worley, interview; J. Pearce, interview, Jan. 4, 1995; Howell, interview.

100. Miller, *Superintendent's Report* (1967), pp. 4, 12.

101. Betty McNabb, "Charm Class Aids Women," *Austin American,* n.d.

102. Eleanor Eisenberg, telephone interview by author, July 30, 1994.

103. Evans, "Care of the Mentally Ill," pp. 108, 109.

104. Ibid., p. 108; ASH, minutes of staff meeting, Feb. 1, 5, 1960, ASH Archive.

105. ASH, untitled report, Nov. 4, 1939, ASH Archive.

106. P. Tobin, "Recreation in the Austin State Hospital," Oct. 1, 1938, n.p.

107. Ibid.; Standifer, interview.

108. Preston, *Superintendent's Report* (1916), p. 4.

109. Stanford, interview.

110. Lewis Brownlow, interview by author, tape recording, June 13, 1990, ATC.

111. Cuthbertson, *Seiders Family History,* n.p.

112. Hurd, *Institutional Care of the Insane,* p. 654.

113. Schultz, interview; E. Brack, interview, Aug. 7, 1995.

114. Hopkins, interview.

115. "Proceedings of the Association of Medical Superintendents of American Institutions for the Insane," *American Journal of Insanity* (1869), p. 150; B. Graham, *Superintendent's Report* (1866), p. 6; Wallace, *Superintendent's Report* (1875), p. 24.

116. Board of Managers of the State Lunatic Asylum, Resolution commending Rev. H. N. Sears, 1915, ASH Archive.

117. Bert Kruger Smith, interview by author, tape recording, July 12, 1996, ATC.

118. Rodney Montfort, interview by author, tape recording, July 21, 1995, ATC.

119. Bill Brammer, "Mental Hospital Shortages Crowd Patients Like Cattle," *Austin American,* Feb. 11, 1955.

## Chapter 6. The Patient's World: Life on the Wards

1. Belknap, *Human Problems,* p. 65.
2. Goffman, *Asylums,* p. 209.
3. J. Pearce, interview, Jan. 4, 1995.
4. ASH, *Daily Schedule 7–3 Shift,* ca. 1950, ASH Archive.
5. Goffman, *Asylums,* p. 16.
6. Ward, *Snake Pit,* p. 34.
7. B. Graham, *Superintendent's Report* (1866), p. 8.
8. ASH, minutes of staff meeting, Nov. 13, 1958, ASH Archive.
9. Worsham, *Superintendent's Report* (1898), p. 4.
10. Committee to Investigate State Departments and Institutions, *Report to the 25th Texas State Legislature,* p. 149.
11. A. T. Hanretta, *A Brief History of the Austin State Hospital 1948–49,* n.p.
12. McCord, interview; Crow, interview.
13. McCord, interview.
14. Hanretta, *A Brief History of the Austin State Hospital 1948–49,* n.p.
15. Miller, *Superintendent's Report* (1967), p. 56.
16. Pat Gooding, interview by author, tape recording, July 17, 1994, ATC.
17. McCord, interview.
18. H. Brack, interview.
19. E. Brack, interview, Nov. 13, 1980; Crow, interview.
20. Anonymous, interview, Aug. 16, 1994.
21. McCord, interview; Montfort, interview.
22. ASH, minutes of staff meeting, Oct. 19, 1959.
23. Committee on Organization and Economy, *Report to the 42nd Texas State Legislature,* p. 60.
24. Belknap, *Human Problems,* p. 58.
25. Ibid., p. 196.
26. Ibid., p. 164.
27. Ward, *Snake Pit,* p. 250.
28. Goffman, *Asylums,* p. 130.
29. Belknap, *Human Problems,* p. 161.
30. Hurd, *Institutional Care of the Insane,* p. 653.
31. Evans, "Care of the Mentally Ill," p. 71.
32. ASH, *Criterion for Determination of Manifest Dangerousness,* n.p., ASH Archive.
33. Schultz, interview; Hopkins, interview; Case, interview.
34. Goffman, *Asylums,* p. 216.
35. J. Pearce, interview, Jan. 4, 1995.
36. O. B. Lloyd, "Insane Negroes Wound Hostages," *Austin American,* Apr. 17, 1955.
37. J. Pearce, interview, Jan. 4, 1995.

38. Lloyd, "Insane Negroes."

39. ASH, *Lecture Course,* no. 4, n.p.

40. Larry Wright, "Suspect in 2 Killings Missing Patient Here," *Austin American-Statesman,* Aug. 22, 1973.

41. Gary Morton, "Hospital Chief Denies Negligence Complaint," *Austin American-Statesman,* Aug. 25, 1973.

42. Lowe, "Austin State Hospital," p. 5.

43. Viola Emmert Roberts, interview by author, tape recording, July 6, 1990, ATC.

44. Fox, interview.

45. Case, interview.

46. Hugh Williamson, "Pierson Remains Free Despite Intensive Search by Officers," *Austin American,* Apr. 17, 1938.

47. Bonnie Gautier, interview by author, tape recording, July 26, 1995, ATC.

48. Al Williams, "Medic Holds Pierson Sane," *Austin American,* Sept. 11, 1963.

49. ASH, minutes of staff meeting, April 11, 1960, Oct. 29, 1958, ASH Archive.

50. Joe Pearce, interview, Aug. 2, 1994.

51. Cynthia Bishop, telephone interview by the author, Nov. 6, 1995.

52. Crow, interview; ASH, minutes of staff meeting, Apr. 4, 1960.

53. Howard, interview; Cranford, *But for the Grace of God,* p. 47.

54. ASH, *Lecture Course,* no. 2, n.p.

55. John Haynes to Preston, Feb. 10, 1916.

56. Texas Dept. MHMR, *Mental Illness and Mental Retardation,* p. 9. Marvin L. Graves, *The Care of the Insane,* pp. 12–13; Committee of the Houston Rotary Club on the Care of the Insane, *Proposed Plan of Caring for the Insane,* p. 18.

57. H. H. Harrington to Springer, Feb. 4, 1926.

58. *Report of the Committee to Investigate Complaints Concerning Austin State Hospital,* pp. 5, 6.

59. Goffman, *Asylums,* p. 165; Montfort, interview.

60. J. Pearce, interview, Jan. 4, 1995.

61. *Report of the Committee to Investigate Complaints,* p. 7.

62. H. Brack, interview; Supak, interview; Schultz, interview.

63. *Report of the Committee to Investigate Complaints,* p. 11.

64. Hughes, *Letters of a Victorian Madwoman,* p. 24.

65. Ernest Stromberger, "Probe on Austin State Hospital Superintendent Resigns," *Dallas Times Herald,* Dec. 15, 1964.

66. Turner, interview.

67. Habbit, interview; ASH, Training film for employees.

68. *Report of the Committee to Investigate Complaints,* p. 8.

69. Goffman, *Asylums,* pp. 267, 313.

70. J. Pearce, interview, Nov. 13, 1980.

71. Schultz, interview.

72. Texas Board for Texas State Hospitals and Special Schools, Department of Biometrics, *Survey of 7896 Newly Admitted State Hospital Patients (September 1, 1951–March 31, 1954),* Austin, Tex., 1955.

## Chapter 7. The End of Asylum

1. Stern, "Our Ailing Mental Hospitals," 69. Staff minutes record she visited ASH for breakfast on Nov. 11, 1958. J. Freemont Bateman and H. Warren Dunham, "The State Mental Hospital as a Specialized Community Experience," *American Journal of Psychiatry* 105 (1948): 448.
2. Committee on State Eleemosynary and Reformatory Institutions, "Report to the 48th Texas State Legislature," p. 1.
3. Ibid., pp. 1, 2.
4. Ibid.
5. Committee on State Eleemosynary and Reformatory Institutions, "Report to the 48th Texas State Legislature," *House Journal,* May 6, 1943, p. 2829.
6. Committee on State Eleemosynary and Reformatory Institutions, "Report to the 49th Texas State Legislature," *House Journal,* Feb. 5, 1945, p. 240.
7. J. Pearce, interview, Aug. 2, 1994.
8. Committee to Investigate State Departments and Institutions, *Report to the 25th Texas State Legislature,* p. 119.
9. Guthrie, *Survey of the Mental Institutions,* 29.
10. H. Brack, interview; J. Pearce, interview, Nov. 13, 1980.
11. Watkins, interview.
12. TRL, *Institutional Services,* p. 7; J. Pearce, interview, Aug. 2, 1994; H. Brack, interview; Jureka, interview.
13. ASH, minutes of staff meeting, Mar. 21, 1960.
14. Monthly Expense Report for Texas Eleemosynary Institutions, Sept. 1926, n.p.; Zilphia Davis, interview by author, tape recording, June 6, 1990, ATC; Bob Lefteau, telephone interview by author, July 26, 1995.
15. E. Brack, interview, Nov. 13, 1980.
16. Greene, "Memoir," n.p.; E. Brack, interview, Aug. 7, 1995.
17. Howard, interview.
18. E. Brack, interview, Nov. 13, 1980.
19. ASH, minutes of staff meeting, Oct. 12, 1959, ASH Archive.
20. Bishop, interview.
21. Ibid.
22. Anonymous, interview by author, tape recording, Aug. 15, 1995, Sarah Sitton Collection.
23. Board of Texas State Hospitals and Special Schools, *Report,* 1960, p. 2.
24. Guthrie, *Survey of the Mental Institutions,* p. 34.
25. Roberson, interview.

26. Leggett, interview.
27. Bert Kruger Smith, *My Brother's Keeper.*
28. Brammer, "Mental Hospital Shortages"; idem, "It Could Be You in Mental Ward," *Austin Statesman,* Feb. 13, 1955.
29. J. Pearce, interview, Jan. 4, 1995.
30. ASH, minutes of staff meeting, May 16, 1958.
31. Ibid., May 19, 1958.
32. Ibid., May 21, 1958.
33. John Middleton, *The Austin State Hospital: Recovery Is Possible for the Mentally Ill,* p. 15.
34. Anonymous, interview by author, tape recording, Mar. 2, 1995, Sarah Sitton Collection.
35. Gary M. Miller and Ira Iscoe, "A State Mental Health Commissioner and the Politics of Mental Illness," in *Impossible Jobs in Public Management,* ed. Erwin C. Hargrove and John C. Glidewell, p. 106.
36. Jean Brightman, "An Historical Survey of the State of Texas' Efforts to Aid the Mentally Ill and the Mentally Retarded" (master's thesis, University of Texas at Austin, 1971), p. 40.
37. Ibid.
38. Ibid., p. 2.
39. Anonymous, interview, Aug. 15, 1995.
40. Ibid.
41. Anonymous to Kinross-Wright, July 1, 1969.
42. Anonymous, interview by author, tape recording, Oct. 26, 1995, Sarah Sitton Collection.
43. Felton West, "Smith Accused of Neglecting Duty," *Houston Post,* April 9, 1970.
44. Norman Baxter, "Petty Politics Did Kinross-Wright In," *Houston Chronicle,* Apr. 19, 1970.
45. Miller, *Superintendent's Report* (1965), p. 1.
46. Texas Dept. MHMR, *Mental Illness and Mental Retardation,* p. 14.
47. John Middleton, "Nursing Home and Follow-up Program Austin State Hospital," *Mental Hospitals* 15 (June, 1964): 1.
48. Evans, "Care of the Mentally Ill," p. 112; Grob, *Mental Illness and American Society,* p. 317.
49. DeMoll, interview.
50. Roberson, interview; "Hospital Units Split by Areas," *Austin American,* July 19, 1968.
51. Sedberry, interview.
52. Eidelbach, interview; J. Pearce, interview, Jan. 4, 1995.
53. Lowe, "Austin State Hospital," p. 25.
54. Otting, interview.
55. Texas Dept. MHMR, *Mental Illness and Mental Retardation,* p. 28.

56. S. Pearce, interview; J. Pearce, interview, Jan. 4, 1995.

57. J. Pearce, interview, Aug. 2, 1994.

58. Goffman, *Asylums,* p. 76.

59. Supak, interview.

60. Ward, *Snake Pit,* p. 275.

61. Anonymous, interview, Aug. 16, 1994.

62. Ibid.

63. Gainer, interview.

64. Anonymous, interview, Aug. 16, 1994.

65. Texas Dept. MHMR, *Mental Illness and Mental Retardation,* p. 30.

66. Denise Gamino, "Mental Health Advocacy Centers Multiply Since '84," *Austin American-Statesman,* May 1, 1994.

67. Ibid.

68. Denise Gamino, "State Hospital Near End of Suit," *Austin American-Statesman,* Feb. 1, 1996.

69. Idem, "Patients declining drugs take fight to medication court," *Austin American-Statesman,* Oct. 11, 1994.

70. Leggett, interview.

71. Miller and Iscoe, "A State Mental Health Commissioner," pp. 121, 123.

72. Ibid., p. 125.

73. Kinnard, interview; Leggett, interview.

74. Grob, "Paradox of Deinstitutionalization," p. 51; Harold M. Visotsky, "Twenty Years of Progress," *Administration and Policy in Mental Health* 21 (1993): 137; Charles A. Kiesler, "Changes in General Hospital Psychiatric Care," *American Psychologist* 46 (1991): 416.

75. Lolita Roberson, interview, Sept. 29, 1995; Anonymous, interview, Aug. 15, 1995.

76. Roberson, interview, Sept. 29, 1995.

# ✄ BIBLIOGRAPHY ∾

## Abbreviations

ASH  Austin State Hospital, Austin, Texas
ATC  Austin-Travis County Collection, Austin Public Library, Austin, Texas

## Unpublished manuscripts

Anonymous. "Austin State Hospital as I Remember in 1912–1913." Unpublished manuscript. ASH Archive, ca. 1950.

Anonymous. Unpublished memoir. San Antonio State Hospital, nd.

Brightman, Jean. "An Historical Survey of the State of Texas' Efforts to Aid the Mentally Ill and the Mentally Retarded." Unpublished master's thesis, University of Texas at Austin, 1971.

Brownlow, Lewis. "Austin State Hospital—formerly State Lunatic Asylum." Unpublished manuscript. ATC, ca. 1995.

Brownson, Chris. "From Curer to Custodian: A History of the Texas State Lunatic Asylum, 1857–1880." Unpublished manuscript, University of Texas at Austin, 1992.

Evans, James. "The Care of the Mentally Ill in Texas." Unpublished master's thesis, University of Texas at Austin, 1964.

Greene, Bess. Unpublished Memoir. ASH, ca. 1950.

Herber, E. "Thoughts on the Austin State Hospital." Unpublished manuscript, ATC, 1995.

Lowe, Hugh. "Austin State Hospital the Winds of Change." Unpublished manuscript, University of Texas at Austin, 1970.

Mapes, Edith. "A Limited History of the Austin State Hospital, 1857–1965." Unpublished manuscript, ASH, ca. 1965.

Shelley, George. "Some Aspects of the Founding Early Government and Incidents of Life in the Old Home Town." Unpublished manuscript, ATC, ca. 1950.

Tobin, P. "Recreation in the Austin State Hospital." Unpublished manuscript, ASH, 1938.

Wilson, J. T. "In Memoriam." Unpublished poem. ASH, 1886.

## Published Sources

*A History of the Historic Administration Building of 1857, Austin State Hospital.* Austin, Tex.: Williams Company, AIA, 1986.

Allison, Wilmer. "What Texas Has Not Done for Her Insane." *Texas State Journal of Medicine* 20 (1925): 479–83.

Anastasi, Anne. *Psychological Testing.* 3d ed. New York: Macmillan, 1961.

*An Outline for the Mental and Physical Examination of Patients.* ASH, 1919, ASH Archive. Adopted from Adolf Meyer. *Outlines of Examinations.* New York: Bloomingdale Pathological Institute Press, 1918.

Association of Medical Superintendents of American Institutions for the Insane. *Report on the Construction of Hospitals for the Insane.* Philadelphia, Pa.: Association of Medical Superintendents of American Institutions for the Insane, 1851.

Austin State Hospital. *Conduct Subject to Dismissal.* Austin, Tex.: ASH, ca. 1950.

———. *Criterion for Determination of Manifest Dangerousness.* Austin, Tex.: ASH, ca. 1970.

———. *Daily Schedule 7–3 Shift.* ca. 1950. ASH Archive.

———. *Duties of Employees.* Austin, Tex.: ASH, ca. 1900. ASH Archive.

———. *Lecture Course for Hospital Attendants. Psychiatric Nursing.* Austin, Tex.: ASH, ca. 1950.

———. *Rules and Regulations.* Austin, Tex.: ASH, ca. 1950. ASH Archive.

———. *Training Outline for New Employees.* Austin, Tex.: ASH, 1948. ASH Archive.

Bachrach, Leona. "Deinstitutionalization: A Semantic Analysis." *Journal of Social Issues* 45 (1989): 161–71.

———. "The State of the State Mental Hospital in 1996." *Psychiatric Services* 47 (1996): 1071–78.

Bateman, J. Freemont, and H. Warren Dunham. "The State Mental Hospital as a Specialized Community Experience." *American Journal of Psychiatry* 105 (1948): 445–48.

Beers, Clifford. *A Mind That Found Itself.* Rev. ed. New York: Doubleday, 1970.

Belknap, Ivan. *Human Problems of a State Mental Hospital.* New York: McGraw-Hill, 1956.

Beveridge, A. W., and E. B. Renvoize. "Electricity: A History of Its Use in the Treatment of Mental Illness in Britain During the Second Half of the 19th Century." *British Journal of Psychiatry* 153 (1988): 157–62.

Board for Texas State Hospitals and Special Schools. *Annual Report.* State of Texas, 1960.

Bockhoven, J. Sanbourne. *Moral Treatment in Community Mental Health.* New York: Springer, 1971.

Brandt, Allan. *No Magic Bullet: A Social History of Venereal Disease in the United States Since 1880.* Oxford, Eng.: Oxford University Press, 1985.

Brownlow, Lewis. "Growing up in Hyde Park." *Pecan Press.* Vol. 13 (December 1987), p. 3.

*By-laws, Rules and Regulations for the Government of the Texas State Lunatic Asylum.* Austin, Tex.: Intelligencer Book Office, 1861.

*By-laws, Rules and Regulations.* Austin, Tex.: State Lunatic Asylum, 1911.

Carson, Robert C., James N. Butcher, and Susan Mineka. *Abnormal Psychology and Modern Life.* 10th ed. New York: HarperCollins, 1996.

Cavness, C. H. *Audit of Austin State Hospital.* Austin, Tex.: Texas State Legislature, 1948.

Coleman, James. *Aesculapius on the Colorado.* Austin, Tex.: Encino Press, 1971.

Committee of the Houston Rotary Club on the Study of the Care of the Insane. *Proposed Plan of Caring for the Insane.* Houston, 1924.

Committee on Organization and Economy. *Report to the 42nd Texas State Legislature.* Austin, Tex.: Committee on Organization and Economy, 1931.

Committee on State Eleemosynary and Reformatory Institutions. "Report to the 48th Texas State Legislature." *House Journal* (May 6, 1943): 2822–30.

———. "Report to the 49th Texas State Legislature." *House Journal* (Feb. 5, 1945): 239–46.

Committee to Investigate State Department and Institutions. *Report to the 25th Texas State Legislature.* Austin, Tex.: Committee to Investigate State Department and Institutions, 1917.

Corley, J. A. *Superintendent's Report for the State Lunatic Asylum.* Austin, Tex.: State Lunatic Asylum, 1870.

Cranford, Peter. *But for the Grace of God.* Atlanta, Ga.: Great Pyramid Press, 1981.

Cuthbertson, Myrtle S. *Seiders Family History 1739–early 1900s.* Privately published, ca. 1980.

Deutsch, Albert. *The Shame of the States.* New York: Harcourt, Brace, Jovanovich, 1948.

Dwyer, Ellen. *Homes for the Mad: Life Inside Two Nineteenth-century Asylums.* New Brunswick, N.J.: Rutgers University Press, 1987.

Earle, Pliny. "The Curability of Insanity." Read before the New England Psychological Society, Worcester, Mass., December 14, 1876. Reprinted in *American Journal of Insanity* 33 (1877): 483–533.

Fischer, Pamela J., and William R. Breakey. "The Epidemiology of Alcohol, Drugs and Mental Disorders among Homeless Persons." *American Psychologist* 46 (1991): 1115–28.

Foucault, Michel. *Madness and Civilization.* New York: Vintage Books, 1988.

Gamwell, Lynn, and Nancy Tomes. *Madness in America: Cultural and Medical Perceptions of Mental Illness Before 1914.* Ithaca, N.Y.: Cornell University Press, 1995.

Goffman, Erving. *Asylums.* Garden City, N.Y.: Anchor Books, 1961.

Graham, Beriah. *Superintendent's Report for the State Lunatic Asylum.* Austin, Tex.: State Lunatic Asylum, 1863.

———. *Superintendent's Report for the State Lunatic Asylum.* Austin, Tex.: State Lunatic Asylum, 1866.

———. *Superintendent's Report for the State Lunatic Asylum.* Austin, Tex.: State Lunatic Asylum, 1869.

Graham, Leonidas J. *Superintendent's Report for the State Lunatic Asylum.* Austin, Tex.: State Lunatic Asylum, 1882.

Graves, Marvin L. *The Care of the Insane.* Medical Series, no. 2, no. 63. Austin, Tex.: Bulletin of the University of Texas, 1905.

Grimes, John. *When Minds Go Wrong.* Chicago: Privately published, 1949.

Grob, Gerald. *The Mad Among Us.* New York: Free Press, 1994.

———. *Mental Illness and American Society 1875–1940.* Princeton, N.J.: Princeton University Press, 1983.

———. "The Paradox of Deinstitutionalization." *Society* 32 (1995): 51–60.

Guthrie, Riley. *Survey of the Mental Institutions in the State of Texas.* Washington, D.C.: National Institute of Mental Health, 1950.

Hamilton, Sam. *A Survey of the State Mental Institutions of Texas.* Washington, D.C.: United States Health Service, 1943.

*Handbook of Texas.* Austin, Tex.: Texas State Historical Association, 1952.

Hanretta, Aloysius T. *A Brief History of the Austin State Hospital.* Austin, Tex.: ASH, 1949. ASH Archive.

Hughes, John S. *The Letters of a Victorian Madwoman.* Columbia: University of South Carolina Press, 1993.

Humphrey, David C. *Austin, an Illustrated History.* Northridge, Calif.: Windsor Publications, 1985.

Hurd, Henry M. *The Institutional Care of the Insane in the United States and Canada.* Baltimore, Md.: The Johns Hopkins Press, 1916.

Isaac, Rael J., and Virginia C. Armat. *Madness in the Streets: How Psychiatry and the Law Abandoned the Mentally Ill.* New York: Free Press, 1990.

Jaco, E. Gartly. *The Social Epidemiology of Mental Disorders: A Psychiatric Survey of Texas.* New York: Russell Sage, 1960.

Jimenez, Mary Ann. *Changing Faces of Madness: Early American Attitudes and Treatment of the Insane.* Hanover, Mass.: Brandeis University Press, 1987.

Kiesler, Charles A. "Changes in General Hospital Psychiatric Care." *American Psychologist* 46 (1991): 416–21.

King, Marian. *The Recovery of Myself.* New Haven, Conn.: Yale University Press, 1931.

Kirkbride, Thomas S. *On the Construction, Organization, and General Arrangements of Hospitals for the Insane.* Philadelphia, Pa.: Lindsay and Blakiston, 1854.

Lamb, H. Richard, and Roderick Shaner. "When There Are Almost No State Hospital Beds Left." *Hospital and Community Psychiatry* 44 (1993): 973–76.

Luchins, Abraham S. "Social Control Doctrines of Mental Illness and the Medical Profession in Nineteenth-century America." *Journal of the History of the Behavioral Sciences* 29 (1993): 29–47.

McCandless, Peter. *Moonlight, Magnolias and Madness: Insanity in South Carolina from the Colonial Period to the Progressive Era.* Chapel Hill: University of North Carolina Press, 1996.

McGovern, Constance M. *Masters of Madness: Social Origins of the American Psychiatric Profession.* Hanover, Vt.: University of Vermont, 1985.

McIntosh, J. A. "The Proper Care and Treatment of the Insane." *Texas State Journal of Medicine* 20 (1925): 483–86.

*Mental Illness and Mental Retardation. The History of State Care in Texas.* Austin, Tex.: Texas Department of Mental Health and Mental Retardation, 1975.

Middleton, John. *The Austin State Hospital: Recovery Is Possible for the Mentally Ill.* Austin, Tex.: Austin State Hospital, ca. 1967.

——. "Nursing Home and Follow-up Program Austin State Hospital." *Mental Hospitals* 15 (June, 1964): 1–8.

Miller, C. R. *Superintendent's Report for the Austin State Hospital.* Austin, Tex.: Austin State Hospital, 1965.

——. *Superintendent's Report for the Austin State Hospital.* Austin, Tex.: Austin State Hospital, 1966.

——. *Superintendent's Report for the Austin State Hospital.* Austin, Tex.: Austin State Hospital, 1967.

Miller, Gary M., and Ira Iscoe. "A State Mental Health Commissioner and the Politics of Mental Illness." In *Impossible Jobs in Public Management,* edited by Erwin C. Hargrove and John C. Glidewell. Lawrence: University of Kansas Press, 1990.

Pearce, Joe. "Past and Present," *The Envoy* 1 (1975): 1–3.

Perry, John C. *Superintendent's Report for the State Lunatic Asylum.* Austin, Tex.: State Lunatic Asylum, 1857.

Pollock, Horatio, and Edith Furbush. *Comparative Statistics of State Hospitals for Mental Diseases.* New York: Bureau of Statistics, The National Committee for Mental Hygiene, 1922.

Preston, John. *Superintendent's Report for the State Lunatic Asylum.* Austin, Tex.: State Lunatic Asylum, 1916.

*Proceedings of the State Conference of Charities and Corrections.* Third annual meeting. Ft. Worth, Tex., Nov. 30–Dec. 2, 1913. Austin, Tex.: E. L. Steck Printing, 1914.

"Proceedings of the Association of Medical Superintendents of American Institutions for the Insane." 23rd annual meeting. Staunton, Va., June 15–19, 1869. *American Journal of Insanity* 26 (October 1869): 129–203.

"Proceedings of the Association of Medical Superintendents of American Institutions for the Insane." 28th annual meeting. Nashville, Tenn., May 19–22, 1874. *American Journal of Insanity* 32 (July 1874): 129–240.

"Proceedings of the Association of Medical Superintendents of American Institutions for the Insane." 30th annual meeting. Philadelphia, Pa., June 13–17, 1876. *American Journal of Insanity* 33 (July 1876): 161–323.

"Proceedings of the Association of Medical Superintendents of American Institutions for the Insane." 39th annual meeting. Saratoga, N.Y., June 17–21, 1885. *American Journal of Insanity* 42 (October 1885): 132–208.

Ray, Isaac. "Observations on the Principal Hospitals for the Insane in Great Britain, France and Germany." *American Journal of Insanity* 2 (1846): 289–86.

Rothman, David J. *The Discovery of the Asylum.* Boston: Little, Brown, 1970.

Rotton, James, and I. W. Kelly. "Much Ado About the Full Moon: A Meta-analysis of Lunar-lunacy Research." *Psychological Bulletin* 97 (1985): 286–306.

Sapinsky, Barbara. *The Private War of Mrs. Packard.* New York: Paragon House, 1991.

Schultz, Otto. *Genesis of a Printer.* Privately published, ca. 1993.

Scull, Andrew. "Psychiatry and Social Control in the Nineteenth and Twentieth Centuries." *History of Psychiatry* 2 (1991): 149–69.

Smith, Bert Kruger. *My Brother's Keeper.* Austin: University of Texas Hogg Foundation for Mental Health, 1953.

Stern, Edith. "Our Ailing Mental Hospitals." *Reader's Digest,* Aug., 1941, 66–69.

Sutton, John. "The Political Economy of Madness: The Expansion of the Asylum in Progressive America." *American Sociological Review* 56 (1991): 665–78.

Texas Board for Texas State Hospitals and Special Schools. Department of Biometrics. *Survey of 7896 Newly Admitted State Hospital Patients (September 1, 1951–March 31, 1954).* Austin: Texas Board for Texas State Hospitals and Special Schools. Department of Biometrics, 1955.

Texas Research League. *Building Engineering and Management.* Report no. 11. Austin, Tex.: TRL, 1955.

———. *Fiscal Administration in the Texas Hospital System.* Report no. 12. Austin, Tex.: TRL, 1955.

———. *For Those Committed to Our Care.* Report no. 1. Austin, Tex.: TRL, 1954.

———. *Institutional Services in the Texas State Hospital System.* Report no. 9. Austin, Tex.: TRL, 1955.

———. *Legal Structure.* Report no. 13. Austin, Tex.: TRL, 1955.

———. *Organizational Structure and Personnel Administration.* Report No. 2. Austin, Tex.: TRL, 1954.

———. *The Program for the Mentally Ill.* Report No. 3. Austin, Tex.: TRL, 1955.

Texas State Legislature. *Report of the Committee to Investigate Complaints Concerning Austin State Hospital.* Austin, Tex., 1970.

Thielman, Samuel. "Southern Madness: The Shape of Mental Health Care in the Old South." In *Science and Medicine in the Old South,* edited by R. L. Numbers and T. L. Lavitt. Baton Rouge: Louisiana State University Press, 1989.

Tomes, Nancy. *A Generous Confidence: Thomas Story Kirkbride and the Art of Asylum Keeping, 1840–1883.* Cambridge, Eng.: Cambridge University Press, 1984.

———. "The Great Restraint Controversy." In *Anatomy of Madness,* edited by W. R. Bynum, Roy Porter, and Michael Shepherd, pp. 190–225. Vol. 3. New York: Routledge, 1988.

Torrey, E. Fuller. "Jails and Prisons—America's New Mental Hospitals." *American Journal of Public Health* 85 (1995): 1611–13.

Valenstein, Elliot S. *Great and Desperate Cures*. New York: Basic Books, 1986.

Visotsky, Harold M. "Twenty Years of Progress." *Administration and Policy in Mental Health* 21 (1993): 133–37.

Wallace, David R. *Superintendent's Report for the State Lunatic Asylum*. Austin, Tex.: State Lunatic Asylum, 1875.

———. *Superintendent's Report for the State Lunatic Asylum*. Austin, Tex.: State Lunatic Asylum, 1878.

Ward, Mary Jane. *The Snake Pit*. New York: Random House, 1946.

Weiselberg, T. F. *Superintendent's Report for the State Lunatic Asylum*. Austin, Tex.: State Lunatic Asylum, 1871.

White, F. S. *Superintendent's Report for the State Lunatic Asylum*. Austin, Tex.: State Lunatic Asylum, 1893.

———. *Superintendent's Report for the State Lunatic Asylum*. Austin, Tex.: State Lunatic Asylum, 1894.

———. *Proceedings of the State Conference of Charities and Corrections*. Nov. 15–17, 1914. San Antonio, Austin: Steck Press, 1914.

Worsham, B. M. *Superintendent's Report for the State Lunatic Asylum*. Austin, Tex.: State Lunatic Asylum, 1896.

———. *Superintendent's Report for the State Lunatic Asylum*. Austin, Tex.: State Lunatic Asylum, 1897.

———. *Superintendent's Report for the State Lunatic Asylum*. Austin, Tex.: State Lunatic Asylum, 1898.

———. *Superintendent's Report for the State Lunatic Asylum*. Austin, Tex.: State Lunatic Asylum, 1900.

———. *Superintendent's Report for the State Lunatic Asylum*. Austin, Tex.: State Lunatic Asylum, 1901.

———. *Superintendent's Report for the State Lunatic Asylum*. Austin, Tex.: State Lunatic Asylum, 1902.

———. *Superintendent's Report for the State Lunatic Asylum*. Austin, Tex.: State Lunatic Asylum, 1904.

Yoakum, Clarence S. *Care of the Feeble-minded and Insane in Texas*. Humanistic Series, no. 16, no. 369. Austin, Tex.: Bulletin of the University of Texas, 1914.

Zwelling, S. S. *Quest for a Cure*. Williamsburg, Va: The Colonial Williamsburg Foundation, 1985.

## Interviews by the author

Anonymous, Aug. 16, 1994, Sarah Sitton Collection; Anonymous, 1995, Sarah Sitton Collection; Basey, V. D., Aug. 6, 1994, ATC; Bishop, Cynthia, 1995; Brack, Ethel, Aug. 7, 1995; Brownlow, Lewis, 1990, 1995, ATC; Case, Margie Worley, July 19, 1995, ATC; Cooper, Jim, June 5, 1994; Covey, Beth, July 21, 1995; Crow, Willie, 1994; Davis, Zilphia, 1990, ATC; DeMoll, Lewis, Aug. 23, 1996, ATC;

Eidelbach, Lillian, Oct. 26, 1994, ATC; Eisenberg, Eleanor, 1994; Fleet, Kay, 1994, ATC; Fox, Margaret Standifer, 1994; Gainer, Lois, 1994; Garcia, Tony, 1995; Gautier, Bonnie, 1995, ATC; Gooding, Pat, 1994, ATC; Habbit, Raymond, 1995; Hopkins, Mary Worley, 1995, ATC; Howard, Ruth, 1994, ATC; Howell, Don, 1994, ATC; Huff, Floyd, 1995; Jureka, Jo, 1994; Kinnard, Tisha, 1995; Lassiter, James, 1994, ATC; Lawson, Doug, June 6, 1994; Lefteau, Bob, 1995; Leggett, Elbert, 1995; Leigh, Erna Wisian, 1990, ATC; McCord, Bess, 1994, ATC; Marks, Penny, 1994; Montfort, Rodney, 1995, ATC; Pearce, Joe, 1994, 1995, ATC; Pearce, Joe, 1996; Pearce, Sue, 1994, 1995, ATC; Pinckney, Mary, 1995; Roberson, Lolita, 1994, ATC; Roberts, Viola Emmert, 1990, ATC; Schultz, Otto, 1995, ATC; Sedberry, Margaret, 1995; Smith, Bert Kruger, 1996, ATC; Stanford, Charles, 1994, ATC; Standifer, Charles, 1994, ATC; Supak, John, 1995; Tedford, Verna Lee Ferguson, 1994; Turner, Dee, 1994; Wade, David, 1995; Watkins, Harvey, 1995, ATC; Worley, Robert, 1994, ATC; Worley, Wendell, 1995, ATC.

## Other interviews

Brack, Ethel, interview with Joe Pearce, 1980, ASH; Brack, Howard, interview with Joe Pearce, 1980, ASH; Bruce, Ida Lou, interview with Joe Pearce, 1980, ASH; Otting, Phillip, interview with Thad Sitton, 1994, ATC.

# ❧ INDEX ❧

CPSIA information can be obtained at www.ICGtesting.com
Printed in the USA
LVOW040141230712

291104LV00006B/1/P